Southern Soul-Blues

Music in American Life

A list of books in the series appears
at the end of this book.

Southern
Soul-Blues

David Whiteis

Foreword by Denise LaSalle

UNIVERSITY OF ILLINOIS PRESS

URBANA, CHICAGO, AND SPRINGFIELD

© 2013 by the Board of Trustees
of the University of Illinois
All rights reserved
Manufactured in the United States of America
1 2 3 4 5 C P 5 4 3 2 1
♾ This book is printed on acid-free paper.

Library of Congress Cataloging-in-Publication Data
Whiteis, David.
Southern soul-blues / David Whiteis.
p.   cm. — (Music in American life)
Includes bibliographical references and index.
ISBN 978-0-252-03479-4 (cloth : alk. paper)
ISBN 978-0-252-07908-5 (pbk. : alk. paper)
ISBN 978-0-252-09477-4 (e-book)
1. Soul music—Southern States—History and criticism.
2. Soul musicians—Southern States.
I. Title.
ML3537.W55   2013
781.6440975—dc23   2012040024

Dedicated to the memories of Ms. Beauty Turner
and Clarence "Little Scotty" Scott

"Must be something, must be something we can do . . .
Keep on moving, keep on moving for what's true"
—Gil Scott-Heron

Contents

"America's Prodigal Son"

Denise LaSalle

I was born in the United States of America, a product of slavery in the Deep South. My mother's name is Heartache; my father's name is Pain.

I was a sad and lonely child. My only sister, Gospel, was very religious and thought she was better than I. So, we traveled in different circles.

Early in my youth my parents found that I had a split personality. I was sad most of the time. But there were times when I would have such an overpowering feeling of happiness that I would have to shout it to the world.

In spite of all my faults, almost everyone seemed to need me around. I had everything going my way. Everybody loved me—or could it be that everybody wanted to use me?

Well, to me it was all the same. If they wanted to use me, that was okay. Because that meant that they needed me, and everyone likes to be needed.

Soon things began to change. It seemed people were getting a bit tired of my hanging around, so they turned to a gal called Rhythm. Well, that backfired on them because Rhythm and I fell madly in love and soon we were inseparable. Ms. Rhythm and I, Mr. Blues, dominated the music industry for years to come.

Things went well until the birth of our first child, Jazz. Jazz grew up to be a very sophisticated young man. He was much like me in physical resemblance. But Jazz possessed elegance and was sometimes a bit complicated and difficult to understand.

As for me, I've always been up-front, uncomplicated, straightforward, and easy to understand. But Jazz and I got along quite well. Sometimes we worked together. My presence gave Jazz a laid-back, moody sound.

The educated, the elite, and those who wished to give the impression that they were upper middle class seemed to attach themselves to Jazz. But when things were not going right for them or they would have one drink too many, they would always return to me for consolation. Oh, I never mind being used this way, for there will always be someone who needs me.

Soon our twins were born, Rock and Roll. These kids were swingers, wild, energetic, and uncontrollable. They turned America out, the young and the old.

There was little tolerance for me and my laid-back beat. I was too slow and old-fashioned. All I had to look forward to were the downhearted people with problems.

Finally, the country had gotten tired of all the "hullabaloo" of the "Rock and Roll" era, and Rhythm and I were in again. But I had lost the ability to stand alone and be accepted. As a duet, we held our own, but alone we were both having our share of problems.

Just when we thought our childbearing years were over, our daughter, Pop, was born. Pop was definitely a city girl, very uptown, polished and sophisticated.

She was almost perfect, but there was something missing. She lacked Rhythm. She pleaded with my beautiful wife to join her.

"What about me?" I cried. "I can help."

"Oh no, Daddy, you're too heavy and old-fashioned. I only want Mom."

"But remember what I did for Jazz?" I argued. "We worked very well together." It was no use. Her mind was made up.

Well, Pop took Rhythm and went on to become everybody's darling. Any other music was secondary. As for me, I was unwanted, outdated, and virtually forgotten.

The radio personalities had labeled me taboo. The American public had found a sense of freedom and well-being and had become intolerant of me and my good ol' "Down Home Blues." In other words, America had moved on up!

I was alone. Even Rhythm had abandoned me for Pop.

I began to experience a bit of self-doubt as those around me—yes, even my own children—urged me to give up. They sought to put me in a retirement home, as most of us do our senior citizens.

They had forgotten how I'd always been there for them; that I had laughed, cried, pleaded, begged, challenged, and even fought for them.

I cried for the voices of runaway slaves across the cotton and corn fields, in ways the old masters couldn't understand, telling others, "I'm Gonna Pack My Suitcase and Move down the Line."

I have pleaded to your secret lovers to "Come on and Steal Away." I have solved many problems when I begged, "Let's Straighten It Out."

I have challenged would-be man stealers: "You'll Never Get Your Hooks in My Man." I have brought messages from the ghetto to Capitol Hill when I told them "Why We Sing the Blues." And when there was joy in your heart, I shouted to the world, "Oh Well, Oh Well, I Feel So Good Today."

Yes, America, I've been in your corner all the way, yet you seek to destroy me.

I have always been a fighter, but what could I gain in trying to fight the whole USA?

However, I'm a tough cookie. When the going gets tough, the tough get going.

I took off to Europe. I remembered that things had been pretty good there when we toured back in the early days. I wondered if they would remember me or if they would be interested in an old, broken-down has-been like me.

Well, indeed they were. They welcomed me with open arms, and they were collectors of all of my oldies. By the thousands they came to be entertained.

They viewed me not as a newcomer, but as a tradition. They were in awe of my longevity. They saw and respected me for the great one that I am, "the father of ALL music."

Even my grandchild, Rap, has to take a backseat to me in Europe. I am held in high esteem by the young as well as the old.

England, France, and Switzerland have become a haven for me. Other nations like Germany, Holland, and Italy are also becoming Blues Metropolises. These countries have pleaded with me to stay.

They can't understand why I keep running back to America, a country that doesn't respect me as one of its pioneers and has little or no regard for me as a part of its culture and heritage.

They may not understand, but America is my home. I'll always love her. Some of the greatest people I know are Americans. While they may have forgotten that I'm the one that helped them through their hard times, shared their failure and their triumphs, I'll always be grateful to America for making me the great music that I am and for accepting my children, Jazz, Pop, Rock and Roll, and my grandchild, Rap.

Only in America could I have been born, nurtured, and flourished as I have. But until America wakes up and accepts me again and gives me the respect that I rightfully deserve, I will be a nomad, a prodigal son, immortal and indestructible.

But, whenever you want me, America, I am just a musical note away.

Acknowledgments

First, I would like to thank Laurie Matheson and her colleagues and staff at the University of Illinois Press for their support and encouragement throughout this project. The readers whom Ms. Matheson assigned to critique my manuscript were prescient and unsparing; their suggestions served to improve both the book's focus and its content. Special thanks to Paul Arroyo for his yeoman's work in helping me with various technological and logistical difficulties. Brett Bonner, editor of *Living Blues* magazine, and Cilla Huggins, of *Juke Blues,* have been invaluable founts of information and encouragement, as well as writing opportunities, for many years. I also thank Scott Barretta, former editor of *Living Blues,* for initiating the contact with the University of Illinois Press that resulted in my first book, *Chicago Blues: Portraits and Stories,* as well as this one. *Living Blues* co-founder Jim O'Neal as well as Chicago-based blues mavens Bill Dahl, Michael Frank (Earwig Records), Bruce Iglauer (Alligator Records), Bob Pruter, and Dick Shurman have shared their knowledge and enthusiasm with me over the years; I hope that their expertise, wit, and tireless advocacy for the music have rubbed off and made me a better and more knowledgeable writer.

Denise LaSalle kindly agreed to let me use her poem "America's Prodigal Son" as the foreword to this book; I thank her for her grace and generosity befitting a queen. My deepest thanks also go out to Denise and every other one of the artists, songwriters, industry representatives, and label executives who consented to speak with me: your openness has reflected a trust and confidence that I cherish with grateful humility. I also thank the photographers whose works grace these pages and help make the music and its people come alive.

Others whose expertise, friendship, support, and encouragement helped inspire and facilitate this project include: Gaye Adegbalola, Steve Balkin, Cicero Blake, Robert Bowman, John Brisbin, Jeneene Brown-Mosley, Holly Bullamore, Ms. Bumblebee, Shelley Chance, Quinton Claunch, Otis Clay, Nadine Cohodas, C. C. Copeland, Tony Dale, Ann Davis, the late Stan "Sarge" Davis, Scott Dirks, Marie Dixon, Barry Dolins, Deitra Farr, Jim Fraher, Paul Garon, Martin Goggin, Robert Gordon, the late Susan Greenberg, Leola Grey, the late Ray Grey, Peter Guralnick, Queen Ann Hines, Dave Hoekstra, Larry Hoffman, Abby Hotchkiss, Bruce James, Patty Johnson, Jackie Lewis, Sharon Lewis, Rick Lucas, Kay Jones, Letha Jones, Bob Koester, Sue Koester, Marc Lipkin, Mama Rosa, Mr. Lee, Ms. Jesi' Terrell, Tony Mangiullo, Charles Mitchell and the Jus' Blues Music Foundation, Janice Monti, Salim Muwakkil, Justin O'Brien, Sugar Mae Owens, Deanie Parker, Judy Peiser and the Center for Southern Folklore, Sterling Plumpp, Sandra Pointer-Jones, Marc PoKempner, Shakila Powell, Mr. A., Mr. Lee (Lee Kirksy), Tim Sampson, Delores Scott, Rosalie Sorrels, Pervis Spann, Peaches Staten, Neil Tesser, Joyce "Cookie" Threatt, Tré, Twist Turner, Amy Van Singel, Pervis Spann, Steve Wagner, Dick Waterman, Kirk Whalum, Robert Jr. Whitall, Flora White, Willie White, Kirk Whiting, Felix Wohrstein, Lynn Wohrstein, the late Carl Wright—and once again, the artists and everyone else who took time out of their lives to talk to me and put up with my pestering questions over the course of interviews and follow-ups for this book.

Southern **Soul-Blues**

"It's a Southern Soul Party"

Got what I got the hard way
And I'll make it better, each and every day . . .
I'm a soul man
  —Sam & Dave, "Soul Man," by Isaac Hayes
    and David Porter

I'm just a Mississippi woman
Got that Mississippi mud on my shoes
I'm just a Mississippi woman
I wanna get back to my blues
  —Denise LaSalle, "Mississippi Woman,"
    written by Floyd Hamberlin Jr.

When "Down Home Blues," Z. Z. Hill's grits-and-pot-likker ode to roots, music, and good times, hit the airwaves in late 1981,[1] it sounded to a lot of blues fans like a call from the Promised Land. Here, arising like an avenging spirit of blues righteousness from amid the mechanized pounding of disco and early rap, was the Real Thing: a voice that sounded equal parts gravel and swamp muck exhorting everyone to "take off those fast records and let me hear some down-home blues" as a fatback guitar chorded and snaked through the mix, a fallen-angel gospel choir added inspirational spice, and an easy-loping blues shuffle pushed everything along.

The reaction was immediate. Hill's label, Malaco, based in Jackson, Mississippi, had been churning out R & B, blues, and soul discs since the late 1960s (they'd scored big with Dorothy Moore's "Misty Blue" in 1976), but they were still a relatively small-scale operation. In the wake of "Down Home Blues," Malaco became a mecca for veteran soul and blues artists, most of whom

Figure 1. Z. Z. Hill, Arie Crown Theater, Chicago, March 30, 1984. Photo by Paul Natkin/Photo Reserve, Inc.

had continued to record and perform since their heyday but had disappeared from the charts. Bobby "Blue" Bland, Denise LaSalle, Little Milton, Johnnie Taylor, Latimore, Tyrone Davis, and Shirley Brown, among others, signed within a few years after Hill's hit; lesser-known figures such as Carl Sims, Stan Mosley, Mel Waiters, and Johnnie Taylor's son Floyd also eventually came on board.

Suddenly, in youth-obsessed America, singers in their thirties and older were hitting the airwaves and the jukeboxes with music that sounded, for the most part, as if it could have been made anytime over the previous twenty or twenty-five years. They were selling albums and packing houses, drawing multigenerational crowds, and pushing those crowds to heights of ecstasy and emotional commitment that seemed to fly defiantly in the face of postmodernist ironic detachment. When Little Milton proclaimed that "the blues is here, and it's here to stay" in 1982 (and then again in 1984), what might have sounded like whistling in the dark just a few years earlier now resonated like a proclamation of victory. "It was felt very strong," remembers Tommy Couch Jr., Malaco's director. "Z. Z. Hill is what got the whole thing going in a big way on the Malaco R & B side. That held up for a long time, through the late nineties."[2]

Although Hill's death in 1984 robbed the putative soul-blues movement of its figurehead, Malaco and other labels continued to issue recordings built around the same style, and the music remained a significant presence on southern radio charts, on jukeboxes, and on stages in nightclubs and show lounges.

Since then, southern soul-blues has occasionally seemed on the verge of breaking out into what's usually called the "mainstream"; other times— most of the time, in fact, at least so far—it's looked destined to remain regional, supported mostly by longtime fans who buy the records (now CDs), attend shows when they come through town, and seem steadfast in their determination to proclaim their allegiance to this "grown folks' music" as a last stand against the predations of rap and hip-hop and cultural dissolution.[3]

But it would be a mistake to think of the soul-blues phenomenon as nothing more than nostalgia, akin to the blues "revival" that took place among whites in the 1950s and '60s. Since the beginning, soul-blues has attracted listeners of all ages; although it remains unique in its embrace of artists and styles spanning multiple generations and although twelve-bar blues still figure in many singers' repertoires, most of its younger vocalists now employ techniques adapted from R & B and neosoul. Their voices, for the most part, are smooth and youthful-sounding. Their songs are often set to spiky 2/4 and 4/4 rhythms rather than blues shuffles or funk, and rapped interludes are becoming more common. Production values increasingly favor synthesized tracks, beats, and other studio effects over sounds more easily reproduced live. At the same time, lyrics have gotten more blatantly sexual, although—as we'll see—this has become a source of controversy within the soul-blues community itself.

More than anything else, though, southern soul-blues' ongoing viability shows that contrary to what some pessimists believe, there is still a place in America for music that appeals to mainstream folks (the audience consists primarily of working- and middle-class African Americans over thirty) but doesn't pander entirely to prefabricated "mainstream" tastes. In other words, regional, historical, and cultural identity still matter; Denise LaSalle's "Mississippi Woman" still has a place to call home, and the party there is still going on.

New Spice for Old Stew: Southern Soul-Blues
and the Living Blues Tradition

Southern soul-blues (also known as soul-blues or simply southern soul; the terms will be used interchangeably in this book) is a stylistic amalgam drawn from influences including postwar urban blues; 1960s-era deep soul and the funk and postfunk that evolved from it; recent and contemporary R & B; and, increasingly, neosoul, rap, and hip-hop. The music's popularity, as its name indicates, is still primarily regional, although its "southern" identity is not defined solely by geography. Its listenership spans roughly the same demographic patterns that traced the diasporic reach of the twentieth-century African American Great Migration (excluding most northeastern cities, as did the primary market for postwar urban blues). Collectively, these patterns represent what former Stax Records president Al Bell once admiringly characterized as "Mississippi River Culture":[4] African American communities in the South and in northern midwestern industrial cities such as Chicago, Milwaukee, and Detroit. To these should be added another longtime migratory route: from the Gulf Coast region to the widely dispersed megalopolis of south-central California. Performers work primarily in these areas along the loosely connected circuit of jukes, clubs, show lounges, theaters, and other venues still sometimes known as the chitlin' circuit.

Thematically, the music combines fervid emotionalism, drawn at least in part from contemporary gospel, with secular, often unabashedly carnal, storylines. It is aggressively danceable (at least when rigorous production values are adhered to), and although the songs usually avoid outright political statements, some address social concerns such as drug use, violence, AIDS, and community breakdown. Most southern soul lyrics evoke the day-to-day realities of working- and middle-class African American life (especially as concerning domestic relationships, both licit and otherwise). The implied message, as it was in deep soul and at least tacitly in earlier R & B and blues, is one of unity through struggle and celebration. This message is further accentuated by the powerful feel of community that permeates many of the venues where the music is featured, most of which are located in the South and attract a primarily African American clientele.

Although sometimes disparaged by critics as overly commercialized and thus not as "authentic" as the deep soul and blues that came before it (a charge that was once leveled at the music of electric bluesmen like Muddy Waters[5] and then later at soul and funk artists in the 1960s and '70s), southern soul-blues, in fact, shares many characteristics with more traditional blues and R & B. A closer examination shows that southern soul, like deep soul before it, is every bit as rooted in the vernacular heritage as the music (or, more accurately, the musics) commonly labeled as blues. It represents, in fact, a revitalized attempt to adapt this diverse heritage to modern popular black culture and, thus—ironically, considering the "inauthenticity" charge—update the "blues" aesthetic to appeal to the evolving tastes of contemporary African American audiences.

Like earlier blues, soul-blues is both a popular music and a living vernacular art form. This dual identity, rather than compromising "authenticity," is precisely what exemplifies it as both a continuation and a reimagining of what's often called the blues tradition. Earlier blues records were commercial artifacts, as are records and CDs today; blues musicians who recorded and performed for a living thought of themselves as professional entertainers, and when they had the opportunity, they marketed themselves that way. Then, as now, success along the blues highway was uncertain; distinctions between local (or regional) celebrity and national stardom could be vague. This wasn't the case only for "down-home" stylists like Howlin' Wolf or Muddy Waters: in the 1950s, even an R & B star like Ruth Brown might work in a prestigious venue like the Apollo or Chicago's Regal Theater for a night or two, then travel to South Carolina and find herself performing in a converted tobacco barn, having endured humiliating and often life-threatening encounters with racist police and other whites along the way.[6]

Today, although the more overt racism may have subsided, touring and performing conditions can still be dodgy, especially in the South. In purely musical terms, as well, the blues/southern soul connection remains strong. A good number of performers, even many who hesitate to label themselves as "blues" singers, slip at least one or two twelve-bar blues into their shows and onto their CDs, and they'll freely throw the term *blues* from the stage as a goad ("Any blues lovers in the house?" "Anybody wanna get down with some blues tonight?"). Song lyrics, especially the popular tales of high times in hole-in-the-wall jukes and after-hours clubs, regularly include references to blues legends like Bobby Bland along with old-school soul performers such as Marvin Gaye and Johnnie Taylor (who are usually accepted these days as members of the "blues" pantheon in good standing). Many of the revues that feature southern soul acts are billed as "blues" shows, and their audiences consist largely of the same fans who pay to see more traditionally labeled blues stars such as Bland or B. B. King. Bland, in fact, often headlines bills that otherwise consist solely of southern soul-blues entertainers.

"The Blues Is Grown"

It's not just critics, and certainly not just whites, who have resisted acknowl-
edging this inheritance. The case for southern soul as a continuation, rather
than a corruption, of the blues tradition is one that needs to be asserted
in the face of considerable resistance, some coming from within as well as
from outside the music industry. For a variety of reasons, the term *blues* has
largely fallen out of favor in the mainstream African American recording
and entertainment world. At least some of this resistance has to do with
marketing: artists have come to fear that the "blues" label might consign
them to second-tier status. The late Tyrone Davis, a 1960s and '70s-era soul
star who became a major figure on the southern soul circuit during the later
years of his career, was uncompromising in his vehemence: "It pisses me
off real bad when somebody come up to me and says 'blues,'" he declared.
"How many blues singers you ever seen get a record to sell three million?"[7]

Blues, in other words, has come to be seen by some as a brand with
unsavory connotations. It's well known that these connotations aren't
merely musical or even commercial; they're rooted in the perceived relationship between the blues and the legacy of oppression. This perception, of course, is based on historical truth, but it has been codified, even
romanticized, over the years, largely by ostensibly well-meaning white
critics and intellectuals who have insisted on stereotyping blues as little
more than music of suffering and sorrow.[8] Vocalist Millie Jackson, in fact,
has suggested that this may be why some whites embraced the blues in
the first place: "Black people don't like the blues normally," she has said,
"because it reminds 'em of a time they don't want to remember. . . . [B]ut
it's also a time that white people *like* to remember. 'Oh, yeah, I remember
the blues, yeah! Let's play the blues! Oooh, boy, I remember how many
slaves I had. Yeah, this is really good; remind me of this! They had the
blues; now I got the blues—they're all gone.'"[9]

Denise LaSalle, a soul-era veteran who now bills herself as the "Queen
of Soul-Blues," is less acerbic in her outlook than her friend Millie Jackson,
but she agrees that for many blacks, "blues represented hard times, [being]
downtrodden." She adds, though, that she sees mainstream African American rejection of the blues heritage as shortsighted, regardless of anything
whites might say or believe: "Here's what angers me. You hear somebody
say, 'White folks tryin' to steal our blues.' But I tell 'em, 'Why would you
say they're stealing it? You gave it away! You don't want it, you didn't want
to have nothing to do with it—we black people turned our backs on our

own music.' I tell 'em in a minute: 'You talkin' about white folks stealing the blues—white folks ain't stole nothin'! You gave it to 'em!'"[10]

Also common is the assumption—again based in some truth, but deadly for sales in a demographics-obsessed marketplace—that the blues appeals primarily to older listeners. Emmett Garner, a veteran of Chicago's blues and soul industry, has remembered the reaction he got when he attempted to break soul-blues vocalist Stan Mosley into the Chicago market: "'How old is he?' First thing they ask. They didn't ask me how good he was or what he got going. 'How old is he?' Girl [at a radio station] told me, 'I seen his record, but I saw it was on Malaco. I didn't even listen to it. I just put it to the side.'"[11]

Ironically, though, such resistance seems more prevalent among industry professionals than fans, a contradiction that many artists and promoters at least tacitly acknowledge. To understand this apparent anomaly, we need to remember that historically the term *blues* has tended to have a broader, more flexible definition within the African American community than outside it. When Sam Cooke made his then-daring transition from gospel to secular music in the late 1950s, he was castigated from the pulpit for singing "blues," even though most of his early secular hits bore little resemblance to anything that even the most open-minded critics might associate with the term. Much more recently, soul-singer-turned-minister Al Green has affectionately referred to his 1977 hit "Love and Happiness" as a "blues"song.[12] Memphis-based songwriter Roosevelt Jamison, as quoted by Peter Guralnick in *Sweet Soul Music*, after initially implying that he saw the blues as reflecting an earlier, less enlightened era (he emphasized that his creations, unlike "that gutbucket stuff," were uplifting and literate), praised soul singer James Carr, his own protégé, as "one of the greatest blues singers of all time."[13]

This ambiguity—or perhaps ambivalence—has continued. Tyrone Davis, despite his fulminations, spent the final decades of his career on the chitlin' circuit, often billed as a "blues" singer on "blues" shows along with other old-schoolers like Denise LaSalle, Latimore, and J. Blackfoot. Sir Charles Jones, a younger singer whose 2001 hit "Is There Anybody Lonely?" achieved the coveted distinction of garnering crossover success on mainstream R & B radio, bills himself as the "King of Southern Soul," but he's also been known to proclaim himself "the world's youngest blues singer" on stage. Then, coming at it from the other direction, there's Sweet Angel, who proudly asserts her devotion to both blues and what she considers genuine soul music yet wants to market herself as an R & B artist and considers the term *southern soul* restrictive, just as Tyrone Davis saw the word *blues*.

These deeply felt, often conflicting desires—to affirm a recognizable cultural identity yet also to escape the commercial restrictions of "regional music" status and be accepted by the putative R & B mainstream—both empower and challenge southern soul as it attempts to carve a niche for itself as a contemporary popular music. Such struggles over identity—racial, regional, artistic, and otherwise—represent yet another link between this music and earlier forms, such as postwar blues, R & B, and deep soul, which contended with similar issues (as well as with one another) on their way to becoming indispensable bedrocks of modern American culture.

"I'll Take You There"

This book is intended both as a snapshot of the current southern soul-blues scene and as an argument for the music as representing a living tradition rooted in the same lineage as earlier soul, R & B, and blues. Rather than provide an in-depth history or analysis of the music or the industry itself (such previous works as Peter Guralnick's *Sweet Soul Music* and *Dream Boogie,* Nelson George's *Where Did Our Love Go?* and *The Death of Rhythm & Blues,* Gerri Hirshey's *Nowhere to Run,* and Rob Bowman's *Soulsville, U.S.A.* have already covered that territory superbly), I have chosen to profile some of the genre's leading artists, both veteran and up-and-coming, and place their work in the historical and musical contexts outlined here. Their stories, of course, also exemplify the concerns facing the business side of the music. As artists, along with label owners, adapt their focus and resources in today's volatile economic and technological environment, their narratives limn a critique of this environment, the changes it is undergoing, and the challenges it presents.

The first section of the book will help set this context by discussing the evolution of modern soul-blues. I will argue that just as soul music, as it arose out of blues and gospel in the 1950s and continued to grow and expand over the following decades, adapted, rather than contradicted or replaced, the core thematic elements of the blues tradition, southern soul-blues represents a further continuum of this heritage instead of a dilution or a corruption of it.

Part of this living heritage has to do with the concept of "soul" as a talisman of identity and solidarity. In "Party Like Back in the Day: Soul Survivors," I profile four veterans whose careers extend back to the deep-soul era, a time when individual struggles and triumphs were symbolically

Figure 2. Tyrone Davis, Arie Crown Theater, Chicago, March 30, 1984. Photo by Paul Natkin/Photo Reserve, Inc.

linked with social and political victories and when friendships and even intimate relationships often symbolized a larger, more global unity (a "soul brother" or a "soul sister" was a comrade in arms as much as a running buddy or romantic companion—or, as Curtis Mayfield famously declared, "The woman that I hold / she's got to have soul").[14] These artists' stories illustrate this meld of personal and community identity, a meld that exemplified—and in many ways still exemplifies—the values represented by both older soul music and modern soul-blues.

"Now Playing Love Games" then focuses on four younger artists, each of whom continues to wrestle with the dual mission of living up to these values and adapting them to fit contemporary standards and tastes. Following the trajectories of their careers so far, we see the challenges they face as they attempt to balance these precariously juxtaposed ideals; we also confront some of the criticism that even many admirers have expressed, in terms of the way the music is being shaped, marketed, and represented. This section also includes a postscript in which I will address one of the most controversial of these issues: the increasing tendency toward what some see as an unsavory reliance on explicit sexual imagery in both the music's lyrics and the stage routines of some of its leading performers (including Ms. Jody and Sweet Angel, both of whom are profiled here). By discussing this controversy in the context of the blues tradition of forthright sexual expression as a coded declaration of independence, I will examine the argument over whether the proliferation of racy (or "raunchy") lyrics and stage acts in recent years bespeaks a corruption of the music or whether it is simply an updating of venerable (and inextricable) blues tropes.

Part IV, "The Crossroad and Further On: Where Do We Go from Here?"[15] will look at the challenges facing southern soul-blues as it attempts to widen its popularity and commercial impact. Among these challenges is finding (or shaping) material that will reflect qualities, such as emotional directness and honesty, long associated with blues and soul, while remaining contemporary enough to attract as wide a spectrum of listeners as possible. Just as important, they include negotiating the contemporary music industry landscape as it struggles to reshape itself in the face of economic, technological, and cultural upheavals. In this context, I will discuss the music of T. K. Soul, a leading exponent of the modernist southern soul-blues aesthetic, to suggest some approaches songwriters and artists might employ to find a balance among what so often seem like conflicting, if not contradictory, pressures.

Finally, in "Soul Stew Revisited," I will provide brief descriptions and synopses of the careers and music of selected soul-blues artists whose music I believe important. The section will be divided into two chapters: "Leading Lights," artists who are (or have been) major figures in terms of their influence on southern soul's development, their recorded legacy, and their popularity; and "Soul Serenade," featuring up-and-coming artists as well as veterans who have contributed to the music and are respected in the field but have not necessarily attained "star" status. This is not a comprehensive list; rather, I intend it as a sampler and an encouragement for readers who want to go further and explore the music more deeply.

As always, I have endeavored to be true to both the spirit and the letter of accuracy; all quotes are from my personal interviews or gleaned from works by established authorities and reliable sources (please check the notes and references for details). I have cross-checked historical facts among multiple sources whenever possible. Unless they are part of direct quotes, all opinions—critical, social, and otherwise—are my own. I take full responsibility for them, as well as for any unintended errors of fact.

Part I

Deep Blues, Deep Soul, and Beyond

The Roots and Development of Southern Soul-Blues

The precise genesis of the term *soul music* is somewhat difficult to delineate, but *soul,* as a secular expression, arose in the mid-twentieth century to symbolize the identity movement that came to life during the postwar years and eventually transformed African American cultural politics. Early on, at least, the concept of "soul" embraced a heritage that had been shaped by history and values of which the blues were an integral part.

"Man, colored people must be somethin' else," author Claude Brown remembered hearing young Harlemites say in the early 1950s. "All those years, man, we was down on the plantation in those shacks, eating just potatoes and fatback and chitterlin's and greens, and look at what happened. We had Joe Louises and Jackie Robinsons and Sugar Ray Robinsons and Henry Armstrongs. . . . Negroes are some beautiful people."[1]

"That was the coming of the 'soul' thing," Brown continued. "'Soul' had started coming out of the churches and the nightclubs into the streets. Everybody started talking about 'soul' as though it were something that they could see . . . a distinct characteristic of colored folks."[2]

Although Brown himself seemed ambivalent about some of the more atavistic elements of this "distinct characteristic" (elsewhere, he disparaged his parents' generation of southern emigrants as "big-city backwoods people"), he also recognized how such shared heritage could represent a continuum of strength and survival worth celebrating: "[Y]ou felt as though you had something strong in common," he wrote. "I suppose it's the same thing that almost all Negroes have in common, the fatback, chitterlings, and greens background. . . . Everybody was really digging themselves and thinking and saying in their behavior, in every action, 'Wow! Man, it's a beautiful thing to be colored. . . . Look at us. Aren't we beautiful?'"[3]

Soul Rising

In music, these values were often exemplified by the dual (if sometimes conflicting) aesthetics of blues and gospel. According to most accounts, "soul" was first used as a musical adjective when the style known as "soul jazz" evolved out of hard bop in the 1950s and early '60s at about the same time as the word was insinuating itself into African American vernacular as a symbol of ethnic pride. Hard bop itself had been at least partly a reaction to what some saw as latter-era bebop's tendency to value technique over emotion (in contrast to early bebop, which bristled with both musical and emotional militance). Hard boppers like trumpeter Clifford Brown, drummer and bandleader Art Blakey, saxophonists Hank Mobley and Johnny Griffin, and trumpeter Lee Morgan grafted the technical dexterity of bebop onto melodic, chordal, and rhythmic frameworks that often invoked the perfervid emotional intensity of a Sunday service along with elements of blues and what was then called rhythm and blues (small-group "jump blues" à la Louis Jordan).

Soul jazz took things even deeper into the alley behind the church. Stripping the music down to its harmonic basics, soul jazz players often incorporated contemporary pop and R & B songs in their set lists along with funk-seasoned originals. Their music came to emphasize groove over melody, and it toughened hard bop's already aggressive thrust with a streetwise, bluesy hipness. The aesthetic dichotomy between this music and its more sophisticated counterparts—cool jazz (abstract, emotionally distant), the so-called Third Stream jazz of ensembles like the Modern Jazz Quartet (more European than Africanist in its counterpoint structure,[4] "bourgie" in both affect and effect)—was often reflected in the demographics of its listeners. As jazz historian Scott Yanow has put it: "While many

young jazz musicians were attempting to redefine jazz as an 'art form'
suitable for concert halls, soul jazz thrived in small black bars and clubs."[5]
Artists such as pianist Horace Silver, erstwhile Ray Charles saxophonists
Hank Crawford and David "Fathead" Newman (to say nothing of Brother
Ray himself), Gene Ammons, Stanley Turrentine, and organists Jimmy
Smith and Shirley Scott were among those who codified the soul jazz
style. Smith, in fact, almost single-handedly made the organ combo the
prototypical soul jazz unit with his 1950s-era recordings for Blue Note.

In rhythm and blues, meanwhile, a similar "Saturday night"/"Sunday
morning" fusion was occurring. And at least at the beginning, it was less
a reaction against the blues tradition than a modernist updating of it. In
fact, what came to be known as "soul music" arose largely out of what
was seen by many at the time as a blues-fueled assault against the very
bastions of mainstream respectability, both black and white.[6] One night
in 1954, Ray Charles and trumpeter Renald Richard were riding though
Indiana when a gospel song, most likely "It Must Be Jesus" by the Southern Tones, came on the radio. Charles and Richard began riffing, playfully
tossing secularized versions of the lyrics back and forth—"I got a woman!"
"Yeah, she lives across town!"—and before they knew it, they had a song.
In November, Charles and his band cut "I've Got a Woman" in the Atlanta
studios of Georgia Tech radio station WGST.[7]

Apocalyptic in every sense of the word, "I've Got a Woman" initially
brought the wrath of both God and man down on Ray Charles's head.
Preachers denounced it as sacrilege; even some blues people were shocked
(no less an authority than Big Bill Broonzy sniped, "He should be singing
in church."). But it spoke to something deep and affirming in listeners,
especially during a time when racial pride and empowerment (i.e., "soul")
were burgeoning sentiments in the African American community.

The record hit the R & B charts in early 1955 and peaked at No. 1;
Charles followed it up with similar updatings of spiritual themes—"This
Little Girl of Mine" ("This Little Light of Mine"), Doc Pomus's "Lonely
Avenue" ("I've Got a New Home"), "Leave My Woman Alone" ("You Better Leave That Liar Alone")—as well as equally fervid but less churchy
outings such as "Drown in My Own Tears" and flat-out barn burners like
"Swanee River Rock (Talkin' Bout That River")." In 1959, he sealed the
deal for all time with "What'd I Say," a paint-peeling ode to raw libido on
which his backup vocalists, the Raelettes, panted and mewed their way
into realms of orgasmic ecstasy that had seldom been approached on
record, let alone radio, before then.

Figure 3. Ray Charles, Star Plaza Theatre, Merrillville, Indiana, May 13, 1983. Photo by Paul Natkin/Photo Reserve, Inc.

Movin' on Up

After Ray—the deluge. By the time "What'd I Say" hit the charts, the new gospel-blues had become a mainstream popular music. Artists like Bobby Bland, Jackie Wilson, Etta James, and Little Willie John, to name just a few, were filling the airwaves and nightclubs with sounds and emotional exultation that had previously been considered proper only in a religious setting, often grafted onto lyrics that might previously have been heard only in a juke joint.

Contrary to the misgivings of some of its critics, though, soul music always kept at least one foot in the church. In performance, both Ray Charles and the soul artists who followed in his wake employed time-tested gospel techniques—call-and-response, the interweaving of sung and spoken texts, carefully choreographed emotional trajectories from intimacy to ecstasy—to get the house. (Bobby Bland adopted his famous "squall" directly from the Rev. C. L. Franklin's recorded sermon "The Eagle Stirreth Her Nest."[8]). Most soul singers got their start in gospel; some—Sam Cooke, Johnnie Taylor, O. W. Wright, and Aretha Franklin, to name just a few—were gospel celebrities before they crossed over into secular music. Although many shied away from maintaining both their secular and religious musical vocations, others continued to cross over, back and forth, throughout their careers. Their musical personas and lyric

JOHNNIE TAYLOR　　　　　**MALACO**

Figure 4. Johnnie Taylor. Malaco publicity photo, courtesy of Malaco Records.

messages often reflected this; inspirational and even devotional songs have been common in soul music almost from the beginning.

And it wasn't only about spirituality. As raw as it might still sometimes get ("soul music," as Peter Guralnick reminds us, "could stink as bad as the nastiest blues"[9]), soul evolved during a time, and at least partly in a milieu (urban and/or northern), characterized by burgeoning middle-class aspirations in the African American community, especially among the youth. What this meant was that by the early 1960s, the music that had been inspired by Brother Ray's chitlins-and-blues-drenched "I've Got a Woman"/"What'd I Say" continuum had become associated with values that seemed, at least on their surface, to represent a new and respectable (if no less celebratory or hip) alternative to the blues.

"In the stuff I was writing," Motown's Smokey Robinson has said, "there was pain, but there was hope, which the blues didn't have."[10] Motown, of course, is known as the label that took soul out of the 'hood and into the 'burbs, as opposed to the ostensibly rawer and more heroically pro-letarian southern "deep soul." But down South, a lot of soulsters were pretty much in agreement with Smokey. At Stax in Memphis—"Soulsville, U.S.A."—songwriters Isaac Hayes and David Porter remained true to the traditional blues trope of lamenting hard times but also echoed Robinson's stated determination to convey "hope, which the blues didn't have" when they created a country-born, hard-loving "Soul Man" who could boast, "Got what I got the hard way" and then vow to "make it better each and every day."

"We wanted to philosophize on the blues," said another Memphian, Roosevelt Jamison, composer of O. V. Wright's deep soul classic "That's How Strong My Love Is" and mentor/manager of the brilliant but troubled vocalist James Carr. Jamison emphasized that both he and Wright wanted to "get away from that gutbucket stuff, that really wasn't very good music in our opinion. Many of our songs had some flavor of God in them, to where you could feel the sacredness."[11]

That's not to say there was nothing rebellious or transgressive about the new music. The tone, however, had changed, and the message had been reshaped. Soul came of age along with the Black Freedom Movement; like the movement itself, soul forged a message that urged both personal striving and social liberation, linking individual betterment with the uplift of "the race." (Curtis Mayfield's creations, both for the Impressions in the 1960s and for himself as a solo artist later on, exemplify this melding of righteous protest with moral and social improvement.) Even James Brown, "Soul Brother No. 1," whose music and persona helped define urban street culture in the '60s just as hip-hop would do thirty years later, endorsed black capitalism as his preferred vehicle for liberation ("I used to shine shoes in front of a radio station. Now I own radio stations. You know what that is? That's Black Power"[12]), and he eventually embraced such figures as Hubert Humphrey and Richard Nixon as heroes.

This point was missed by some white counterculturists, who saw in soul music's uninhibited sensuality and emotional expressiveness a rejection not merely of oppression and the legacy of slavery, but of conventional middle-class aspirations, if not propriety itself (a faux nihilism that many had read into the blues as well). But that was a misunderstanding on the part of privileged youths who could afford to scoff at the sedate lifestyles and comforts that poor and minority kids had only recently begun to even dare dream of acquiring. "Some young white folks," mused Joe Brown, James's father, "run *away* from America. They ashamed. Black folks, they run all over, up North, everywhere, tryin' to get *into* America."[13]

It was an America far removed from the cultural and class values the blues now seemed to represent. "We used to laugh at the blues," Chicago doo-wop veteran Maurice Simpkins asserted. "We were going to school every day and these blues singers hadn't even gone to grammar school."[14]

From today's perspective, however, it's apparent that soul was less a rejection of the earlier blues aesthetic than a savvy updating of it. In fact, in many ways the "soul" movement honored roots much deeper—and extending much father back into history—than even many of its own advocates acknowledged at the time. By seeming to violate the long-standing theological/ideological divide between the sacred and the secular, Ray Charles and his followers weren't just throwing down a challenge to "bourgie" primness, they were throwing down a challenge to the Eurocentric Cartesian dualism that whites had attempted to impose on Africans since the dawn of slavery.

"It's All Blues if It Comes from the Heart"

The blues is rooted, in its deepest essence, in a tradition in which spirit and flesh mingled closely together: dance, rhythm, melody, and prayer—body and soul—interwove into a single celebration.[15] Within this context, many of the dualisms taken for granted in the Western cultural worldview— "individual" versus "collective"; "serious" versus "playful"; "supernatural" versus "worldly"; "spirit" versus "flesh"—were not so sharply drawn. Carnality did not, in and of itself, represent an oppositional force against the holy or the good, a religious ritual of ecstatic transcendence incorporated many of the same elements as its secular counterpart, and vice versa.[16] "I've Got a Woman" and the soul music that followed simply reaffirmed (or perhaps finally admitted) this connection.[17] As Mark Anthony Neal has pointed out, the art of a soul singer like Aretha Franklin "constructed blackness as a medium for the black church tradition, and vice versa. . . . [H]er ability to secularize her gospel training [was] an exchange that travels both ways and reflects the broad and diverse sensibilities of the African-American diaspora."[18]

At the same time, the blues as a musical idiom—again, contrary to stereotype—was never entirely repudiated. Some of soul's most important hits—Aretha Franklin's "Dr. Feelgood," Wilson Pickett's "Mustang Sally," any number of James Brown's dance-groove anthems—were structured on the twelve-bar blues form. Moreover, straight-ahead blues singers such as B. B. King, Albert King, and Little Johnny Taylor continued to enjoy R & B chart success during and after the soul era, and their recordings increasingly featured the same kind of hard-booting horns and funk-flavored rhythm lines that characterized the music of soul stars such as Otis Redding, Aretha Franklin, and James Brown.

In retrospect, then, it seems clear that many of the commonly accepted dichotomies between blues and soul, valuable though they may have been to both critics and demographics-savvy marketers, represented ideology more than aesthetics—and that in many ways, they still do. When Stax, the label that virtually created deep soul in the 1960s, closed its doors in 1975, its sound had evolved into diverse and apparently contradictory, but actually complementary, directions. Stax didn't just popularize soul music during its run; it also played a major role in keeping the blues contemporary—or, more accurately, Stax helped blur the distinction between "soul" and "blues," a blurring that set the stage for the hybrid called "soul-blues" to assert itself among fans of both genres in the wake of Z. Z. Hill's early 1980s hit.

At Stax, veteran bluesman Albert King's smoky baritone and taut, string-bending guitar style garnered him eleven chart hits between 1966 and early 1974. Johnnie Taylor, though known as a soul man throughout most of his Stax tenure, was almost as successful with blues or blues-based material ("I Had a Dream," "Steal Away," "Cheaper to Keep Her") as he was with soul testimonials like "Who's Making Love."[19] And, as Sam & Dave's "Soul Man" exemplified, the prototypical soul stance of hard-won triumph charged with hard-loving sexual prowess ("Comin' to you on a dusty road / Good lovin',' I got a truckload") was rooted in imagery and mythos closely related to long-standing blues themes.

Meanwhile, though, Stax had begun to seek a more sophisticated alternative to what president Al Bell sometimes referred to as "that 'Bama music."[20] "Soul Man" co-writer Isaac Hayes's landmark *Hot Buttered Soul* LP in 1969 and his Grammy Award-winning *Shaft* soundtrack two years later helped set the new tone with their extended cuts, jazz-funk stylings, and overall feel of hip urbanity. Arrangements at Stax (strings, background vocals) became lusher; in the wake of its falling-out with Atlantic, which had handled its distribution until 1968, and then the demise of Booker T & the MGs in the early '70s, Stax began to rely more heavily on outside studios, session musicians, and songwriters. The result of all this, as historian Rob Bowman has suggested, may well have been that by the late 1960s "the idea of a readily identifiable [Stax] sound was beginning to recede into history."[21] The upside, though, taking the long view, was that a lot of stereotypes and purist ideologies had to do the same thing. The definition of soul authenticity began to loosen; the citified, street-savvy John Shaft and the brokenhearted California dreamer fleeing a doomed relationship in Hayes's epic reading of "By the Time I Get to Phoenix," by their very appearance in songs on the Stax label, were revealed as soul brothers with roots as deep and down-home as the titular "Soul Man" of Sam & Dave's hit.

At the same time—Bell's misgivings about "'Bama music" notwithstanding—Stax, and by implication, soul music itself, refused to abandon its roots. In fact, as times got harder, it seemed to embrace them with new determination. The Soul Children, co-fronted by J. Blackfoot, signed on after Sam & Dave left Stax in 1968, and they stayed around until the label's final days; their fusion of sanctified ecstasy, backstreet grit, and erotic heat was as "deep-soul" torrid as anything their predecessors had ever envisioned. Stax also continued to release gutsy-sounding sides by blues and deep-soul stalwarts like Little Milton ("If You Talk in Your Sleep," 1975), Johnnie Taylor ("Try Me Tonight," from the same year), and, perhaps most excitingly, Shirley Brown, a singer of apparently unlimited vocal prowess who'd been brought to the label by Albert King and was envisioned as a possible competitor for Aretha Franklin. Brown's Stax debut, "Woman to Woman," infused the pop-softened sound of the "new" Stax with the sanctified emotional fervor of the deep-soul tradition; it spent two weeks at No. 1 on the R & B charts in 1974. Unfortunately, the doomed label was unable to support her career, even though she scored a minor hit the following year with "It Ain't No Fun." She ended up pretty much going down with the ship. Today, along with other veterans like Denise LaSalle and Latimore, she's a premier attraction on the southern soul-blues circuit.

Figure 5. Shirley Brown, Ovens Auditorium, Charlotte, North Carolina, February 2010. Photo by Gene Tomko.

This process of evolution and stylistic melding continued after Stax folded. In fact, it's apparent in retrospect that "Down Home Blues" didn't create a market in 1981 and 1982 as much as it unearthed one that was already there. During the years following the collapse of Stax and the attendant decline of deep soul, artists such as Little Johnny Taylor, Ted Taylor (no relation), O. V. Wright, and McKinley Mitchell, along with Stax soul survivors like Shirley Brown and Johnnie Taylor himself (to say nothing of bluesmen like Albert King) soldiered on; most of the others who eventually signed on with Malaco in the wake of "Down Home Blues" also maintained careers during this time. But this went on mostly under the radar, in the lower regions of the R & B charts (Johnnie Taylor never saw the Top Ten again after he hit with the bluesy "Love Is Better in the A.M. [Part 1]" in 1977) and at largely unheralded chitlin' circuit venues.

As soul morphed into funk, postfunk, and eventually neosoul, rap, and hip-hop, mainstream African American popular music moved farther away from both the blues form and deep soul's churchy, horns-and-keyboards embellishments on it. At the same time, however, the influence of the newer sounds became increasingly evident in the work of those who still billed themselves as "blues" or "soul" artists (the distinction became increasingly hazy as time went by). In fact, by the early and mid-1980s, quite a few deep-soul veterans had begun to reinvent themselves as "blues" or "soul-blues" entertainers, usually purveying much the same kind of material as they'd been offering all along. Younger singers eagerly joined the party, adapting and embellishing the old sounds to suit their own styles and ambitions. Sensing a fresh market, new labels arose to accommodate them.

Labels and Sounds: A Brief Overview of the Post–"Down Home Blues" Southern Soul Recording Industry

Malaco was not the only recording company to set off on the soul and blues trail. Not long after "Down Home Blues" changed the southern musical landscape, Stax veterans Homer Banks and Lester Snell, along with another Memphis-based musician and producer named Chuck Brooks, launched the Sound Town label. They scored with J. Blackfoot's "Taxi" in 1983, and they also recorded Stax expatriate Shirley Brown, who managed four modest hits for Sound Town in 1984 and 1985. Johnny Vincent's Ace imprint out of Jackson, Mississippi, first made its mark in the 1950s with New Orleans R & B artists like Earl King ("Those Lonely, Lonely Nights"), Huey Smith and the Clowns ("Don't You Just Know It"), and others. After a disastrous distribution deal with the doomed Vee-Jay label drove Ace into bankruptcy in the mid-1960s, Vincent dropped out of the record business; he attempted a comeback in the 1970s, but it wasn't until the early '90s that he truly revitalized Ace with southern soul-blues artists such as Cicero Blake, Willie Clayton, and Pat Brown. Vincent sold the company in 1997; he then initiated a new imprint, Avanti, which continued to record soul-blues artists, such as Willie Clayton, with moderate success. Johnny Vincent passed away on February 4, 2000.

In 1985, an Englishman named John Abbey began to issue R & B, soul-blues, and rap records on his Atlanta-based Ichiban imprint. Ichiban's biggest claim to southern soul fame was "Strokin,'" Clarence Carter's ode to backseat, bedroom, and sofa sex that breathed new life into Carter's career in the 1980s and has since become a standard. Ichiban has been faulted by some for lowering the bar on southern soul production and songwriting: it helped usher in the synths, prefabricated backing tracks, and overall mechanical feel that detractors say have diluted the music; its cover art often looked low-rent; and some of the songs its artists recorded relied on the kind of cheap-joke double entendre humor that has now become a contentious issue. Nonetheless, artists such as Willie Clayton, Chick Willis, Trudy Lynn, Francine Reed, harmonica player Jerry McCain, vocalist/guitarist David Dee, Artie "Blues Boy" White, Bobby Rush, and Tyrone Davis enjoyed at least moderate success on Ichiban. The label folded in the mid-1990s.

Warren Hildebrand's New Orleans–based Mardi Gras label has made some significant noise in the soul-blues field; the late Senator Jones's Hep' Me imprint, closely affiliated with Mardi Gras, also did well before Jones's death in 2008. Former Stax songwriter and vocalist William Bell has been active with his Wilbe label in Atlanta since 1985. The Miss Butch label, owned by former Ray Charles collaborator Jimmy Lewis, was responsible for Peggy Scott-Adams's "Bill," a slyly smoothed-over riposte to down-low brothers (closeted gay men who maintain relationships with unknowing women), which made the national R & B charts in 1997. In early 2007, Dylann DeAnna, an online journalist who goes by the *nom du Net* "Blues Critic," established the CDS label in Carlsbad, California; CDS has already become an important player in the field, largely by luring artists who had formerly been affiliated with labels such as Malaco or Ecko. Various other independents record local and regionally based singers in the South or the Midwest, and an increasing number of artists are self-producing and/ or distributing their own product.

Far more important to southern soul-blues over the long haul, though, has been Ecko, which was founded in 1995 by songwriter/guitarist John Ward after he was turned down by both Malaco and Ace when he tried to pitch them "I'll Drink Your Bathwater, Baby," a song he'd written and recorded featuring vocalist Ollie Nightingale. The Ecko facility on North Hollywood in Memphis has a history that goes back to the final days of the Stax era. In 1976, the novelty hit "Disco Duck" was recorded there, originally for the Fretone label, which was owned by former Stax co-owner

Estelle Axton. Not long after "Disco Duck" became a hit, former Stax engineer and session musician Bobby Manuel built a new studio in the building so he could make records for his Black Diamond imprint; his partner in this project was Axton's brother, Jim Stewart, who had launched Stax as Satellite Records back in 1957. They recorded Shirley Brown's "If This Is Goodbye" for Black Diamond in 1989; they also cut some sides on her that ended up on her early Malaco albums. The facility went through several names, including Daily Planet and High Stacks Records. Finally, in 2002, Ward, who'd been running Ecko out of his house until then, purchased it and moved his company in. The original studio where "Disco Duck" was recorded is now subdivided into office space; the old "Daily Planet" logo is still visible on one of the glass doors in the building.

For all that, though, Ecko's sound is decidedly un-Stax-like. Almost entirely synthesized except for the occasional lead guitar or sax solo, Ecko productions also feature plenty of lyric naughtiness, much of it from Ward's own pen (e.g., Carl Sims's "Coochie Key" and Sweet Angel's "The Tongue Don't Need No Viagra"), along with the usual boudoir ballads and celebrations of all-night partying at the local hole in the wall. Although, like Ichiban, Ecko is sometimes criticized for hit-and-miss production and song quality, it moves product effectively, its roster includes some of the most popular artists on the circuit, and it has played an important role in southern soul's ongoing attempts to bring its sound into line with mainstream contemporary R & B.

Let the Music Play

In the face of all this competition, Malaco also did its best to modernize its sound in the 1990s and early 2000s, even if some thought its recordings remained too rooted in "that down-south blues flavor," as Johnnie Taylor's son Floyd has put it, to cross over into the mainstream. (The point may be moot; by 2011, in the wake of declining CD sales and the exodus of many of its biggest names, Malaco had all but pulled out of southern soul in favor of gospel and contemporary R & B.) But as younger singers and producers, raised on the modernist, technology-intensive sounds of post-1980s R & B and hip-hop, have entered the field, they have updated southern soul still further. Today, in fact, by any objective standards, the stylistic difference between an R & B superstar like Jay-Z or Usher and a southern soul artist such as Sir Charles Jones, Floyd Taylor himself, T. K. Soul, Mr. Sam, or Simeo (a songwriter, singer, and producer for the CDS label in California, whom online critic Daddy B. Nice has dubbed "the hiphopper lost in the land of southern soul")[22] may be more a matter of marketing than music; the stories told, the overall vocal and musical approach, and the production values have become so similar as to make critical distinctions difficult.

Nonetheless, southern soul-blues retains its identity as a subgenre. It's still primarily a singer's showcase: vocals are usually mixed well out in front, they tend to be relatively straightforward and devoid of flowery melisma, and they're seldom distorted or tweaked electronically. Guitar and sax solos remain prevalent, even if the rest of the accompaniment is almost entirely synthesized (and "accompaniment" is usually what it is, instead of the techno-spiked ambience sharing primacy with the singer's voice that's common in R & B). And for all the complaints about "raunchy" lyrics, the subject matter is usually mild by contemporary standards, and plenty of songs still praise "country" virtues like faith, family, and perseverance through hard times.

Probably for theses reasons, the music continues to attract a fan base somewhat older and more socially conservative, probably more solidly working-class, and more defined by region than the mainstream R & B listenership (although the two audiences definitely overlap). It's a sizeable demographic, and southern soul can't afford to lose it, but to remain viable in today's marketplace, it needs to appeal to younger, trendier, and more shopping-savvy listeners as well as the old-school vanguard that makes up its primary base. The conflicting desire to go "mainstream" while remaining true to stylistic and regional roots (perhaps "cultural identity" would be a more accurate term) thus remains one of southern soul's most significant challenges.

As we'll see, this challenge impacts virtually every facet of southern soul-blues activity: the music the artists choose, the style in which they deliver it, how they package and promote themselves, and the ways in which it is distributed and marketed. It's reflected in the ongoing debates about nomenclature ("blues" versus "soul-blues" versus "southern soul" versus "R & B"), the appropriateness of various musical styles and lyrics, and the role of the music in influencing and reflecting the lives and values of its purveyors and audiences alike. It is, in short, the overriding theme that shapes, impels, motivates, and sometimes haunts the southern soul-blues world and the artists who keep that world alive.

Part II

"Party Like Back in the Day"

Soul Survivors

1

Latimore

"I Capture the Feeling"

Sit yourself down, girl, and talk to me,
Tell me what's on your mind . . .
Let's straighten it out,
Baby, let's straighten it out
   —Latimore, "Let's Straighten It Out"

Benny Latimore reigns as the Sweet-Loving Philosopher King of Southern Soul.[1] Whether he's preaching transcendence through sexual ecstasy ("Take Me to the Mountaintop"), spinning out parables that equate conjugal devotion with spiritual enlightenment, if not salvation itself ("Dig a Little Deeper"), extolling the redemptive power of free love ("It Ain't Where You Been"), or even playfully mocking his own aging-roué persona ("I'm an Old Dog"), his aphoristic meld of romantic fervor, life lessons, and self-deprecating irony continues to melt hearts and elicit screams, no matter how predictable his set lists may become, no matter how tirelessly he keeps his show on the road, year after year and decade after decade, in show lounges and theaters across the dwindling but still potent chitlin' circuit.

"Let's Straighten It Out," Latimore's career-defining No. 1 hit in 1974, codified his persona as a tender-hearted sensualist, flawed yet penitent, ready by any means necessary to win or redeem his lady's affections and fortified with wisdom by the experience. He never again hit the top of the charts, but once he claimed

Figure 6. Latimore, Greensboro Coliseum, Greensboro, North Carolina, February 2009. Photo by Gene Tomko.

the image he never abandoned it. In fact, he's cultivated and honed it over the years.

What he projects when he gets on stage is a little tougher (after all, he's also a man among men) but no less seductive. Sporting gold earrings and with a shiny pendant dangling around his neck, he stands with regal nonchalance behind his electric keyboard, clad in a suave-looking black sweater or a sleeveless leather vest that highlights the sweat glistening on his biceps. He mostly eschews the soul man's macho strut, preferring to sway hypnotically over his instrument with eyebrows raised and head cocked at a rakish angle, his white-bearded countenance softened by a grin that stops just short of being lascivious. His fingers tease, tickle, and caress the keys as he croons his tales of sensitive-guy empathy in a muscular baritone laced with vulnerability.

It's an image that could easily seem silly or even pathetic for a man in his seventies. But Latimore, who was born in rural Tennessee in 1939, gets away with it. It's not just that he's sharpened his showman's chops to a fine edge over the course of a fifty-plus-year career. His longevity, he insists, is also rooted in his determination to inspire and even uplift his audience, rather than merely tantalize or entertain them. He's convinced that the sincerity he projects keeps his music and his message fresh, and, in the process, saves him from self-parody. "I try to tell the truth," he says, "and try to be honest about it. Positive kinds of songs—it's not a contrived kind of thing. Most of those things that I do and say on record, I believe it." And sensing this, his listeners believe it, too.

A manifesto like that may seem quaint, if not disingenuous, in our irony-besotted times. After talking with Benny Latimore, though, it's easy to believe him. His conversation, contemplative yet laced with wit, reflects the same blend of thoughtfulness and playfulness that permeates his music, bespeaking a man who takes life seriously even as he celebrates it. It's a legacy he inherited from his father, Eddie Lattimore (Benny later dropped the second *t*), a hardworking country man who moved with his wife, Edna, and their family to the small town of Charleston, Tennessee, when Benny was about ten years old. "We were on this farm," he remembers. "My granddaddy and all of 'em worked [there], and then my granddad and the rest of 'em moved closer to town. I'm the oldest; I have a sister two years younger than I am, and my brother was four years younger than me, and my baby sister is ten years younger than me."

Eddie and Edna Lattimore had high aspirations for their children. Post-war boom-era optimism was burgeoning, even in southern working-class black communities, and the Lattimores felt it strongly. Although segregation continued to haunt everyday life, there were signs that the racial caste system that had tormented the South for so long might be challenged. In 1954, *Brown v. Board of Education* declared public school segregation unconstitutional; in December of the following year, Rosa Parks, E. D. Nixon, Dr. Martin Luther King Jr., and their allies in Montgomery, Alabama, launched the historic bus boycott that spearheaded the modern civil rights movement. A striving black family like the Lattimores could dare to believe that the future might finally be brighter than the past. Their eldest son became determined early on that it would be so for him. "I wanted to set the world on fire!" he says today, the old enthusiasm undiminished.

My mother and father worked hard for their money, and my father said he never wanted me to have to work as hard as he did. He and my mother, neither one had a lot of education. My mother was a very, very intelligent woman. She didn't have a lot of education, fourth grade, but she could read; she read everything we brought into the house. She learned everything right along with us. I was a straight-A student, and they just thought, well, he's going to be some big professor or something like that. I dreamed of doing that, too.

Music, meanwhile, served primarily as either a relaxing diversion or a means of praising the Lord. "First I remember," Latimore reflects, "is my mother singing to me and playing guitar, out in the country. Just songs, folkie kinda songs and some religious songs."

When I was coming up, we mostly heard country music, poppish kinda music. Blues was considered music that you'd hear in bars and beer joints and juke joints and stuff. The church people, anything that's secular, they framed it as [blues]. They thought it was a sin to be doing this. The first place I ever sang was in church, when I was about thirteen, fourteen. When I first started singing on talent shows and stuff in high school, it was a bit of a conflict because I went to church and sang in church. When I started hearing blues music, was on a station out of Nashville, Tennessee, called WLAC. Late at night they played blues. Randy's Record Mart.[2]

WLAC at that time was probably the nation's most important outlet for black popular music. A powerful station whose 50,000-watt signal could be heard at night throughout most of the eastern U.S., it started broadcasting blues and R & B (or "race music") in the mid-1940s, when disc jockey Gene Nobles began to take requests from college students attending Fisk University and Tennessee Agricultural and Industrial State College (later Tennessee State) in Nashville. In 1947, a businessman from nearby Gallatin named Randy Wood became one of the station's major sponsors; his mail-order record business, the now-legendary Randy's Record Shop, soon became the nation's largest enterprise of its kind.

On WLAC, disc jockeys such as Nobles, John R. (née Richbourg), and Bill "Hoss" Allen spun records by the likes of Etta James, Muddy Waters, Howlin' Wolf, and Lightnin' Hopkins, which they overlaid with jivey hepcat banter so smooth that many listeners actually believed they were black. The station's primary market was its widespread southern African American listenership; however, untold numbers of white teenagers also got their first taste of the sensual rhythms and erotic heat of blues and R & B by closing their bedroom doors and jamming their ears against radios turned down low. The music and the disc jockeys' madcap rants infiltrated and bent their consciousness—"soft driving, slow and mad, like some new language," as Jim Morrison would put it years later.

Such goings-on were nearly as unheard-of in a conservative black family like the Lattimores as they were in most white households. Nonetheless, the music began to seep into Benny Lattimore's awareness, although for a long time it wasn't much more than a backing track. "We had a piano in the house; my sister took music lessons. Every now and then I'd sit down there and try to bang out something, played blues changes and doo-wop changes. I was learning how to do that, [but] I was more interested in sports than I was in taking music lessons and stuff like that."

In any case, young Benny had loftier goals in mind than spending the rest of his life singing for his supper. "I did it in church, and that was a thrill, but I didn't even consider the possibility of doing it for a living. I come from a working-class family, and you 'worked' for a living. You didn't 'play' for a living. People, still, most people think of being an entertainer or a musician, they think of it as 'playing.' They take the word *play* literally. It's not just a figure of speech, 'playing.' I was planning on being a teacher, an English teacher. I was the first in my family to go to college."

College, however, opened new vistas for the serious-minded young man. In 1957, Benny Lattimore arrived at Tennessee A & I in Nashville, the same school whose students had helped spur WLAC into adopting its revolutionary playlist over a decade earlier. There he encountered young men his own age who had no problem at all envisioning themselves "playing" music, even if at that point it didn't seem there would be much money in it. In Benny's case, the experience seems to have unleashed aspirations he'd been harboring, mostly unacknowledged, all along. "I got up there," he says with a rich chuckle, "and I got interested in that doggone music."

> I'd see guys harmonizing, you know, doo-wop, the guys standing on the corner. I started talking to them and harmonizing with them. [Then] I went to this little bar near the campus, and these guys were back in there, drinking beer and harmonizing, and I got up enough nerve to go over and introduce myself to them, and said "I sing a little bit, too." And they said, "Well, come on, man." So I hung with them, and boy, I'm telling you. I really, really got into it then. It just kinda took hold of me and consumed every waking hour. I was hooked, man. It was almost like I was on some sort of drug or something. It was just the pleasure of being able to sing and have people appreciate it.

The name the group eventually took, the Neptunes, arose out of a characteristic Latimore blend of playfulness and erudition. "We narrowed it down," he remembers.

I was always interested in the planets. I memorized when I was a kid in school, all the planets and their positions, and I can still do it now: Mercury, Venus, Earth, Mars, Jupiter, Saturn, Uranus, Neptune, Pluto. I was doing a takeoff on [the idea] that we were going to be "stars," but we were going to be actually somewhere in the system, the sky, like the planet Neptune. And the word *tune*, we thought it was clever, the word *tune* for "The Neptunes." Nineteen fifty-eight, I think it was. We went around town, we made a little something; we'd get a few bucks, we'd get on shows in some clubs.

What had once been a casual hobby had suddenly exploded into a forward-thrusting vortex of ambition. It became so all-encompassing, in fact, that he did the unthinkable: "I dropped out. I did not want to be going to school and not be totally absorbed and interested in my studies, because to me that would have just been throwing away my parents' money, and I did not want to do that. They were disappointed, but they respected me for coming to them and not just going on and going through the motions: 'It's your life, and you go ahead and do what you have to do, and when you find out'—not '*if* you find out,' but '*when* you find out'— 'that this is just a pipedream, you can always come back home. We'll see what we can do to support you, get you back in.'"

His musical horizons, though, kept expanding. "One of the guys had a brother-in-law who sang or played with a group called Louis Brooks and the Hi-Toppers. And Brooks had told him that their vocalist [Earl Gaines] was going to be going off on his own, and they were looking to have another vocalist. So the guy said, 'Why don't you try for it?'"

Louis Brooks[3] was a burly-toned tenor sax honker who recorded several sides for the Nashville-based Excello label in the 1950s, including "It's Love, Baby (24 Hours a Day)," with Gaines on vocals, which hit No. 2 R & B in 1955. Even though the Hi-Toppers were primarily a regional act (Brooks is said to have limited his touring because he didn't want to give up his day job at Nashville's First National Bank), a gig with them meant instant celebrity and, at least in theory, a lot more money than Benny had been making with the Neptunes.

Brooks's shows would feature his hit song, of course, but like most working bands, then and now, the Hi-Toppers tailored their act for audiences who wanted party music that was both danceable and familiar. "We did stuff that was out then," Latimore affirms. "Some bluesy things, some ballad things. This is late '50s, '59 and '60. You did blues, you did a variety of things."

"They were very patient with me," he admits. "All the guys were old enough to be my dad."

With the Hi-Toppers, Benny entertained at private parties in Nashville ("We'd have to put on the white dinner jackets. Have this big old vest too big for you") as well as in venues ranging from VFW clubs and fraternal lodges to rough-hewn country jukes.[4] Before long, he found his role in the band expanding. Dissatisfied with the group's regular piano player, Brooks made the newcomer an offer: "Louis came to me and said, 'How would you like to [both] play and sing? You can get paid more money.'

"I was very nervous. They were doing a lot of different kinds of things, some jazzy things and stuff. Louis Brooks was an excellent musician. I said, 'I can't play the chord changes to these songs that you guys do.'"

But braced by the work ethic he'd absorbed from Eddie and Edna Latimore, Benny rose to the challenge.

> I had a knack for hearing something and then going and finding it. Trial and error: I'd play something, and I'd add a note here, and I'd add a note there that sounded good to me. And [Brooks] worked with me. I'd go to his house, and he'd work with me, go over the entire repertoire. The lady that I rented a room from had a piano, and I'd practice on that piano every day, all day long, just trying to learn the songs. That was my job. Sat there and played 'til my fingers got raw.
>
> I got to where I was doing quite well with him. Of course, he never told me that until I put in my notice to leave. [Then] he told me he was proud of me and proud of the progress that I had made. I said, "How come you never told me?" He said, "Because I was afraid you might let your ego get too big and think you were good, and once you get to the point where you think you're good, you don't have a lot of room to grow. You think you got it." He said, "You will never ever stop learning."

Praise, in fact, was a rare commodity in those days. Latimore chuckles wryly as he remembers his first encounter with Ernie Young, owner of Excello, the label for which Louis Brooks had recorded his hit. "We went to the studio," he recalls. "I went to the men's room, and I came back out, and old man Ernie was talking to Louis, and I heard him say, 'Louis, that boy can't sing.' He said, 'I'm not gonna record this.'

"And it killed me. It killed me! Louis just [told me], 'Well, Mister Ernie didn't like the song, so we have to try to see if we could write something else.' But it was *me* he didn't like." He chortles again, then concludes: "I've often, over the years, I was hoping that he was still living, that I could go and say 'Yah, yah-yah, yah, yah!'" (Young died in Nashville on June 8, 1977.)[5]

It was time to move on, anyway. When not gigging with Brooks, Benny had been doing various one-off studio jobs around Nashville. He sang on demos for aspiring songwriters, and he also remembers being on a few legit country-and-western sessions in bands that included the likes of Jerry Reed and Ray Stevens. Another young vocalist, an erstwhile gospel singer named Joe Henderson,[6] was "hanging around the studios" as well. The two became friends, and in the timeless spirit of young blood brotherhood, they made a pact: "If you make it, you give me a job. If I make it, I'll give you a job."

In 1962, Henderson broke through with the bluesy "Baby Don't Leave Me" on Paul Cohen's New York–based Todd label, which he followed up immediately with "Snap Your Fingers," a deft fusion of R & B, pop, and country that stayed on the R & B charts for sixteen weeks, peaking at No. 2 (it also reached No. 8 on the Pop charts). "He called me up," Latimore relates, "and said, 'Okay, you ready?' I said, 'What do you mean, am I ready?' He said, 'You know the pact that we had made? I'm living up to it.' So I put in my notice to Louis and went on the road."

This time, it really was "the road," not merely the regional circuit Benny had traveled with Louis Brooks. Ironically, though, this also meant dealing with more musical uncertainty. A singer like Joe Henderson, with a couple of records out but not a fully established star, usually couldn't afford to carry an entire band. Instead, he might take one accompanist who knew his material or, at best, a core rhythm section. Local show bands would provide the rest of the backing. It's not that different from what often goes on along the southern soul-blues circuit today, and then, as now, it could take some savvy musicianship and quick thinking to make things work.

"I was his musical director," Latimore explains. "I learned all the parts. I knew all of his stuff. I knew all of his moves. We had charts; the horn players just read their parts. Then we pieced everything to the rhythm section. I kinda watched everybody to make sure that everybody watched me, and I got pretty good at it. He depended on me; I knew his stuff as well as he did. He didn't even have to go to rehearsals."

Henderson and his trusted pianist/musical director traveled widely, stringing along one-nighters "from one end of the country to the other," playing shows with such luminaries as Ben E. King, the "5" Royales, and Jackie Wilson. Benny also did some instrumental work on Henderson's 1962 LP *Snap Your Fingers,* which featured Boots Randolph on tenor sax, and he recalls that DeFord Bailey Jr., whose father had played harmonica on the original Grand Ole Opry and remained with the otherwise all-white revue until his controversial firing in 1941, played bass for Henderson for a while.[7] He still remembers the thrill of "makin' as much money in a night as my father used to make in a week." But Henderson, who died in 1964 at the age of 27,[8] was ill suited for the stresses and temptations of the traveling musician's life.

"Joe kind of had emotional problems," Latimore remembers, "and he was getting more and more into pills and stuff. He was my friend, and it was too much for me. I couldn't deal with him in that state." After getting "stranded in Indiana during a very, very cold winter," and with Henderson's behavior becoming increasingly erratic, Benny decided it was time to pull out.

A ready escape route was at hand. Some time earlier, after playing a show in Miami, Benny had dropped in on a club called the Knight Beat, located in the Sir John Hotel in the city's Overtown community (then known colloquially as "Colored Town"). A talent contest was under way, and on a whim he decided to enter. He sang Jackie Wilson's "To Be Loved" and brought the house down, but after the judges discovered he was a professional musician he was disqualified from winning. The club's owner, Clyde Killens, liked what he heard, though, and he gave the young singer his phone number and advised him to say in touch. Now, looking for a graceful exit from his situation with Henderson, Benny took Killens up on his offer. As luck would have it, the organ player in the Knight Beat's house band had just gotten sick. Killens, needing a quick replacement, bought Benny a plane ticket to Miami.

But Benny had been used to calling the shots on the bandstand. At the Knight Beat, working under someone else's authority, he got in trouble the first week. The Orlons, a pop-soul group from Philadelphia that had a string of hits in the early 1960s, had been booked into the club. The house band's vocalist had been doing some of their material in his own act and was being uncooperative. Benny, who'd encountered similar situations with local prima donnas while touring with Brooks, intervened and tried to smooth things out ("I'm thinkin' I'm making points, you know?"). The upshot was that the singer/bandleader complained to Killens—"This new guy is trying to take over my band"—and Killens responded by firing the man he'd just flown down to Miami at his own expense.

Whether out of sympathy or fiscal probity, though, he hired the youngster back, this time to perform solo during intermissions. "That was the best thing that ever happened to me," Latimore says now. "I was playing the organ, and I had a drummer. I was playing thirty minutes a night, just regular songs, R & B songs that were out at the time. I started making more money than I'd made with [the house band]. And I stood out—got to meet all the stars and all that, hang out with the stars."

He also found a mentor who taught him to think about music, as well as play it, in new ways. "His name was Joe Watson," remembers Latimore. "His nickname was Black Magic. World-class keyboard player. He encouraged me to sing songs like Broadway songs and some jazz songs, 'Bye, Bye Blackbird,' 'Fly Me to the Moon,' 'What Kind of Fool Am I'—he said, 'You got good phrasing. That'll make you better at the other things.'"

Watson helped Benny develop his keyboard technique, but he cautioned him against falling into the trap of overrelying on it. "He said, 'Technique doesn't mean anything; it's what you use that technique for. Technique is like having a Jaguar or a Ferrari in your driveway. If you can't drive it, if you can't get from point A to point B, you might as well have a Yugo.'"

Some of Watson's lessons were couched in the kind of aphoristic lyricism Benny would eventually embrace as his own. "All notes have been played," Watson told him. "All words have been spoken. Sometimes people talk fast, and they ain't sayin' shit. Then you got a person of few words, can really get the idea across. Jazz is improvisational; you're creating all the time, as you go. In the now. You gotta live in the now. Just go on, work on it, and learn how to sing through your fingers."

Benny eventually took his solo act into other venues, and before long he was playing with full bands again. This, in turn, led to his association with a pair of unlikely white hipsters whose combined efforts ignited the spark that eventually propelled him onto the charts.

No discussion of the independent record industry in the United States would be complete without including Steve Alaimo and Henry Stone, both of whom have managed the seemingly impossible feat of insinuating themselves directly into pop music's mainstream while retaining their cred as freethinking mavericks. Alaimo's résumé includes everything from hitting the pop charts as a balladeer (1963's "Every Day I Have to Cry") and hosting the mid-1960s teen-dance TV show *Where the Action Is* to producing sides on artists ranging from pre-Stax Sam & Dave (1961's "My Love Belongs to You" on Marlin) and pre–Allman Brothers Duane and Gregg Allman (in a band called the 31st of February) to the pop group Mercy ("Love [Can Make You Happy]" in 1969). Through the years, he's also owned or co-owned some of the most important indie labels in the business.

Alaimo's longtime business partner, Henry Stone, may come on these days as an aging down-home hepcat Buddha, but he's actually an urbane Bronx expatriate who dabbled in jazz trumpet as a youth before hustling his way into the record business in Los Angeles after being discharged from the military in 1946. By the late 1940s, he'd settled in Florida, and he's remained active there ever since, virtually creating the entire Sunshine

State recording industry in the process. He's probably best known for his T. K. label, which launched the career of KC and the Sunshine Band, among others, and garnered over twenty gold and platinum records in its disco-era heyday. But he has also been at the forefront of such less-famous but musically significant labels as Rockin,' Marlin, Glory (a gospel imprint), Alston, Brownstone, Cat, Chart, Dash, Blade, Dade, and Glades.

Any artist in southern Florida trying to break into the business in the early or mid-1960s had to cross paths with Stone and Alaimo at some point. In Benny's case, the connection was direct. He was co-leading a band with a drummer named Freddy Scott[9] when Alaimo hired them to back him up on shows and do some studio work (including, according to Latimore, some of the backing tracks Alaimo used on *Where the Action Is*). "Some of the places we would go and play behind [Alaimo]," he remembers, "the club owners would have us back, just us. We did that all around South Miami. I started playing on a lot of recordings, then they decided they'd record me. I played on all of Betty Wright's recordings; I played on Little Beaver's things,[10] Gwen McCrae and George McCrae, these are all T. K. people. Then later on, I played on Bobby Caldwell's 'What You Won't Do for Love' [issued on T. K.'s Clouds subsidiary in 1978]."

Benny's own early sides for Henry Stone,[11] first on the Blade label and then on Dade, showcased what was already a remarkably supple and nuanced vocal delivery. From the beginning, he could craft an emotional trajectory with precision. His 1965 debut, "I Can't Go on Anymore," was a minimalist gem of pop storytelling as he moved, over the course of less than two-and-a-half minutes, from a breathy near-whisper through a pleading midrange into a melodramatic ascent reminiscent of the Righteous Brothers, whom he has cited as early favorites.

Benny's organ accompaniment and a robust gospel choir lent churchy fervor to his reading of Doc Pomus's "The Power and the Glory," and again he displayed his mastery of emotional control as he built from an intimate croon into a house-wrecking finale, teasingly modulating his intensity at various points along the way. He infused Charlie Rich's "Life's Little Ups and Downs" with the kind of edge-of-tears urgency that might have drowned a lesser vocalist in bathos, but which he negotiated with the élan of a seasoned pro.

Alaimo's bass-heavy production and an accelerated tempo saddled Benny's take on the Bobby "Blue" Bland standard "I Pity the Fool" with a jarringly hyped-up feel, but the singer still summoned vocal pyrotechnics, including a few atypical gospel screams, that came close to rivaling Bland's own sanctified intensity. On the B-side ballad, "I'm Just an Ordinary Man,"

Benny summoned a world-weary resignation that again belied his relative youth. Although it never charted, "Fool"/"Man" was strong enough that Atlantic eventually picked it up and issued it on a disk that's now a collector's item.

But what probably ended up breaking him through as much as anything was Henry Stone's decision to upgrade his equipment. The sound coming out of Stone's studio was pretty primitive even by 1960s standards; by the early 1970s, it was downright atavistic. "Some of 'em were [recorded] upstairs on a little eight-track thing," Latimore recalls. "It was all kind of trial and error; we just didn't have the machinery to do it. Later, they got a nice board, still had to be somewhat creative with everything we did, but everything got a little bit better, and the engineering got a little bit better."

Along with the slick new sound, Benny adopted a slick new moniker—simply "Latimore"—and in October 1973, he released a jazzy, up-tempo cover of the T-Bone Walker blues classic "Stormy Monday," from his eponymous debut album on Glades. It hit the R & B charts and stayed there for sixteen weeks, peaking at No. 27. "Stormy Monday" hadn't been intended as the hit single from the album (Stone was betting on "Jolie," a pop-sweetened Al Kooper confection that might well have been the most lightweight offering Latimore had yet served up), but when disc jockeys played the song, the listener response was so enthusiastic that Stone decided to go with it. The sound was roomy and clear, and there was a newfound slickness to both Latimore's piano work and his vocals, although it didn't compromise the emotional immediacy—he was putting Joe Watson's tutelage to good use. The emotion this time, though, was jubilance, tempered by a hip insouciance that might have seemed at odds with the passionate sincerity that had been Latimore's calling card until then. Although it harked back to a similar treatment that Lou Rawls and pianist Les McCann had given the song back in 1962 (as the title song of a Blue Note LP), its propulsive, pop-tinged groove and Latimore's own jubilant vocal directness made this incarnation of the classic entirely his own.

The follow-up, "If You Were My Woman," an answer to Gladys Knight and the Pips' "If I Were Your Woman," returned him to his Lothario-with-a-heart-of-gold persona (as well as the throat-ripping deep-soul fervor he'd evidenced on "I Pity the Fool" a few years earlier). Then came the hit that would define his career:

We were doing an album [1974's *More More More Latimore*], and we needed another song. This was a song that I had kicking around in my head. It was inspired by a lot of different things—personal experience, and I get a chance to talk with a lot of people, being in this business, and people tell me things that they go through in life.

And I was always under the impression that until you sit down and talk about [something], nothing's gonna get done. You can't solve anything without sitting down and talking about it, and you gotta straighten it out. As long as it's crooked and going back and forth, back and forth, it ain't going anywhere. So just the whole idea, if you're having any kind of a relationship with another person, whether that's with a spouse, a girlfriend or boyfriend, a friend, or employer/employee, whatever—there's gonna be times when you're going to have some wrinkles and some ups and downs, and they have to be straightened out, or that particular relationship ain't going anywhere.

Clocking in at over five minutes, "Let's Straighten It Out" was too long for radio play; Stone and Latimore cut it by over two minutes for release as a single. But even on the longer album version, there wasn't a note wasted. Perhaps remembering Joe Watson's admonition to "sing through your fingers," Latimore crafted an extended keyboard intro that told the story as vividly as his lyrics. After building tension over the course of a twenty-eight-bar improvisation set to a single minor chord, he arrived at what sounded like the beginning of the actual song—only to fall silent, wait a moment, and then plunge into a new melodic theme (the refrain, as it turned out), before finally starting to sing: "Sit yourself down, girl, and talk to me . . ."

It was all intentional. "The whole idea," he explained to *Living Blues* in 1975, "is that he sees something is wrong. She's not really sayin' nothin' about it, you know, but she's givin' off all kinds of vibes. . . . [T]here's a part in there where you think that I'm gonna start to sing, and I don't. He's gettin' ready, now, here's these two people, sittin' around, lookin' at each other, and then one starts to—but then they don't, 'cause they don't know whether I should say it, or what."[12]

Latimore's supple baritone depicted a tenderhearted masculinity no doubt calculated to be both seductive to women and nonthreatening to men, but his lyrics amplified the emotional turmoil conjured up by the introduction. His protagonist alternately demands answers ("Now how in the hell do you expect me to understand / when I don't even know what's wrong?"), promises understanding ("If you're tired and you don't want to be bothered, baby / Just say the word, and I'll leave you alone"), vents his pent-up frustration ("Instead of layin' there, cryin' your eyes out, baby / you and me ought to be gettin' it on"), and pleads for a chance to set things right ("Let's straighten it out—baby, let's straighten it out").

Here, in one masterstroke, Latimore had both codified his musical persona and declared—perhaps to himself as much as to his listeners—his declaration of artistic intent. "I feel that it's my responsibility to have some sort of integrity in my work," he says today, echoing a theme he returns to often. "I just try to tell the truth and what I see as the truth—maybe to cause you to think about something a little bit deeper."

That's not to say he suddenly became sanctimonious. His hits over the next decade and a half included such fare as 1975's funkified "There's a Red-Neck in the Soul Band" (a shout-out to white guitarist Joey Murcia, a longtime musical partner); "Qualified Man," from 1976, with its burbling synth-funk rhythm track, good-natured lyric machismo, and wink-wink references to "Let's Straighten It Out"; and 1979's "Discoed to Death," a somewhat quixotic but pointed fulmination against the prevailing musical fad of the time.

But the die had been cast. So powerful was the image Latimore created with "Let's Straighten It Out" that it's been the context for virtually all of his success since then. It's an image he's expanded upon, both in his own songs and the ones he's accepted from others, until what began with a simple tale of romantic atonement has grown into something close to an all-encompassing philosophical stance. Carnality and transcendence, earthly pleasure and redemptive grace—Latimore melds them as ardently as he fused eroticism and penitence in "Let's Straighten It Out."

"Take me to the mountaintop!" he exhorts his lover in the song of that title; "I don't care / let me die"—bringing biblical fervor to erotic desire (and, perhaps, throwing a bit of Mosaic signifying in the direction of Al Green's baptismal "Take Me to the River," also recorded in 1975 by Syl Johnson, who scored a hit with the song). To a woman wrestling with guilt and memory, he offers reassurance: "It ain't where you been," he sings, backed by a percolating dance groove, "It's where you're going . . . Don't start feeling guilty, baby / 'bout the things you might have done / Let not your heart be troubled / you're not the only one." It's all a pickup line, of course ("I don't care about your past," he assures her, "I don't have to be the first one / as long as I'm the last"), but so deft is his blend of rapture and reassurance that it's almost impossible not to be seduced.

Turning his attention to the men (and knowing, of course, that the women are still listening), he warns them that they'd better take his hard-won advice, "stop half-loving these women," and "keep the home fire burnin.'" "Dig a little deeper," he preaches, "You might find what you're looking for, right at home."

Figure 7. Latimore, 2004 Sunflower River Blues and Gospel Festival, Clarksdale, Mississippi. Photo by Gene Tomko.

Even when he gets more graphic, Latimore manages to stay gallant; he tries to make all the women within the sound of his voice feel sexy and admired, while assuring each one that if she were his, she'd be cherished forever. Even songs like "Whoop That Thang on Me" and "'Nanna Pud-din'" turn out to be celebrations of shared ecstasy rather than wham-bang sexual release. He may show his lascivious side in a girl-watcher's anthem like "Pretty Women," but more characteristic is "The Only Way Is Up," in which he promises his lady that despite hard times, they're in it together for the long haul.

Perhaps his most explicit boast is his aging player's anthem "I'm an Old Dog," a grinding, guitar-heavy blues from 2000's *You're Welcome to Ride* on Malaco (reprised on his 2011 LatStone CD *Ladies Choice*). "I can make that little bitty man in the boat / stand up and salute!" he proclaims. "I may be old, but I ain't cold / I still know how to bury the bone." Even here, though, and especially in live performance, the outrageousness of his claims, his uncharacteristically mannered delivery, and his cartoonish leer make the song seem more like fantasy, if not self-satire, than the droolings of a dirty old man.

In a sense, it hardly matters anyway—everything he does is merely prelude to the inevitable. "Let's Straighten It Out" is the obligatory climax of any Latimore show, and he's mastered the craft of contouring his performances to build up to that moment. This leads, inevitably, to a certain sameness over the long haul. Like most soul-blues artists who enjoyed at least some success in the soul era, Latimore hasn't had a major hit in years. Although he charted fifteen times between 1973 and 1991 and has continued to record strong material since then—on Malaco, whom he joined after leaving Henry Stone's shop in the early 1980s and more recently on LatStone, the label he and Stone co-founded in 2008—most of his releases since the early 1990s have sold moderately, even by the relatively lenient standards of the southern soul-blues market. What this means is that, aside from the addition of a newer offering or two that may have made some regional noise in the South, a Latimore show in 2013 probably looks and sounds a lot like a Latimore show from five, ten, or maybe even fifteen years earlier.

"Sometimes it's frustrating," he admits. "When I'm doing shows myself, just me, and I got plenty of time, I can get to a lot of other stuff. But if the people have not heard it, if it was never played on the radio, the general crowd will say, 'Hey, why did you do that, and you didn't do so-and-so?' I mostly have to do the ones that were the most popular."

He tries his best to keep it fresh. "'Let's Straighten It Out,'" he knows, "is the song that they always are waiting on."

> I have different introductions that I use on it. Even when I do my talking and stuff, I don't say the same thing every time; I might add some subtleties. I do that with all my songs. When you're in person, that's the time to work the story, get the people involved in it, headwise, with their attention. If you can leave the people with a good taste in their mouths,

then you've accomplished your job. The melody that they hear in their head when they leave is what's most important.

But if lack of chart recognition and the threat of stagnation get discouraging, he doesn't show it. It would be easy to write off as disingenuous his insistence that "I'm not one of these people who enjoys being everywhere, traveling, and going from place to place. I enjoy being at home," but he was saying pretty much the same thing at the height of his success as a hit maker. In his 1975 interview with *Living Blues,* he complained about the "hassles" of touring and even suggested that "I was probably happier [before stardom] than I am now, in a sense."[13]

Today, as he warms to the subject and begins to offer up his philosophies on life, art, career, and family, it becomes even easier to take him at his word. "I enjoy the fact that people appreciate my music in different places," he asserts.

> But if I could do like they did in *Star Trek,* when it's time for me to go on, say "Now, ladies and gentlemen, Latimore"—and I'd step in this thing and they'd beam me up, I'd do my little thing, and when I'm done, I take my little bow and step into the thing and beam me back, I'd love that. Unfortunately, that's not the way it is. The reality of it is that I have to be out. But I come back home as quickly as I can, and I try to keep home at the forefront. In other words, I don't let show business completely consume me. It's what I do and not necessarily what I am. I try to keep that balance, as much of a balance as I can.
>
> I live out in the country, about a hundred and twenty miles from Miami. I enjoy not having a lot of traffic and not having to stand in line for everything, and it's inspirational, too. I can sit down by my pond and write songs; come home, don't have a schedule. I just want to get up and enjoy the day.

Benny Latimore, the "Miami Sex Machine," as a country squire jotting down his musings in Emersonian pondside solitude? "That's how I keep my head together," he affirms. "I don't go out and have to be seen. In fact, I'd rather not even be that guy 'Latimore' when I'm out. I'm happy just having a nice, comfortable home, being quiet."[14]

When he's not writing songs by the pond, he's often reading Khalil Gibran, the Lebanese-born philosopher/poet whose book *The Prophet* became a New Age touchstone in the 1960s and '70s. Latimore likes to point out that contrary to the "roving bluesman" stereotype, he's been married to his wife, Yvonne, for over forty years, despite the toll taken by his frequent absences and the pitfalls of a traveling musician's life.

The key, he says, may lie partly in one of his favorite Gibran passages—which, not coincidentally, draws an analogy between musical and conjugal harmony:

> The thing he did on marriage and relationships says to stay together, but not too close together, "for the strings of the lute stand apart, though they quiver with the same music." Two notes right together make a dissonant sound. But if you split it just a little bit and put something in between it, it can be harmonious. If you're too close together, you know, you're doing everything the same way. My wife is not that impressed with what I do, as a fan or anything like that. She sees what I do, and she appreciates that, but I don't have to impress her. We just kick back here, watch a little TV, some popcorn or something, or we have some people over, some friends of ours, the same friends that I've had for years. Just relax.
>
> I don't like being stereotyped. Sometimes they think of a "blues" guy as like an older guy who is basically rural, and very little sophistication. They feel that they can predict what you're going to do, and what you can do, and what you're able to do. There's very few stereotypes that a person can really put me into. I can come from a lot of different directions.

It's probably not a stretch to suggest that this same reflective outlook has played a role in the consistency of his music through the years. In an age when southern soul-blues is increasingly criticized for assembly-line production and unimaginative or clichéd lyrics, he remains steadfast in his determination to create work of artistic as well as (he hopes) commercial value. The results have been varied, of course (his 1983 Malaco remake of "Let's Straighten It Out," he believes, "failed to capture the real feeling of the song," and most listeners would probably agree), but it's difficult to find anywhere in his legacy a single track that sounds thrown together, sloppily produced, or otherwise in violation of what he holds as his aesthetic and ethical standards.

Unlike many of his generation, for instance, Latimore has made the transition from "live" to synthesized recording techniques with a minimum of discomfort and little noticeable change in quality. "Technology is a terrible master," he says. "But it's a good slave, if you know how to handle it."

> Too many people think they can go in the studio, "Oh, I can do this, I got Pro Tools. Oh yeah! Pro Tools!" These guys go in there, and it sounds like they did it in their kitchen or something. I [use] the new technology, but we're all musicians; we don't try to just turn the machine on and let it play a drum track and this or that. We *play* it with that; we *play* our stuff. In other words, we let [technology] do the heavy lifting. It's our slave.

Always conscious of his image as well as his professed dedication to integrity, he takes a similar moderation-in-all-things approach toward lyrics, even his more explicit ones. He continues to insist that music, at least for him, is most meaningful when it both touches the heart and stimulates, even challenges, the imagination. And, of course, if he can't believe in what he's doing, he'd rather not do it at all.

> I can say things for an adult group, because if you're adult enough you will understand what I'm talking about. [But] I think it shows a lack of class when you just go for, "Let's see if I can get dirtier than the other guy." There's less artistry. It's like underestimating the intelligence of the audience, and it appeals to the lowest common denominator.
>
> There's a lot of people that's attracted to that. But with me, if that's what I have to do, I wouldn't be honest. 'Cause that's not what I would personally feel. I'd just be doing it to get a rise out of people. To me, I feel good when I can go on the stage and do my thing, and I can get up there and I can get just as much response when I tell my little stories on the stage, and I don't get up there and do a lot of cussing and all that fuss. I try to tell what I see as the truth and be honest about it.

"You see," he concludes, "I capture the essence of the thing. I capture the feeling. That's what I try to do—I capture the feeling."

2

Denise LaSalle
Still the Queen

"I had a problem when it come time to become an artist," Denise LaSalle reflects as she relaxes over coffee in the spacious kitchen of her ranch-style home in Jackson, Tennessee. "I had to fight with Satan on that one."

The year, she remembers, was 1963,[1] and Chicago was emerging once again as a hotbed of black pop music. The Delta-tinged blues of the 1950s had faded in popularity, but a new, more upbeat, youth-oriented sound was rising. Nurtured in the church tradition of rich vocal harmonies but usually conveying a less fervid emotionalism than most gospel, it was a buoyant, often lushly arranged style (dubbed "soft soul" in later years), reflecting the optimism and aspirations of 1960s-era urban youth. Artists such as Gene Chandler, Jan Bradley, the Dells, and Jerry Butler and the Impressions were among its major figures. A host of independent record companies were scouting the city for new hopefuls and trying to break them into the market. The redoubtable Chess label, as usual, was among those leading the chase.

On the South Side, a barmaid at Mix's Lounge near

the corner of Fifty-First Street and Calumet Avenue had been watching all this with mounting interest. Ora Denise Craig, recently married and even more recently separated, had come to Chicago from Belzoni, Mississippi, a few years earlier. She had musical talent—she'd sung gospel most of her life—and she also had literary ambitions: she'd already placed stories in the magazines *Tan* and *True Confessions*. Freelance writing, though, was a gamble. "I got eight manuscripts returned," she remembers today, "and that's when I started thinking about writing songs."

Fortuitously, one of the regulars at Mix's was in a position to help. Pianist and vocalist Billy "The Kid" Emerson was a veteran of Ike Turner's Kings of Rhythm who had recorded in both Memphis (on Sun) and Chicago (on Vee-Jay and Chess, among others) and was also a respected songwriter. His credits included "When It Rains It Pours" (eventually popularized by Elvis as "When It Rains, It Really Pours") and "Red Hot," which Billy Lee Riley recorded for Sun in 1957 and has since become a rock-and-roll classic. When Emerson came into Mix's one afternoon, she showed him some of her songs. He liked what he saw (in more ways than one; the two became lovers), and he offered to record a demo for her.

The song she sang for him, "Tears" ("I can't see the clock for the tears"), never made it onto an actual record, but when Emerson took the demo to Chess, the company was sufficiently impressed to invite her in. For her audition, she laid new vocals over the backing tracks of some recordings that Chess vocalist Mildred Cummings, better known as Miss Cornshucks, had already made. As Denise remembers it, Chess offered her a contract almost immediately after that. But an unexpected barrier arose: Denise—who'd been proudly independent all her life, who'd left home as a teenager against her mother's wishes to get married, who'd been pursuing her dream of becoming a writer undaunted by turndowns and disappointment—found herself stricken with fear. "I would not sign a contract," she recalls. "I was scared to death of that."

> I had never sung by myself; I had always sung with a group. With the gospel group, I was singing tenor and never led a song and all that, so I refused to do it.
>
> I'll tell you what happened, and this is truth as ever I've told. All the jobs I had had been on my feet. And I was having problems down in my stomach and my back all the time [from] standing on my feet, working on concrete. I had been running back and forth to the doctor, and I had been praying about that. And [after] I turned that down, I was in my bed one night. I'm sleeping—I'm by myself, had no man, just a little basement apartment, [a] house my godmother lived in—and I felt a weight on the side of the bed, as though somebody had sat down. And a voice said to me, "You asked me

Figure 8. Denise LaSalle, LaMont's Entertainment Complex, Indian Head, Maryland, August 26, 2006. Photo by Ron Weinstock.

for a better way to make a living. Now I've shown you, you won't take it."
I'm struggling, trying to wake up and see who is this talking to me? You
ever have a dream like that, where you're dreaming, and you're struggling to
wake up and you can't? Like somebody was holding me down. The minute
I felt the weight get up off the bed, my eyes opened and I got up.

   I kept walking around the house, looking for somebody. And I said,
"Now think about what was said to you." I started thinking about, evaluat-

ing the words that were said to me. And I went to work at the lounge the next day. A young man [there], used to talk God to me all the time. He was a very devout Christian. He'd come in, and we'd talk all the time. I asked him about that dream. I said, "But I'm scared to do that. I've never sung by myself; I've always had someone on the stage with me." He gave me, to read, he gave me some books. *The Power of Positive Thinking* by Norman Vincent Peale and [a book] by Napoleon Hill. I read those books and I said, "I'm ready. I'm ready to go see Chess Records." I went to see Chess Records, and the rest is history.

• • •

Even as a girl growing up in Belzoni, Mississippi, Ora Denise Allen felt destined to go her own way. Born on July 16, 1941, in rural LaFlore County, she moved to Belzoni with her family when she was about seven years old. She sang in church ("Oh yes—my mom wouldn't have it no other way"), but in Belzoni she also heard the earthier sounds of R & B and early rock and roll emanating from a jukebox in a cafe across the street from where she lived. She remembers being thrilled by the sensuality and life force she could feel in the voices of such artists as Dinah Washington, the Dominoes, Hank Ballard ("Work With Me Annie"), and Chuck Berry.

But it wasn't dreams of musical stardom that compelled her to leave home. "Dr. King's movement had started," she remembers. "People were very mean, very violent in those days."

> I knew that I would probably be one of the dead ones, because I know I couldn't take what a lot of people took, and I would have to be sassy and fight back. Probably end up getting killed, so I just wanted to make sure I got out of there as soon as possible. My mother said the only way I would get out of the house, I would have to be married, and if I had a baby she'd put me out. I didn't want her to put me out about having no baby, so I wouldn't do that. She took me to Chicago on vacation; my oldest brother was there, and my sister was there. And while I was up there I met a boy. I came back home, and I tried to get my mom to let me go [back] to Chicago, stay with my brother. And she said, "No way—ain't no way you gonna leave here. You have to get married if you're going to go away." And I ran off and married that guy.

As she remembers it, she was only thirteen at the time, although she also says she heard Chuck Berry's "School Day" while she was still in Belzoni, and that record didn't debut on the charts until 1957, so it's possible she was closer to sixteen. She was underage, in any case, which explains the confusion that's arisen over the years about exactly when she was born. "We were all born out in the country to a midwife," she explains, "and there was no record of our birth. My baby brother was the only one with a birth certificate." That made it easy for her to falsify her birthdate when she got married. For years, she says, both her Social Security card and driver's license gave the year as 1934; these days most accounts suggest 1939 instead of 1941.

The woman who would eventually become famous for calling out no-good men in her songs doesn't seem to have taken her own first husband very seriously. "He ain't even worth talkin' about!" she snorts. "I won't even call his name. I just ran off and got married—a means to an end. I only did that for one reason, so I could get the hell out of Mississippi. I didn't stay with him. I went to my brother's house and moved in with my brother."

Determined to forge a life for herself, the newly renamed Ora Denise Craig attended night school, sang in a female gospel group called the Sacred Five, and found work at various places—in a dry cleaner, in a bakery—before finally landing the barmaid job at Mix's, which brought Billy Emerson into her life and led to her first break as a recording artist. That break, though, didn't come overnight.

"Chess asked Billy Emerson to get me started," she recollects. "He started taking me, entering me in contests and all that, and I started winning first place and stuff. I got a job at this place called the Trocadero [Lounge, on South Indiana Avenue], fifteen dollars a night. Three-night weekend. I worked there for almost two years. And [my] price went up, and I started branching out to other places. Billy was taking me around to all of the clubs, and I was singing with his band and other people's bands and stuff like that. And that's how I got started."

Meanwhile, though, what had looked like a career opportunity at Chess wasn't turning out that way. "Chess never recorded me," she relates. "They kept me under contract for a whole year. They had Jackie Ross, they had Mitty Collier, and they had Etta James at that time. They didn't need me. So when the year was up, I wrote them a letter asking for a release from the contract. Then they want me to come down there and record! 'We'll have a record cut on you in two weeks.' I said, 'I've been here one year, you didn't record it. Now I'm gone.'"

Looking back, she believes that gender politics had something to do with what happened. "I could have been real big," she muses. "Matter of fact, I think I could have recorded that first year with Chess, had I been the kind that they could take advantage of. I used to go down there, and they want to know why did I bring Billy with me every time I come; I never would go by myself. It looked like they wanted me to come by myself so they could talk me into some couch action or whatever they wanted. But

I wasn't for nothing [like that]. I just stayed out of that position, never let them get me in that predicament. So the year went by, I never cut nothing. I always felt that this was probably the reason."

She continued to work locally under Emerson's tutelage, and in 1967 he finally issued her debut single, "A Love Reputation," on his newly formed Tarpon label. For the occasion she created yet another name for herself: "My first name is Ora. I told nobody that name, because I didn't want it used. My daddy gave me that name, and I hated that name. So I just dropped Ora altogether and went for Denise." Contrary to some previous accounts, she also says that "LaSalle" was her idea ("I named myself; Billy Emerson just called me Denise"), adapted from a character she'd seen in a *Mary Worth* comic strip.

Although rather crudely produced by today's standards, "A Love Reputation" exemplified Chicago soul at its most buoyant. But it was not, strictly speaking, an entirely new creation: once again, Denise laid her vocals over someone else's previously recorded accompaniment. Emerson, credited as co-writer, lifted the instrumental track from "Just Like the Weather," which had been cut by Chicago-based vocalist Nolan Chance and released on the Constellation label in 1965.[2]

It was still an impressive debut. Pushed by a throbbing bass line and a robust horn section, the song was both propulsive and sprightly (in contrast, for instance, to the raw, driving attack then coming out of Stax). Its blend of streetsy energy and touch-of-class sophistication was clearly designed to appeal to young African American listeners reveling in their newfound status as "American teenagers," declaring their independence from the lifestyle and values of their country-born, working-class parents.

The singer, though, sounded bent on arousing more primal passions. Affecting a disarmingly girlish mewl, Denise proclaimed herself a red-hot young seductress on the prowl ("I'll steal your man, little girl. . . . I can't help it 'cause I know how to love / Mama says it's in my blood"). Over the next few years, as her voice matured, she'd abandon the baby-girl–sexpot image (it never really fit her in the first place), but "A Love Reputation" was nonetheless a tantalizing foretaste of the musical persona she would eventually claim as her own.

Chess eventually picked up "A Love Reputation" and reissued it under their own imprint, but it still never charted nationally. Tarpon wasn't going very far as a company, either, and Denise began to suspect that it was coming time for her to make another getaway. Not long after "A Love Reputation" broke, Chicago disc jockey E. Rodney Jones put her on the bill for a Jackie Wilson show he was bringing into the Regal Theater—

probably her biggest opportunity up to that point. A dispute with Emerson over who'd accompany her ("Red Saunders's band was playing for everybody, and Billy wanted to play for me") resulted in her being taken off the show. "I ended up falling out with Billy over that," she says. "I told him, 'Well, I tell you what. You can't be my man and be my manager. So we just gonna have to let that go. You got me started out here; I thank you for what you've done, but that's it.'"

Not long after that (or possibly a little before), Denise met a local businessman named Bill Jones, whom she married about two years later.[3] She has said that "A Love Reputation" kept her pretty active during that time, but she wasn't about to settle for being a one-city, one-hit wonder. In 1969, she and Jones launched Crajon Productions ("Cra-" from "Craig"; "-jon" from "Jones"). Operating out of their South Side home (and later out of the new Chess headquarters at 320 East Twenty-First Street),[4] they incorporated their own publishing company, Crajon Music, and set up three labels: Gold Star, Parka, and Crajon itself. Obviously, they were thinking big; this wasn't going to be just a vanity operation for self-produced Denise LaSalle records.

Denise's first few attempts at coming up with a follow-up to "A Love Reputation" failed. Then she heard a record that astounded her. In 1969, a Detroit disc jockey and would-be singer named Al Perkins had a hit with "Yes, My Goodness, Yes" on Atco. "Al couldn't sing," Denise says. "He couldn't stay in tune and couldn't keep time. And when I heard Al's record—'Who could do this? If he can make Al Perkins sound good, and Al Perkins can't stay in tune or in time, what could he do for me?'"

"He" was Willie Mitchell, the producer who would eventually go on to create some of the most influential music in all of R & B out of his now-legendary studio at 1320 South Lauderdale in Memphis, Tennessee (Al Green, Ann Peebles, and O. V. Wright are among the artists whose careers he helped launch). A year or so before Perkins's unlikely hit, Denise had discovered a tough-voiced soul shouter named Bill Coday at a South Side club called the Black Orchid. With an eye toward building her label as well as her own career, she brought him along on her first trip to Memphis to record for Mitchell. "And then," she chuckles, "he got a hit, and I didn't."

At least not right away. Coday's first two Crajon releases made some noise around Chicago; his third, "Get Your Lie Straight" (credited to "O. Denise Jones"), broke nationally in 1971. Another Crajon act, a Chicago-based girl group called the Sequins, scored with "Hey Romeo" (an uncharacteristically teen-dreamy Willie Mitchell production) on Gold Star in 1970. Meanwhile, "The Right Track," the first side Mitchell produced on Denise, showcased a much more mature-sounding vocalist than the Lolita-like temptress of "A Love Reputation." Digging into her gospel roots on this remake of a 1966 Billy Butler hit (and trying a bit too obviously to emulate Aretha Franklin), she sounded on the verge of transcendence as she sang of keeping the faith through hard times ("I've been trying to reach my goal too long / to give up on my journey now"), melding spiritual and worldly aspiration in the deep-soul tradition. The production was clean and roomy; Mitchell's arrangement, with its swaggering horns and driving bass, exploded with energy yet retained his trademark unhurried feel. Crajon was unable to capitalize on it at the time ("We didn't have no money, didn't know nothing about distribution," Denise has said;[5] it was eventually issued on Parka in 1972), but "The Right Track" was without a doubt her most fully realized effort to date.

She followed it up with "Hung Up Strung Out," which also didn't chart but opened some important ears. Detroit-based Westbound Records, which had entered into a distribution deal with Crajon not long after its own inception in 1970 (and would go on to include on its roster such R & B legends as the Ohio Players and Funkadelic), sensed a hit-maker in the making and offered Denise a contract. This put her in the odd position of competing against her own record company, but the arrangement seemed to work, at least for a while. In 1971, her "Trapped by a Thing Called Love" on Westbound made it all the way to No. 1, and Denise LaSalle was a national recording star at last. Again produced by Mitchell, with his signature easy-rolling, "lazy" horn lines impelling the rhythm, "Trapped by a Thing Called Love" showcased Denise's youthful yet worldly sounding mezzo-soprano testifying to a romantic entrapment so delectable that the prisoner couldn't help but loving her own chains. Even when singing about being tied down, Denise managed to sound like a free spirit.

Most of her other Westbound output was even more assertive. The hard-charging, blues-inflected "Now Run and Tell That," her follow-up to "Trapped by a Thing Called Love," found her telling off a "two-timin,' four-flushin,' street-talkin' John" as the horns laid on an appropriately rigorous ass-kicking; "Man Sized Job" was her first in a long line of sexual throw-downs to players whose prowess doesn't live up to their promises; titles such as "My Brand on You" and "What It Takes to Get a Good Woman (That's What It's Gonna Take to Keep Her)" were pretty much self-explanatory.

But Denise was more than a signifying party girl. In "Married, but Not to Each Other," for instance, she brought a rare emotional complexity to the well-worn "cheating song" theme. Neither a sinner's confession nor an adventuress's boast, the song laid bare the emotional maelstrom endured by a woman willing—or perhaps compelled—to "hurry up and love him, hurry up and please him," only to go back home and "make believe that you've been good / give your love to the one you should / but you can't," as the specter of personal and emotional ruin looms closer with each illicit tryst.

This was knowing, sophisticated pop, worldly beyond run-of-the-mill Top Ten fare, yet delivered with Denise's paradoxically youthful panache. Even as her voice seemed to toughen and deepen with each release, it retained the life-affirming brightness that had characterized it since the beginning. Although she wasn't working with Willie Mitchell anymore ("After Willie got a hit on Al Green, everybody was running to Willie. He was busy every time I wanted to go into the studio"), she continued to use Memphis session talent. Trumpeter Gene "Bowlegs" Miller arranged and/or produced most of her Westbound output after "Trapped by a Thing Called Love." The results were often stunning, even on records that weren't major hits. "Get Up Off My Mind" only reached No. 96 in 1974, but its stylistic blend—a Delta-fried blues guitar intro that segued into a bass-heavy rhythmic and melodic line borrowed from Motown, seasoned by congas and punched by JB-derived horn blasts—bespoke the kind of roots-rich yet forward-looking exploratory zeal that was already becoming rare in an increasingly homogenized pop milieu.

But on the home front, things weren't going so well. Crajon wasn't thriving. The Sequins never again charted nationally after "Hey Romeo," and Coday's success with "Get Your Lie Straight" had proved a mixed blessing. "I leased Coday to Galaxy," Denise remembers. "'Get Your Lie Straight' got so hot and so big, and we didn't have the distributorship for it to keep up the pressing. Galaxy asked us for the master, and we leased it to them. And that's where he stayed, with them." Coday hit again in 1971 with Denise's song "When You Find a Fool Bump His Head," again issued on Galaxy. But despite the power of his gospelly baritone, and although he enjoyed something of a southern soul comeback with a series of CDs on Ecko and his own B & J imprint in the 1990s and 2000s, he never had another chart hit. He suffered a stroke and died in Memphis on June 7, 2008.

By 1974, both Crajon and the Joneses' relationship had run their course. Denise knew what had to be done, but as her fellow Willie Mitchell protégé O. V. Wright would sing a few years later, there was no easy way to say goodbye. "I divorced my husband, and I went to Memphis. I loved Chicago. I didn't want to come to Memphis, but I had to put some miles between me and that man, or I'd've been gone back to him. And I was determined I was not going back."

Not long after she moved, her contract with Westbound expired (1975's country-styled *Here I Am Again* was her swan-song LP for the label), and she signed with ABC. With the notable exception of Ray Charles, ABC had never been known as a deep soul stronghold, and it's questionable whether Denise ever really felt at home there. She insists that she still produced all of her own material, but for the most part, little of her trademark soulfulness came through. She didn't chart for almost a year after "Married, but Not to Each Other," and when she did, it was with "Freedom to Express Yourself" from *Second Breath,* her ABC debut LP (which she describes as "a dud, as far as I was concerned"). The song scraped to No. 100 in April 1977.

As if stung by the tepid reaction to *Second Breath,* Denise stormed back in 1977 with an album that, at least on its surface, looked like her most audacious effort yet. The front cover portrayed her poolside at what could have been either a Grecian or Roman bath, standing triumphantly atop a tiger-skin rug. Clad in a slinky black gown with a slit that revealed a muscular but soft-skinned thigh emerging from its folds, she was smiling in apparent ecstasy as she clutched herself, looking both consumed with desire and inflamed by her own touch. On the back cover, a shaven-headed hunk emerged from the pool to run his palm up her leg as she snapped herself erect in a pose of victory. In case anyone still missed the point, the LP's name drove it home: *The Bitch Is Bad!*

Even for a self-proclaimed envelope-pusher like Denise, it was a daring move. If this wasn't the first time the "B-word" had been used in main-stream black pop music, it was almost certainly the first time it had been displayed so openly.[6] "I didn't think nothing about it," Denise maintains today. "Richard Pryor was using it all the time." But she confirms that "when I cut *The Bitch Is Bad!*, that was sorta the beginning. Millie Jackson came right back with *Feelin' Bitchy* [the same year]."

She also says that her seemingly newfound brazenness was the result of a natural progression that had begun with her very first single: "I did kinda raunchy lyrics in the beginning. I shied away from [some of] the words, but really I could've gone there at any time. On my shows I went there, but I didn't do it on the records. . . . Even when I started out in Chicago, I went as far as the law allowed, without going over."

Musically, though, *The Bitch Is Bad!* blazed no new trails, and in fact much of it sounded like a disco-era compromise. Even the title tune, a strobe-bedazzled tale of dance-floor intrigue, failed to live up to its bill-ing: the "bitch" turned out to be the singer's rival, not the singer herself.

Significantly, "Love Me Right," the LP's biggest hit, was a throwback. Set to a slow-rolling ballad cadence, it allowed Denise to summon her old erotic fire; she managed to make lines like "Do it to me right" and "Let me be your dessert" sound like assertions of erotic power, and her orgasmic gasps at the end were nothing less than aural aphrodisiacs. The song peaked at No. 10. But the other single culled from *The Bitch Is Bad!*, "One Life to Live"—a bride's testimonial of devotion, eloquently written but smothered under billowing cotton-candy strings—only made it to No. 87. Denise would never reach the Top Fifty again.

By this time, she'd remarried and moved to Jackson, Tennessee, where her husband, James Wolfe, was a celebrity disc jockey known as "Super-Wolf" on WDXI. As she struggled to stay on the charts, her creativity seemed to falter, or at least change direction. "Workin' Overtime" in 1978 was a gutsy, gospel-tinged, deep-soul testimonial, but the following year's "P.A.R.T.Y. (Where It Is)" saddled her blues-toughened delivery with a burbling disco backdrop. The slick disco sheen of 1980's "I'm So Hot" couldn't hide the fact that the song was pitched too high for her vocal range (apparently an attempt to make her sound younger), and the message, such as it was, never went any deeper than "I'm so hot, so upset / you've got me soaking wet." It was a long way down from gems like "Married, but Not to Each Other."

At least some of this probably reflected commercial dictates more than creative decline. Judging from the live version of "Trapped by a Thing Called Love" on her 1979 LP *Unwrapped* (in a medley that also included the 1967 Bettye Swann hit "Make Me Yours" and Jackie Moore's "Precious, Precious"), her stage act never lost either its emotional directness or its soulfulness. And buried on various B-sides and tracks from her LPs during these years was evidence—"Think about It," from *Unwrapped*, "Sometimes" and the proto-soul-blues "You'll Never Get Your Hooks in My Man" from *I'm So Hot* in 1980—that her songwriting muse also remained strong.

At this juncture, though, she "did something messed up" that torpedoed any future she might have had with her record company. In the wake of "I'm So Hot" (issued on MCA, the conglomerate to which ABC now belonged), Denise's husband asked her for a copy of the backing track so he could use it to create a theme for his radio show. "I made him a track and he rapped on it: 'Super-Wolf Can Do It.' I should've offered it to MCA, but I didn't. I put it out on our own label, Ordena. Joe Robinson from All Platinum Records, Sylvia Robinson's husband, he came to me and asked me to lease it to him. So to get that money, I leased it to him [the Robinsons issued it on Sugar Hill, thereby ensuring it immediate respect in the rap world]. When I got ready to go back into the studio and called for my budget, they said, 'Well, we changed our mind. We think we won't do any more records.' They released me from my contract." Her final MCA album, *And Satisfaction Guaranteed,* appeared with little commercial fanfare in 1981.

It was time to move on, anyway. By the early 1980s, not even the most titillating lyrics could hide the fact that Denise's style and sound no longer represented the mainstream of contemporary R & B. Soon, though, the success of "Down Home Blues" would revitalize the fusion of bluesy deep soul and modernist lyric signifying that represented her strongest suit.

It was almost as if they saw her coming. Not long after MCA released her, Denise received a call from legendary promo man Dave Clark, now ensconced at Malaco, asking her to write a new song for Z. Z. Hill. Clark wanted a "Down Home Blues" soundalike. The song Denise wrote, "Someone Else Is Steppin' In," was set to the same changes and the same rhythm as Hill's smash. It was also a classic LaSalle tale of erotic combat that allowed Hill to inhabit the persona of a wrongdoing man paying for his transgressions—a surefire selling point in a market where women have traditionally been the major consumers.

Malaco "fell so in love with that song, they called me back and asked what was I doing," Denise recollects. "I said, 'I'm not doing anything right now. I've been without a record company for about a year.'"

> They said, "Well, you want to cut something?" I said, "I don't sing the blues." I thought blues singers had to have curly voices, y'know, like the way they throw their voice out and curl it all around. But they said, "Well, you write the blues real well. We're willing to try it, if you could write yourself something." So I wrote "You Can Have My Husband, but Please Don't Mess with My Man." I had never done no hard-core blues. [But] when I did "Don't Mess with My Man," I went raw. And it turned out to be a smash, instant smash. So I said, "Well, okay. This what y'all want, I'll go for it." So I started cutting using guitar solos, the style that they did as blues. I stayed at Malaco sixteen or seventeen years.

In many ways, this was a strange new world for Denise to work in. For one thing, it was a market where one didn't necessarily need a major chart hit to be successful. In fact, the very notion of what a "hit" might be was somewhat vague ("You Can Have My Husband," Denise's "smash," never charted nationally). But an artist with sufficient appeal could still move enough records and garner enough exposure to keep her name in the public ear and maintain a consistent touring schedule. If a lot of the venues now felt more like earlier-era chitlin' circuit show lounges than the theaters and nightclubs a Top-Ten veteran like Denise might have been used to, and if success on this new circuit might mean embracing a "blues" aesthetic that many still denigrated as passé—well, the former Ora Denise Allen from Belzoni, Mississippi, was used to turning stumbling blocks into stepping stones.

In 1985, she broke into the charts again, this time with her cover of Rockin' Sydney's 1984 zydeco offering, "My Toot-Toot." It's unclear why what was basically a nonsense song brought Denise back after a five-year hiatus—cynics might suggest that at a time when thinly veiled drug references such as Laid Back's "White Horse" and Kurtis Blow's very name were inserting themselves into pop culture, "My Toot Toot" fit right in[7]—but she delivered it with customary aplomb, and it remains one of her showstoppers.

Still, she chafed at how difficult it was becoming for her and many of her colleagues to get airplay. She decided it was time to trouble the waters a bit. The singer who'd balked at recording "blues" just a short time earlier now decided to embrace the word as a badge of identity—but with a twist:

"I got on the case. I'm the one coined the phrase *soul-blues*. That came from me."

> Everywhere I stood on the stage, I talked about it, and I asked people [to] join the National Association for the Preservation of Blues, NAPOB. I'd sign autographs for 'em, and they would join the organization, and we started bombarding all those people with letters. I wrote to NARAS [the National Academy of Recording Arts and Sciences, sponsors of the Grammys] and everybody. Every big radio station, every program director, everybody got those. I said, "Don't call us 'blues.' The blues people say we're not blues; you can't put us in the category of Muddy Waters and Koko Taylor and John Lee Hooker. And R & B said we're not R & B. Call us soul-blues." I started sending it out there. "Soul-blues" stuck.[8]

Whether the new nomenclature actually affected radio playlists is questionable, but after launching her crusade, Denise never looked back. As a "soul-blues" artist, she has since made some of her finest recordings, including several that have become standards, including "Your Husband Is Cheatin' on Us," "Drop That Zero," and her own definitive, R-rated version of "Down Home Blues." Her voice has coarsened over the years, but in most cases that only accentuates the bluesy toughness of her material. She has also cultivated her bawdy image, especially in performance. Although she proclaims in another of her signature songs that she's a "lady in the street, freaky in the bedroom," her language and subject matter these days often seem designed to catapult her boudoir persona to the front of the stage, if not into the street itself; "Snap, Crackle, and Pop," a paean to cunnilingus in which she demands that her man "just treat it like a lollipop" and then pops her tongue and smacks her lips to imitate the sound of a satisfied "coochie," is not atypical.

But there's purpose behind the pose. Even at her most scabrous, Denise charges her routines with a righteous undercurrent of sisterly solidarity. Like her contemporary Millie Jackson, she makes it clear that she's speaking and singing (and cussing) on behalf of women who've been dissatisfied and betrayed and aren't going to take it any longer. Thus her indictment of macho poseurs who think a woman should be glad just to "have a dick in the house" and her insistence that satisfying a woman—sexually, financially, and emotionally—is the first duty of a husband or a lover. "Real women would like you lick it before you stick it!" she declares, and if a man isn't doing it right, it's time for the woman to "drop that zero, and get yourself a hero." Such proclamations bespeak a powerful ethic—if not exactly a moral center—underlying her rowdy onstage persona. Profanity, even promiscuity, in the service of justice, is no vice.

Few were prepared, though, for Denise's attempt to transform herself into a gospel singer. It began when she decided to insert a gospel interlude into her act after the initial success of her gospel CD, *God's Got My Back,* which she released on her Angel in the Midst imprint in 1999. "I had a smash hit record with [the song] 'God's Got My Back,'" she explains. "I said, 'It's as big a hit as any of the other ones I had, so why not sing it?' I would wait until the end of my show, and I would do a little talk about it: 'One thing that I always know. I wrote this song; I've been through a lot; I've been here for many years, been through a lot of trouble and pain. A lot of 'em dead and gone on that started after I did. It's not because I'm such a great singer that I'm still here. It's because God's got my back.' And that was my testimony."

Her blues fans, she maintains, took it all in stride; the gospel community was more skeptical, especially when she decided to take the plunge and actually promote herself as a gospel artist. "I thought my husband was planning to go full-scale into the ministry," she explains, "and I was going to support him." It probably didn't help that in the insular, gossip-besotted music world, some suspected that both Denise and her husband had decided to embrace ministry more as a midlife career move than in response to a divine calling. As it turned out, in fact, both Denise's crossover experiment and James Wolfe's ministerial vocation were short-lived: "Because he didn't get a church that he was trying to get, he just went

Figure 9. Denise LaSalle, House of Blues, Chicago, November 19, 2006. Photo by
Paul Natkin/Photo Reserve, Inc.

back to radio and started doing whatever else he wanted to do and wasn't interested in trying to do nothing else. He'd go to our church and wouldn't even get in the pulpit with the other preachers. I said, 'I'm not gonna be missin' no gigs! I can't live like this. I got to have some work.'"

Characteristically unrepentant, she made sure that her reentrance into soul-blues was as flashy and brazen as she could make it. "I went back," she recalls, "because everybody, all the young girls coming up, was saying, 'I'm Queen of the Blues now; Denise LaSalle's gone.' So I just came back, and I wrote me a song called '[I'm] Still the Queen.'"

That song, which warned any "soul-blues mamas" within the sound of her voice that "The Queen is back, kickin' ass and takin' names," became the title track of her 2002 debut for Ecko. (Her last secular album up to that point had been 2000's *This Real Woman*, on her Ordena imprint, which had included her now-standard "Lick It before You Stick It.") If she'd lost any momentum during her brief crossover attempt, it wasn't evident. *Still the Queen* and its successors on Ecko, *Wanted* and *Pay before You Pump*, were well received, and her touring schedule never flagged. Nor did at least one old-school principle that she still tries to honor despite pressure from producers and her own awareness of changing tastes and trends: "I believe in live instruments," she attests. "At Ecko, most of my stuff was done live. Everybody said, 'You're the only one at Ecko sounds different.' I cut with a live band, and I don't like programmed music—fake horns, fake drums, everything. When you hear my new album on Malaco [2010's *24 Hour Woman*], you'll be able to tell the part that I did from the part Malaco did. You'll be able to tell the difference."

As she warms to her topic, Denise broadens her range to take on some other aspects of the contemporary scene that concern her. She's disturbed, she says, by the extremes to which some artists have been taking their sexual explicitness in recent years. This may sound strange, even disingenuous, coming from the woman who made "lick it before you stick it" a modern-day blues catchphrase and who has been known to introduce her band on stage by proclaiming, "Do they sound good? They fuck good, too—I auditioned 'em myself!" But she insists that some of the things going on in soul-blues today offend even her sense of propriety.

"Okay," she says, "Denise LaSalle is the woman with the mouth, that does all the talking. Me and Millie Jackson, right? So they got to outdo us; they got to go further than we go. And I think we go a bit too far sometimes, so I don't think it should be any further, any more explicit than we do. Anything else is just downright dirty, just ugly. These gals going up on stage with dildos and stuff, that's something neither Millie nor I, neither one, have ever done. That's just ugly. If that's what they wanna be, then go ahead, but I don't deal with that. They have all surpassed me. And I refuse to go any further."

Her attitude isn't as incongruous as it may seem. As easy as it might be to raise eyebrows at some of the apparent contradictions she's straddled over the years, Denise's core approach toward both her work and her life is undergirded by a seriousness at which it's impossible to scoff. When asked why she thinks so many of her contemporaries resist the "blues" label—or even, by implication, why she herself was wary of embracing it for so many years—her answer is immediate and uncompromising: "I know why. Because blues represented hard times, [being] downtrodden. I wrote a poem about it, called 'America's Prodigal Son.' It tells the story of how they had a baby and they named the baby 'Blues,' [and] when they got down on Blues in America, Blues went to Europe and became the toast of the European countries; yet when it comes back home, it's being kicked around."

She's even more forthright in some of her other writings. Her poem "Cry of the Black Soul" depicts the horrors that have been visited upon African Americans since the Middle Passage, making it clear that many of the modern-day crises that threaten the black community are direct linear descendants of slavery and Jim Crow:

Today America's a different place
And Jim Crow now has a different face
Lynch mobs are still in hot pursuit
Dressed up as men in business suits

No hoods, no ropes, no hanging tree
Let the Niggar think we set him free
Put a gun in his hand and fill him with dope
He'll kill himself we don't need no rope

But true to the redemptive spirit she embraces in both gospel and blues, Denise concludes in a spirit of hope and resilience:

But I wouldn't change one single hair on my head
My nose, my skin, I'd rather be dead
I'm black and I'm proud, and I don't give a damn
As long as you respect me for who I am[9]

On a more prosaic level, it's clear as well that many of her blues and soul-blues lyrics also come from the heart. Her stance as a self-proclaimed "bad bitch" who refuses to accept mistreatment has been hard-won. One early boyfriend, she remembers, "beat me up within an inch of my life. Almost cracked my ribs, stomped me in the chest . . . picked up an ashtray off my coffee table and hit me [she still carries the scar on her face]. And [then] he went to the police station and told 'em I pulled a knife on him, and he had to beat me up."

More happily, "I'm Loved," from her 1990 Malaco release *Still Trapped*, arose out of a spontaneous moment of romance between Denise and James Wolfe. "One day," she recalls, "he walked out of the house without kissing me goodbye. And I said, 'Wait a minute. I didn't get my kiss. You come back here and give me my kiss.' He turned around and came back in the house and kissed me, and he said, 'I want you to know one thing. Whether I kiss you or don't kiss you, I want you to know you're loved.' And when he said that [she squeals girlishly], 'I'm loved! I'm loved! Okay, okay! I'm loved!' I said, 'I'll have it written when you get back.' He came back home that night, I made him get in the bed, when he got in the bed, I straddled him in the bed, on my knees, and sang that song to him."

Denise has also continued to proclaim her religious faith, albeit in her own personalized and sometimes confrontational style. Her 2001 CD single "There's No Separation," which she released on Ordena (it also appears on *Still the Queen* and her more recent gospel disc *Still Talkin' bout a Man*), warned Americans that the 9/11 terrorist attacks had been a wake-up call to the nation to change its sinful ways, among which she included legalizing same-sex marriages, teaching *Harry Potter* in schools, and taking prayer out of them. Her conclusion? "There's no separation of churches and state." That's not necessarily a message that even some of her more godly blues fans might want to hear—if nothing else, a theocratic regime would probably outlaw most of her own recordings, to say nothing of her stage show—but with her usual resourcefulness, Denise finds a way to graft even her most apocalyptic visions onto an aesthetic framework that encompasses the full spectrum of her music.

"We don't know what tomorrow's going to bring," she maintains, evoking a scenario that sounds like a cross between an End Times prophecy and a Green Party policy paper.

> Who knows what's going to happen from one day to the next? I think people ought to face facts. Something may go down, it'll be years before we'll have electric again. You never can tell. Nobody ever expected the [2010] earthquake in Haiti. We don't expect nobody to drop an atomic bomb over here. If it happens, how long do you think it'll be before we get our electricity back? And meanwhile, who's gonna play the music, and whatcha gonna use?

I think you ought to prepare yourself. You ought to learn how to play a guitar, acoustic piano. I think that these young people are losing out on a lot by not going to school, music school, getting a good musical education. I have a baby grand sitting in my living room, don't require no electricity. Horns don't need no electric. I think we need to get back to basics. At least learn.

Meanwhile, though, there's still plenty of good music to be made with the aid of electricity, whether it's powering traditional instruments or synthesizers. Like most soul-blues entertainers, Denise performs with a full band, even if she grudgingly accepts prefabricated backing tracks on at least some of her recorded material. Although the recent economic downturn has had its impact on gigs, she continues to be a popular draw along the southern circuit as well as in northern outposts like Chicago and some other midwestern cities.

And, as always, there's her spiritual mission to attend to. A Web site in her name, *Denise LaSalle's Inspirational Site,* is dedicated to promoting *Still Talkin' bout a Man,* which includes most of the songs from *God's Got My Back,* along with "No Separation" and a couple of newer offerings. The site describes *Still Talkin' bout a Man* as representing "a journey for us of our faith, the changes within our lives, and our dedication to help those in need." "This CD project," it continues, "arose out of our desire to help organizations and communities working to assist families, children, and individuals in obtaining food, supplies, shelter, employment, and sustainability. We are committed to do our part in helping others." There's also a list of charities to which the CD's proceeds will be donated.[10]

Denise has obviously toned down her rhetoric since "No Separation," but she included the song on the new disc nonetheless. Is she harboring second thoughts, then, after all these years, about straddling the line between the sacred and the secular? "It doesn't really matter to me," she insists, again deftly dodging land mines both ideological and theological. "I don't see no separation, and I don't worry about it. I'm going to just sing whatever I want to sing."

3

J. Blackfoot
"Don't Give Up—Tighten Up!"

All it takes is an audience, and their reaction is what gets
you back into the song, right where you belong.
    —J. Blackfoot, 1978

"That's what makes me mad!"

J. Blackfoot's emery-board rasp sounds even more
corrosive and forceful than usual as he revisits the
theme he'd broached in that 1978 interview: his ability
to win over a crowd and wreck a house.[1] Now, though,
more than thirty years later, the topic seems to upset
more than inspire him:

> Man, here these people love me like this, and here's
> these disc jockeys, they halfway don't want to play
> your record. Listen to my albums—nothing but
> hits in those albums. All I want 'em to do is play
> my stuff. But I ain't gonna stop trying. I'm just go-
> ing to keep doing what I'm doing; I don't give a
> shit what they do.

Our conversation up to that point had been about
his triumph at the 1997 Chicago Blues Festival, where
his Saturday evening performance elevated—or maybe
rammed—a mostly white, boogie-sodden crowd from
apathy into ecstasy. Craftily inserting a medley of familiar soul standards into his set to grab their interest,
he engaged his longtime singing partner Queen Ann

Hines in a series of churchy call-and-response exchanges, slowly building both the tension and the heat, until there was virtually nothing left but for all that energy to explode. By the time he was through (he closed, of course, with "Taxi," his career-defining 1983–84 hit), the audience at the Petrillo Music Shell was on its feet, screaming for a singer many had probably never heard of before that night. It was as masterful a job of crowd-conquering as any I've seen, even at the hands of such legendary showmen as Buddy Guy or James Brown—perhaps more so, because this audience had to be won over.

Foot, as he's known to his friends, appreciated my compliment. But reminded again of his gifts as an entertainer, he seemed unable to let go of the frustration that grips him whenever the subject comes up, whenever he thinks about those gifts in light of the slack commercial success and meager radio play most of his latter-day recordings have garnered while he's still active, still ambitious, and still thinks of himself as a contemporary R & B artist with plenty to offer. The man who made "Taxi" a southern soul standard, and who remains capable of igniting fires of emotion in an audience that few others outside of gospel can summon, now staggers under the shockwaves emanating from a convulsed recording and broadcast industry. His defiant tone can barely mask the plaintiveness of his query as he pleads: "Why won't they play a good song?"

· · ·

J. Blackfoot, born John Colbert Jr. in Greenville, Mississippi, in 1946, does not comfortably wear the mantle of self-pity. Although he's an affable man capable of great charm, his conversation still reflects the fighting temperament he had to adapt early on to negotiate his way through a hardscrabble, poverty-scarred youth. "You had to be tough in the neighborhood I grew up in," he has remembered. "You had to fight. The only guys I knew were crooks."[2] That pugnacity often explodes in his forceful language, and it's accentuated by the corrugated timbre that remains his most distinctive vocal asset. Like his voice, his disposition is marked by richness and complexity, but also by an insistent, sometimes inflexible bluntness. Whether it's notes or his own will, J. Blackfoot will not easily bend.

"Well, I was staying there, and it wasn't real bad for me," is how he sums up his early years in the town of Panther Burn, about twenty miles southeast of Greenville, where he moved to live with his grandmother when he was about two years old. "My daddy's mother, me and my oldest brother was staying with her. My grandfather—well, he wasn't my grandfather; he was married to my father's mother, so I would say he was, like, my grand-stepdaddy—we called him Daddy Bud. I don't know his real name; they separated. But we called him Daddy Bud."

Panther Burn was a rather auspicious hometown for a boy who would someday become famous for his vocal intensity. According to legend, it got its name after early settlers set a marauding wildcat on fire. The resulting screams of feline anguish, so the story goes, seared so indelibly into the region's collective memory that the people eventually named their community for the sacrificed beast—an almost archetypical southern gesture, equal parts memorial and expiation.[3] Blackfoot's recollections of living there reflect both the simplicity and the dark undercurrent of oppression that characterized rural Mississippi life at the time.

"We used to go to school in a wagon. My oldest brother George, he was in the first grade or the kindergarten. We was so close. . . . I would cry and cry until they would just let me go to school with him. Mama—Grandmother—had the food, our food in the wagon and took us to school. I would sit in the class with him, and I didn't supposed to be there."

In pre–civil rights Mississippi, a black family's well-being often hinged on whether they could make themselves valuable to wealthy and powerful whites. Fortunately, Daddy Bud had managed to do just that. "They like him a lot, 'specially the white folks. He was working for the white guy that owned, that run the town. We used to play with his daughter—white guy's daughter. I remember we used to go to the movie free; we used to play with her. And you know, at that time, I mean you ain't supposed to be playin' with no white girl. But we did."

Even for a man like Daddy Bud, though, opportunities were drying up as the old southern farm economy bent to the changes of mechanization and the postwar urban boom. When John Jr. was about four years old, Daddy Bud moved the family to Memphis, Tennessee, where they eventually reunited with at least some of their relatives (John Sr. had made the trip a few years earlier). It probably wasn't much later that the boy literally walked into what would be his lifelong nickname and professional moniker. In Mississippi, he has recalled, "It was all dirt roads, and most kids didn't wear any shoes. Up in Memphis, I still didn't care to wear shoes, but now my feet would go black from the tar, so people started to call me 'Blackfoot,' and it stuck with me."[4]

It's an arresting, even poignant image: the barefoot country boy, stepping into unforeseen dangers on pitiless city sidewalks. The rube-in-Babylon theme is one that Blackfoot, whether self-consciously or not, has returned to at various times throughout his career (it provided the guiding motif for his debut CD, 1983's *City-Slicker*). At the time, though, the newly nicknamed arrival from Panther Burn probably felt more thrilled than intimidated. It was during these early years in Memphis that his ears were opened to music. "One song I heard," he enthuses, "I never will forget. 'Greyhound, Greyhound, bring my baby back home.' I don't know who sung it; one of them old back-time old guys, back then. It seems like that was the first song I ever heard."

The song was "Greyhound," by pianist and vocalist Amos Milburn, issued on Aladdin in 1952. That was the era, of course, when blues and jump-blues (usually subsumed, at least on the charts, under the rubric of "rhythm and blues") were evolving into what would soon be known commercially as rock and roll. Within a few years, Milburn's suave croon and swinging, horn-seasoned rhythms would, indeed, sound "old-time" to young listeners like Blackfoot, who could now keep up with the latest trends simply by switching on the radio. Memphis station WDIA had hired Nat D. Williams, its first black disc jockey, in 1948; by the end of the following year, it had converted to its groundbreaking all-black format. In the wake of 'DIA's success, other stations also began to program more black music. Soon, over the course of any broadcast day, a Memphian could turn on the radio and hear everything from gospel through blues and jump-and-jive R & B to the newer sounds being aggressively pitched to the new teenage market.

Along with this demographic-driven marketing came a new emphasis on branding; the name of the music one listened to was becoming as much a badge of identity as the music itself. "When they said 'blues,'" remembers Blackfoot, "it was B. B. King, down-home blues. What I was hearing, at the time, they never said 'blues'; you'd say 'R & B.' Rhythm and blues. Had a little rhythm to it. It was more uptempo-ish. Like Jackie Wilson, Sam Cooke; those were my influences. Roy Hamilton, Chuck Berry, and James Brown, even Frankie Lyman—all those guys was R & B to me."

It may seem strange to hear B. B. King typecast as "down-home," since he was one of the seminal influences in the urbanization of postwar blues. He was also, of course, an important figure on the R & B charts while Blackfoot was growing up, and he'd stay that way for a long time (he actually had more R & B chart hits between 1960 and 1969 than in the 1950s). Plenty of younger folks were still buying King's records and attending his shows. Nonetheless, Blackfoot's recollections, as well as his pantheon of early influences, highlight the generational differences that were becoming increasingly significant in popular music during his formative years. As the decade wore on, that generation gap intensified. Movies and the proliferating new medium of television also began more aggressively to court the teenage market. Alan Freed, the Cleveland disc jockey who eventually moved to New York and is usually credited with popularizing the term *rock and roll,* is famous mostly for his importance in exposing white teenagers to black music (as well as for the payola scandal that eventually brought him down). Blackfoot, though, remembers being as enthralled as his white counterparts by what Freed was doing.

"I used to go to the movies a lot," he says. "I was a movie fanatic. I used to see this white guy, Alan Freed, had four, five movies out.[5] I used to look at all these movies. Frankie Lyman and the Teenagers, Clyde McPhatter, Jackie Wilson, Little Richard, Chuck Berry, all those guys was on these movies. I used to see Frankie Lyman; he was a young little young boy singing like that, and, 'Boy,' I said, 'Lord, I wanna be a singer just like them.'"

There was plenty of inspiration closer to home as well. Memphis was one of America's epicenters of gospel music at that time. Composers like the Rev. W. Herbert Brewster ("Move On Up a Little Higher," "Surely God Is Able") and Lucie E. Campbell ("Jesus Gave Me Water," "He Understands"), as well as vocal groups such as the Spirit of Memphis and the Sunset Travelers, were instrumental in developing the modern gospel sound: rich harmonies, inherited from the quartet tradition, infused with energetic rhythms (often, and not without controversy, borrowed from secular blues and R & B) and perfervid emotionalism. The music was in the air, on the radio, everywhere. It was as natural for young people in Memphis to form impromptu gospel quartets as it would soon be for them to stand on street corners and sing doo-wop. In fact, there was a direct connection between the two.

The Dixie Nightingales, led by vocalist Ollie Hoskins, were a popular gospel group who first recorded for the Pepper label in 1958. In later years, Hoskins would enjoy moderate R & B chart success as Ollie Nightingale, leading a group he called, somewhat redundantly, Ollie and the Nightingales.

"They used to rehearsal at my friend's house," remembers Blackfoot. "I was staying up over a store; it was a family, we still close, right today. I used to go downstairs in this store. June McGee, we used to call him 'Junior,' he was working, him and his mother was running this store, and they was behind the meat counter, and we used to harmonize together. He was showing me how to harmonize and sing in harmony. He was with a group called the Redemption Harmonizers,[6] and they used to rehearsal, him and Ollie and the [Dixie] Nightingales, they used to rehearsal at his house. They used to come down the street singing harmony, and I'd listen."

Blackfoot, determined even then to go his own way, soon embraced the secular stepchild of the quartet gospel singing he absorbed in the McGee family store. And in the great tradition of 1950s-era African American urban youth, he did it on the street corners.

"I was a star in the streets," he recalls without braggadocio. "Oh, we had a great group. It was three or four, five of us, and we was harmonying, learning harmony behind the liquor store. We would go in the liquor store and buy us some wine and come out, and be drinkin' wine, and we singin' behind the liquor store. My name, if I came on the street, I could draw eighty, ninety people just listening to me sing a cappella. People wouldn't believe it, but—and I'm not exaggerating—that happened to me."

Naming themselves the Intruders (this was years before the popular Philly soul group), they sang "in talent shows, in school, and mostly on street corners," but on at least one occasion they performed in a more legitimate setting. "We went to a place, I didn't supposed to be in there, but they let us come in and sing, gave us five dollars and let us come in and sing at a place called the Flamingo Room; it was downtown, I believe off of Fourth and Vance, down the street from Club Handy, off of Beale. That was the first kinda professional date for me. It was just like Amateur Hour, but I was singing in front of grown people. That was the first time." In the late spring of 1964, he also got the opportunity to sing at a high school concert at Ellis Auditorium on North Main Street. That show was notable for another reason: the headliners were a doo-wop–styled vocal group called the Emeralds, who would soon find fame on Stax as the Mad Lads.[7]

Despite the thrill of local celebrity, life was not easy for Blackfoot. Although postwar prosperity had trickled down somewhat into black communities in Memphis and elsewhere, many newcomers from the country found themselves struggling more desperately than ever. Foot and his family were among them.

> It was a lot of us. With my mother, it was ten of us. So I was what you call a bad boy. I sung on street corners, and at night or sometime during the daytime, I would burglarize, break in folks' houses, I mean, not in folks' houses, but break in buildings. I was a thief. I used to go downtown, and I used to pick pocketbooks, ladies' pocketbooks. I did all of that. Because I was trying to get money for, we could eat, my brother could—I mostly focused on my brother going to school. My brother was a good basketball player, and he didn't have no clothes, so I used to get money, and I used to get money for him, so he could go to school. So I was stealing and making money, good money at it, and buying food for the house, buying clothes for me and my brothers and sisters.

I graduated to the tenth grade, and I didn't go back. I never finished school. I got all of my education from listening and learning that way. As a matter of fact, I can read words I can't spell. I'm just telling the truth. I can read some words I can't spell. I've never been a great speller, but like I say, I can read words, but you ask me how to spell it, I couldn't spell it.

Blackfoot did latch onto at least one opportunity to launch a singing career during these years. O. V. Wright, a former gospel singer who had recently crossed over and was recording for Quinton Claunch's Goldwax label in Memphis, heard him sing, possibly on the streets near the Le-Moyne Gardens housing project where Wright's mother was living at the time. "He said, 'Why don't you go to Goldwax and go down there and see? You know, you might could get a record deal.'"

But life and payback intervened. "By the time Quinton Claunch came looking for me, I was in the pen doing three years."[8]

It must have been a devastating blow, but even when he learned that some childhood friends of his had become recording stars while he was doing time, Blackfoot responded with determination, not despair. "I got a paper in prison," he remembers. "The Bar-Kays, I knew them as kids, and they was on the front of it. And I said, 'Man, that band, the guys I know, here's a drummer, [Carl] Cunningham, he was in my classroom.' I said, 'Man, when I get outta here, I'm going to make it.'

"All the old cats that was in prison, they said, 'Man, the way you sing, you ain't got no business here.' They was just amazed about my singing talent, for a young kid. Everybody used to say, 'Hey, man, you don't need to be in this prison. Don't come back here, man.'"

Among Blackfoot's fellow inmates at Tennessee State Penitentiary in Nashville was a vocalist named Johnny Bragg, who had formed a singing group in the prison in the mid-1940s. By the early 1950s, as the Prisonaires, they had earned the rare privilege of being allowed out to perform regularly on two Nashville radio stations, WSOK and WSIX. They also issued four records on the Sun label. One of their songs, "Just Walkin' in the Rain," became a major hit when vocalist Johnny Ray covered it in 1956.[9]

Bragg was released from prison in 1959. But he was back the following year, and he put together a fresh group of Prisonaires. Several years later, the Nashville label Sur-Speed approached prison officials for permission to record the group. "That's when I made my first recording," Blackfoot confirms. "Some people came in and they recorded Johnny and his group, and they recorded me. They let us out to go to the studio. They took us in, y'know, in one of those vans. They took us to record and brought us back to the prison. Two songs I had written: one was called 'Surfside Slide,' and one was called 'Congratulations.' Only thing we was playing was a piano, a bass guitar, and drums."

The record, credited to John Colbert, was issued on Sur-Speed in 1965. "They ain't even sold two copies," he admits. "It was just really for my ears." (He also recorded a third song for Sur-Speed, "Recipe for Love," which has since appeared along with the other two on some collectors' anthologies.)

But there were opportunities awaiting in Memphis. Not long after he got out of prison, Blackfoot began hanging out at a joint called Payne's Café (not the well-known Memphis barbeque restaurant), near the Stax studio on McLemore Avenue. "People would put money in the jukebox, find a record they liked, . . . and the people would have me sing it over and over again." It was more of a hustle than a gig: "The people would fill up my table with whiskey and beer to hear me singing their favorite song."[10]

Stax songwriter David Porter got wind of the talented stranger singing for drinks down the street, and he dropped by Payne's to check the fellow out for himself. This time, Blackfoot paid for his own backing track. "I put some money in the jukebox, and I sang over Wilson Pickett's 'I'm in Love' and a song that Otis Redding wrote called 'Shout Bamalama,' by a guy called Mickey Murray. Well, I blew David's mind, and he told me to come to Stax for an audition."[11]

Blackfoot remembers that when he went there a few days later, Otis Redding and Stax co-owner Jim Stewart were listening to a tape of Redding's now-legendary "Dock of the Bay" session. Redding was preparing to go on tour, with Blackfoot's old friends the Bar-Kays as his opening act and backup band. Blackfoot auditioned later that same day.

> David and Isaac Hayes took me in the studio. Jim Stewart and [drummer] Al Jackson and Booker T. and the MGs and Otis was there. Otis was such a nice guy; that was my first time meeting him, and my last time. David was telling, him and Isaac was jivin' Otis, saying, "Hey, we got a young guy fi'n' to cut your head, Otis," you know. Booker T. and the MGs played, and I did "I'm in Love" by Wilson Pickett and "A Change Gonna Come" by Sam Cooke.
>
> David asked [Redding] in the studio, said, "Hey, could you take him on the road? We can get him some two or three suits right quick, if you could take him on the road with you, so he can get some training out there." And Otis told us, "Well, you know, I won't be able to take him on this trip, . . . don't have enough room." But he said, "When I come back and I go back out the next time, I can take him." And David said, "Well, when you go back out the next time, we probably done cut a record on

him." And Otis said, "Well, if you done cut a record on him, I'll take him out on the road with me." And that's the last time I saw Otis [before] the plane crash happened.

On Sunday, December 10, 1967, at about 3:30 in the afternoon, Redding and four of the six Bar-Kays were killed when Redding's twin-engine Beechcraft H18 plunged into the icy waters of Lake Monona in Wisconsin, just minutes before their scheduled landing in Madison. (Bar-Kays bassist James Alexander wasn't on the plane; trumpeter Ben Cauley managed to cling to his floatable seat cushion until he was rescued.) For the survivors, it felt as if the bottom had fallen out of the world, but the show had to go on. Alexander and Cauley fought back their grief and hastily assembled a new group of Bar-Kays. They chose Blackfoot as their lead singer.

Although he'd virtually never performed a professional engagement in his life, and despite the pressure of stepping into a show that would inevitably feel haunted by death and legend, Blackfoot insists he wasn't intimidated. "Honest to God," he avows, "I was professional before I even hit the road. Jesus just gave me that—the power to know how to handle myself on stage. I was telling myself, 'I can handle it.' And when I first went out with the Bar-Kays, I was a hit."

Meanwhile, back at Stax, the blows kept raining down. On April 4, 1968, Dr. Martin Luther King Jr. was assassinated as he stood on the balcony of the Lorraine Motel in Memphis. The city erupted in flames and violence. About a month later, while everyone was still reeling from both Dr. King's assassination and Otis Redding's death, the label's long-time distribution deal with Atlantic ended acrimoniously. In the process, Stax lost Sam & Dave, one of their hottest acts, to their larger and more powerful former partner. David Porter and Isaac Hayes had been thinking for a while about putting together a new act in the wake of Sam & Dave's success. This time, though, they wanted two men and two women, to deepen the vocal texture and allow for a wider range of expression. Now, with Sam & Dave gone, the idea became more urgent.

Blackfoot, already working in the studio with Porter and Hayes, was an obvious candidate for the new group. The other three singers Porter and Hayes recruited all turned out to be acquaintances of his. He'd known Shelbra Bennett since childhood, Anita Louis was a background singer at Stax, and he knew Norman West from the Memphis club scene. The quartet was christened the Soul Children.

Although he has said that he considered himself a solo act and was reluctant to share the mic, Blackfoot's early gospel and doo-wop training

Figure 10. The Soul Children (left to right): J. Blackfoot, Anita Louis, Shelbra Bennett, and Norman West. Stax publicity photo, courtesy of Concord Music Group, Inc.

had prepared him perfectly for this new assignment. He had a finely honed harmonic sense, and his choked, passion-scarred vocals contrasted dramatically with the others' more varied deliveries, creating a tension that gave rise to a riveting emotional intensity. Even at their most romantic, the Soul Children sounded like a pent-up fire ready to surge out of control at any second.

It's immediately evident from their first two releases. The hard-driving "Give 'Em Love" features Blackfoot and West taking the lead in deep-pocket harmony obviously patterned after Sam & Dave. But it's the women who are the revelation: their orgasmic squeals ("Ooh, baby, let's do it!" "Ooh, baby, I like it!") amplify the lyrics' call for erotic gender equity ("You can get what you want / just give it to the girl"), creating a forward-looking anthem that boldly melds sexual and social liberation yet still manages to sound like good, if not entirely wholesome, fun. It peaked at No. 40 in 1968.It should have charted higher, but maybe the vocal mix took some getting used to for listeners weaned on Sam and Dave's exuberant but unrelenting machismo.

The follow-up, "I'll Understand," ranks with James Carr's "The Dark End of the Street" and Luther Ingram's "(If Loving You Is Wrong) I Don't Want to Be Right" as among the most wracked cheating songs of all time. It's the story of two tormented lovers obsessively pursuing their illicit affair in the face of danger, condemnation, and worse ("My mama said, 'Go somewhere else and eat!'"). Blackfoot opens the ballad in as mellifluous a croon as he's ever summoned, then gradually toughens into his trademark rasp; Anita Louis answers him in a clarion-toned wail of desperation infused with desire. The tension builds to an almost unbearable tautness, and it never really dissipates; the protagonists continue along their doomed path, still shouting hopeless reassurances to each other, as the song fades out. The record peaked at just No. 29, but by now it was clear that the Soul Children were for real.

Their early career trajectory made it even more obvious. The group's first live engagement was at a Memphis club called Down Under. Then, in 1969, "The Sweeter He Is," their fourth single, broke into the Top Ten, peaking at No. 7. In the wake of that record's success, the Soul Children landed their first out-of-town gig, at Harlem's fabled Apollo Theater. The exhilaration still fills Blackfoot's voice as he remembers: "Straight from that to the Apollo Theater! Oh, come on! The Apollo Theater? First time? Knowing the history of the Apollo Theater? It was the greatest thing that ever happened in our life, to go to the Apollo Theater. Straight! And then we did it six times in a span of a year. By popular demand. 'Cause we was tearin' 'em up."

The Soul Children charted six more times during their first Stax run, but their trajectory was eventually impaired by business reversals, the most significant being the demise of the label itself. In June 1975, as Stax was entering its final death throes, the Soul Children left to sign with CBS in New York. CBS put them on its Epic subsidiary and enlisted erstwhile Stax producer (and Motown expatriate) Don Davis to work with them. Davis's slick production values and brusque personal manner ("He just rubbed me the wrong way," Blackfoot says) had never been entirely commensurate with deep soul's down-home, grits-and-gravy aesthetic; according to some sources, there were also disputes with him over royalties for some the new Soul Children material.[12] Now a trio—Shelbra Bennett had left to pursue a solo career—the Children reached No. 49 in 1976 with "Finders Keepers," but that was their only hit of any consequence during their tenure at CBS.

Nonetheless, it seems mostly to have been a good-faith effort on everyone's part. The company even let Blackfoot recruit David Porter to produce the group's second Epic LP, with material provided by veteran Stax songwriters. The main problem was probably that, by this time, R & B was moving in a glossier, more aggressively produced direction (Motown had established itself as "The Sound of Young America" among both black and white audiences, and disco was on the horizon). The fervid emotionality of groups like the Soul Children was no long speaking as deeply to "young America" as it had just a few years earlier.

In 1977, Fantasy Records, which had acquired Stax's assets, commissioned David Porter to revitalize the Stax imprint. The new Stax landed nine chart hits over the next year and a half or so, including the Soul Children's disco-tinged "Can't Give Up a Good Thing," which made it to No. 19 in 1978. But the project lasted for only about eighteen months, perhaps because Fantasy lost interest in sustaining it. Porter has even questioned their commitment in the first place.[13]

Both the Epic and Fantasy/Stax disappointments were unfortunate, but they were hardly unique in the notoriously volatile recording industry. Blackfoot, though, has come to see them as symptomatic of an almost conspiratorial pattern of neglect. Having endured, scraped, and scrapped his way into the music business with few tools other than his own determination and protean talent, and then having achieved something close to overnight (and untutored) success, he seems to have been unprepared for the inevitable setbacks that would arise, setbacks that he couldn't surmount by either toughing them out or fighting them down. Even today, as he rails against the betrayals and subterfuges of the recording industry and its shyster moguls, his fulminations often sound laced with the bewilderment and hurt felt by a man who, for all his finely honed intelligence and survival skills, still struggles to master the labyrinthine machinations necessary to succeed in the corporate world, a world of which the music "industry" is indelibly (if still somewhat disingenuously) a part.

"They promised us a whole lot of things to get us to sign with them," he says of CBS and Epic, "but they was full of jive."[14] He believes they simply hung the group out to dry. "You can have a great record, but if you don't have promotion, you just got a record sitting on a shelf. I was younger then. They just mistreated us."[15] He likewise scoffs at the idea of any goodwill on the part of Fantasy. "They really didn't want Stax to happen," he insists, his voice rising as his anger mounts. "That was some [tax] write-offs. That's why I don't have no respect for Epic or none of them ol' labels. They didn't do nothing! Weren't going to do nothing, didn't try to do nothing, didn't want nothing to happen. Act like people don't have to eat! Don't starve me to death, man. I have to eat, too. Got to feed my family. That pissed me. I don't have no good taste in my mouth for 'em."

The Soul Children split up not long after "Can't Give Up a Good Thing."[16] Blackfoot, with a recognizable voice and a still-marketable name, could have gone solo at that point, but he says he was simply burned out. "I just didn't have the spirit." he maintains, although he's quick to add, "I never gave up. I just bided my time, and it worked. The Lord know when it's time, and he let me know when it [was] time. And I did it at the right time."

That was two or three years later ("would've been about '80, '81, somewhere like that"), when his old Bar-Kays compatriot Ben Cauley tracked him down and talked him into working a few gigs. They didn't pay much, but they were enough to give Blackfoot the bug. When he learned that former Stax songwriter Homer Banks had returned to Memphis from New York, he got in touch, and before long he was singing on some of Banks's demos. He released a single on the Prime Cut label in 1983, but it went nowhere. Then came the song that would define him for the rest of his life.

Banks had originally written "Taxi" for Johnnie Taylor. Blackfoot dutifully sang the demo so Taylor could hear what it sounded like. He maintains, though, that he always knew his version was something special; as evidence, he points to his cab-hailing whistle at the beginning. "The Lord had that song for me," he says. "I told Homer, 'Man, if you're gonna send Johnnie a demo, don't send him my whistle! I don't want him to have that. Cause that's the key to it.'"

Taylor passed on the song. "The Lord closed Johnnie's ears," Blackfoot explains, "so he couldn't hear. But I knew it was a smash."

Blackfoot's subsequent version, co-produced by Banks and Chuck Brooks, fully substantiates his claims. He brings it in with that now-famous whistle, which he inserts perfectly into the final measure of the intro on the upbeat just before the dramatic stop-time break that makes way for the opening verse. The song itself is a classic deep-soul parable; images of transgression ("Like a fool, I broke her heart in two"), atonement ("I've got some patching up to do"), and redemption ("She's my reason for living") swirl through Banks's story line, and Blackfoot's voice, rent with his trademark angst but sweetened with a feeling of desperate ntensifies, portrays a man in the throes of crises both

__al.

n, meanwhile, is a minor masterwork of focused yet re-
__alism. The song's melody line, with its rounded contours
__lescents, is set to an easy-flowing ballad tempo and framed
__ aural dreamscape (complete with thunderstorm sound
__ing a sense of brooding melancholy even as Blackfoot's
caustic voca. timbre intensifies the emotional charge. Here was the balance of modernist pop sheen and old-school soul rawness that Blackfoot needed to span the generation gap he now found himself confronting, to sell his song to post-disco sophisticates as well as tough-minded deepsoul survivors. "Taxi" broke in November 1983 and stayed on the R & B charts for twenty-four weeks, peaking at No. 4.

So what happened? Why did Blackfoot chart only seven more times before disappearing from the listings forever after his cover of the Staple Singers' "Respect Yourself" struggled to No. 58 in 1987 and early 1988? And why did none of those other seven climb any higher than No. 28, which is where "Tear Jerker" peaked in 1987 (with Ann Hines, not Blackfoot, on lead vocals)? For that matter, why (or *how*) could a ballad like "Just One Lifetime," his and Hines's aching testimonial to conjugal devotion from his 1991 LP *Loveaholic*, never chart at all? And why haven't his more recent, lushly produced collaborations with younger vocalists ("I'm Just a Fool for You" with Lenny Williams in 2006, the follow-up "I'm Just a Fool for You Part 2" with Sir Charles Jones the following year) garnered anything more than modest regional recognition along the southern soul circuit?

"Because they're assholes!" Blackfoot barks, blaming radio disc jockeys and station managers who he feels unjustly ignore his music.

> That's what it is. Why wouldn't you play a good song? Come on, now! You got to ask them disc jockeys, them asshole-ass disc jockeys why. Talkin' 'bout my record don't fit that format—that's just an excuse. They say that to keep from playing you. And I know this. They wouldn't have a job if it wasn't for folks like us, if it wasn't for groups like the Soul Children, if it wasn't for a guy like me as a single artist, J. Blackfoot, a lot of them wouldn't be doing nothing now. But the disc jockeys, the young disc jockeys, they act like our music ain't worth a dern, [even] if they halfway want to play it. Play my music! How you gon' tell me what don't fit your format if you don't play it there?
>
> They'll play other people, but hey, man, my records fit your station! You just got to play J. Blackfoot and see. If you don't play it and get behind it, you can't tell me nothing. Because you ain't played nothing. Play it like

you play them other records. Don't just play it every once every seven hours [referring to stations that include occasional "blues" or "southern soul" segments in their formats]. Play it like you play Mary J. Blige! Play it like you play these young artists! Play mine like you play theirs. And see what happens.

There's more to it, of course. While plenty of evidence exists to suggest that the music variously known as soul-blues, southern soul, and southern soul-blues is capable of reaching a much wider audience than it's usually given credit for, and while the corporate consolidation of radio in the years since passage of the Telecommunications Act of 1996 under President Bill Clinton has undoubtedly hurt, it's also undeniable that Blackfoot's style, like that of other gifted but idiosyncratic "classic" stylists—Howlin' Wolf, James Brown, Wilson Pickett, even Otis Redding or Aretha Franklin—is resolutely and inflexibly of an era, if not a cultural milieu, that has for years been consigned (albeit sometimes tacitly) to the realm of nostalgia. Among modern artists geared toward the contemporary African American market—even the few southern soul singers still willing to embrace the "-blues" suffix—Blackfoot's brand of housewrecking rawness is no longer, for the most part, in vogue.

The dilemma may have been best summed up by critic Daddy B. Nice in his combined blog/fanzine *Daddy B. Nice's Southern Soul RnB.com*. In a characteristically sympathetic yet prescient commentary, he concluded that although Blackfoot's work continues to have plenty to offer, "listeners accustomed to the 'urban smooth' sound of contemporary R & B should proceed with caution. As sophisticated as Blackfoot's music may sound to an 'insider's' ear, 'outsiders' may find it as cracked and wrinkled as folk art—the aural equivalent of a sepia-toned, Depression-era photograph."[17]

In fact, even in his heyday Blackfoot shone best when he was afforded material and production crafted specifically to highlight his unique strengths. The Soul Children gave him a context where other voices, more supple and tonally varied, could serve as foils for his relentlessly linear and aggressive attack. The best of his solo work has likewise surrounded him with leavening elements, whether the atmospheric production of "Taxi" or the interweaving of his hoarse rasp with Ann Hines's mellifluous warble on sweet-harmony workouts like the unjustly neglected "Just One Lifetime." This, most likely, is what his producers have been attempting more recently by pairing him with crooners like Lenny Williams and Sir Charles Jones, duets that nonetheless unintentionally lay bare Blackfoot's elder statesman status (to say nothing of his unreconstructed Greenville/Panther Burn patois) alongside the younger artists' more youthful-sounding voices.

They're still impressive outings, though, even if they deal in the kind of straightforward romanticism that's also largely fallen out of favor in the irony-drenched, postmodernist pop mainstream (and that increasingly seems to have a difficult time succeeding even in southern soul). Blackfoot throws himself into them with his customary gusto; ironic detachment is not in his repertoire. And if it might seem like a desperation move to pair him with men young enough to be his sons or nephews solely because they happen to be bigger names at the moment (Sir Charles even addresses Blackfoot as "Uncle J." at one point), his dignity and sense of hard-fought pride make it impossible to dismiss him, even as he improbably entreats his youthful co-stars for advice on matters of the heart.

Another relatively recent release, "Two Different People," again show-cases Blackfoot's enduring strengths, albeit paired with more of those throwback tendencies he can't seem to shake. Cast as a midtempo ballad, it features some spirited call-and-response with his longtime singing partner Queen Ann Hines. The arrangement recalls "Just One Lifetime," and again the voices complement each other well. This time, though, the words signify a more dramatic and ominous disjunction between the protagonists. Affecting a breathy little-girl mewl, Hines sings the role of a stand-by-her-man loyalist who "wouldn't get upset" even if she "saw you in another woman's arms"; his response is to threaten that if he ever catches her doing such a thing, she'd better "run for cover . . . call 911." "I'm an old-fashioned woman," she promises him, to which he replies that he's "a jealous man," and she'd better watch herself and act accordingly. It's a gripping portrayal; the scenarios are drawn with almost cinematic vividness, and in the end, we can almost believe it's all in fun ("We make such a lovely pair," Hines croons in her ironic teen-dream warble). Once again, though, modern listeners may find themselves struggling to get past the anachronism to savor the artistry.

Then there's "Meow" or, as Blackfoot euphemistically calls it, "my 'cat' song." Ever since Billy "Soul" Bonds's oddball double-entendre ballad "Scat Cat, Here Kitty Kitty" broke in 2006, soul-blues songs about men's "dogs" satisfying, craving, attacking, subduing, or otherwise impressing themselves on women's "cats" have been proliferating at an astonishing rate. Blackfoot might seem an unlikely candidate for this trend; from the beginning, his persona has been that of a life-hardened adult (he was a soul "child" in name only) with meaningful stories to tell. Even today, he insists that for southern soul to remain viable, "they got to come on back to . . . songs with great stories. You know how writers used to write? They got to write 'em like that. I want strong stories, a good hook, and nice rhythm."

Figure 11. J. Blackfoot, Greensboro Coliseum, Greensboro, North Carolina, April 2010. Photo by Gene Tomko.

So how to explain "Meow," his 2009 entry in the "dog/cat" sweepstakes? "Even I jumped into that," he admits. "Although mine was a little different. My 'cat' song is different from any other of 'em out there. The rhythm, the whole thing. And the story is strong, even though it's a 'dog and cat' song, but the story, you listen to the story. It tells a story."

In fact, "Meow" is pretty much a nonstop boast from a player whose opening voice mail message proclaims, "You've reached K9-12-Woof-

Woof-Meow" and who goes on to inform us that "I'm a dog, I'm genuine, I'm canine, I'm pedigreed / If you got cat problems, baby just call me," to a lurching minor-key synth groove. The CD it's from, 2009's *Woof Woof Meow*, also features a "Taxi" spinoff called "Mr. Bus Driver" (this time the protagonist is leaving his woman, not trying to get her back) as well as two more "Cat" ditties, both apparently set to the same backing track as "Meow": "No Ordinary Pussy Cat" finds guest vocalist Ms. Jody fronting off the dog man with her characteristic aplomb ("This ain't your ordinary pussy cat . . . I'm gonna make you tuck your tail and run"); "Meow (Pussy Cat Remix)" is yet another dialogue between Mr. Woof-Woof and a panting female beset with "cat problems."

Given the limited subject matter, there's plenty of imaginative wordplay in these songs, and their tough, bass-heavy production gives them a contemporary urban R & B edge. But although "Meow" made some noise around the southern circuit, it's difficult to see songs like these becoming the kind of classics audiences will be calling for years from now, the way they still demand "Taxi" or "Just One Lifetime"; more important, probably, as far as Blackfoot is concerned, it's hard to see such fare helping him fulfill his ambition to return to mainstream R & B radio rotation alongside the likes of Mary J. Blige or her younger successors. Admirers of Blige's spirit-driven, feminist-tinged poeticism would most likely find these "cat" songs embarrassingly lowbrow (to say nothing of sexist); conversely, hardcore hip-hoppers would scoff at their puerility.

It's all the more frustrating because even when his material betrays him, Blackfoot's own powers remain undiminished. Regardless of how silly some of the "cat" lyrics may be, or how retrograde his threats in a minidrama like "Two Different People," he delivers them with a grittiness that makes his macho boasting sound utterly genuine. And he can still infuse a ballad with longing so desperate that it's almost overwhelming. His rubbed-raw vocal timbre only heightens the pathos; it bespeaks a hard-bitten soul survivor crumbling under the burden of heartbreak.

And if nothing else, in live performance Blackfoot can erase any lingering doubts about his prowess as a soul man. In late 2004, he appeared on a tribute for a critically ill Tyrone Davis, an event that had inexplicably failed to draw much of a crowd to the spacious Harold Washington Cultural Center on Forty-Seventh Street in Chicago. Joined by fellow soul veteran Otis Clay, he eased into a low-key but fervid reading of Al Green's "Love and Happiness." Over the course of the next fifteen or twenty minutes or so, Blackfoot and Clay ramped up the tension and stoked the heat with secularized gospel fire until the sparse audience was on its feet screaming. By the time the song's climax came around, it felt as if the walls and ceiling of the auditorium were about to blow out. Once again, as he'd done at that Chicago Blues Festival seven years earlier, J. Blackfoot had come into a situation that could have been disastrous for him, bent it to his will, his talent, and his showman's acumen, and transformed it into a triumph.

"I know what to do, how to do it, to make it happen," he proclaims, relishing yet another memory of how he had gotten into the house and conquered an unsuspecting crowd. And, he emphasizes, this shows how capable he still is of going head-to-head against any soul or R & B star anyone might care to throw at him, past or present, if only the system would relent and give him the opportunity:

> If I could put it together like I really wanted, had the money to do what I really want, it'd be too tough. I'll stand up with Usher and all of 'em. You give me the right shit, put me on a show with 'em, and see what happens. They can just go on, do what they wanna do. I'll tear their ass raggly! I'm gonna have a show for 'em! If I got the right money, I'm gonna have four or five horns, I'm gonna have the whole nine yards. And I'm gonna kill 'em.
>
> You just got to hold on, man. It's coming. I don't fall into that "giving up" kinda thing, or "it's drying up." Ain't shit drying up. Just keep on doing what you're doing until it open back up. You got to keep on hanging in there. You don't give up—you tighten up! That's what I'm gonna do. I'm gonna tighten it up.
>
> They still can't get away. They can't get away from J. Blackfoot.

• • •

Epilogue: "Just One Lifetime"

On Wednesday, November 30, 2011, one of the toughest hard-soul voices of all time was silenced when J. Blackfoot passed away at Methodist Hospital in the Memphis suburb of Germantown, following a long battle with cancer. Resolute to the end, he had given his final performance in West Memphis the previous Friday.

His funeral, on December 10 at Christ Missionary Baptist Church in Memphis, was a true homegoing celebration, rich with affirmation as well as grief. Stax veterans David Porter and Eddie Floyd, among others, spoke in Blackfoot's memory; Bobby Rush contributed a characteristically wry meditation on aging, along with an improvised song that he delivered a cappella followed by a harmonica solo—both structured around the changes of the blues standard "Sitting on Top of the World," which itself is based on the spiritual "You've Got to Move."

Norman West, Foot's partner in the original Soul Children, was too overcome to sing at first, but he later came through with a heartfelt reprise of "Taxi." Memphis-based vocalist Toni Green and Blackfoot's longtime musical companion Queen Ann Hines also sang; Queen Ann sent chills down spines with her rendition of "Just One Lifetime," accompanied by her fellow New Soul Child Katrenia Jefferson, with longtime Blackfoot back-up vocalist Warren Miller standing in for him. Most memorable, though, was Shirley Brown's transcendent "Amazing Grace." She brought the congregation to its feet, and by the time she was through the church was resonating with shouts and applause.

Most of the speakers that day recalled Blackfoot's determination, his love for his music, and above all his unquenchable will. As a singer and as a man, he exemplified what soul music, at its essence, represents: the bluesy grit of the survivor, leavened with the faith and hard-won dignity of the striver and spiritual seeker. "I just gotta keep going," he told me when we spoke, and that's exactly what he did until he simply couldn't go any more.

Looking through various online tributes, I've come across several references to the old Soul Children lyric, "The sweeter he is, the longer the pain is gonna last."[18] That pretty much sums it up for those of us who were privileged to know J. Blackfoot, whether personally or through his music. I regret that he left us before he could have the opportunity to see this chapter and this book.

4

Bobby Rush
Behind the Trickster's Mask

Eleggua [the Yoruba trickster deity] dressed himself in a garment
that was red on the right side and black on the left. Thus attired, he
walked between two friends. One of the men remarked to the other
on the handsome black suit the Orisha had been wearing. The second man looked at his friend in disbelief. "Are you color blind? That
man was dressed in red!" The argument grew to such proportions
that they were soon at each other's throats.
—From González-Wippler, *Tales of the Orishas*

Soul star Bobby Rush remembered . . . three women getting in a
fight over Muddy [Waters]. "I instigated it just to get them fighting,"
said Rush. "Willie Mabon was playing the piano, his hands never
stopped. He said, 'Let 'em fight, me and you will fuck 'em all.'"
—From Gordon, *Can't Be Satisfied:
The Life and Times of Muddy Waters*

One of the most widely occurring characters in the
folklores of the world is the trickster. A deity or demi-
god who usually (but not always) takes a male form,
he's a complex and often-misunderstood figure who
acts as both challenger and guardian of a society's most
sacred values. He presides over festivals and carnivals
as Lord of Misrule, symbolizing a temporary freedom
from everyday moral and ethical constraints. On the
other hand, as the tale of Eleggua demonstrates, he may
simply wreak havoc for the sheer joy of doing so and
thus must be appeased through prayer, ritual, and song.

The trickster, irreverent and untamable though he
may be, is not merely an anarchist. He's both wise

teacher and holy fool. He deflates pomposity and challenges authority in the name of preserving, rather than destroying, social harmony. The trickster of the Lakota people of the North American Great Plains was represented in human form by a shaman known as the thunder dreamer or *heyoka*, who had a special dispensation to do things in reverse order. When a fight or some other unpleasantness threatened a community, he might make a dramatic—and highly comedic—entrance, cavorting backward through various burlesques of everyday human activity, until the tension dissipated. He could heal sickness, reverse misfortune, even change the weather. He was both revered and feared for his strange visions and uncanny powers. Lakota writer and medicine man Archie Fire Lame Deer has called him "sorrow and laughter rolled into one, sacred and ridiculous at the same time."[1]

If that sounds a little like the blues, it probably should. Nowhere has the trickster in all his guises been more prevalent than in the cultures of the African diaspora. As Eleggua, he served the Yoruba people of West Africa as Guardian of the Crossroads, governing the portal between this world and that of the spirits. He was also Monkey, direct ancestor of the Signifying Monkey of blues and street lore, the sassy rascal who tied Bush Cat's tail to a tree and then fled to the treetops to escape the cat's revenge. He inspired dancers and drummers; he opened the way to visions and insight for those brave and respectful enough to invoke his powers and earn his trust; he cavorted merrily—and a little ominously—through life and dream, wreaking his havoc and teaching his lessons along the way.

During the long nightmare of slavery in North America and its seemingly endless aftermath, the trickster evolved into a real-world hero, a necessity for people to believe in—and become—in order to survive. In the day-to-day struggle for survival, he (and she) learned to don masks of subtlety and deception, sometimes "playing the fool" with guileful purpose, sometimes remaining concealed behind a facade of ambiguity or inexpressiveness. As the wily slave known as "John," he outfoxed Ol' Massa to win his freedom; as Br'er Rabbit, he engaged in Olympian battles of wit with other legendary tricksters like Br'er Fox. Even nihilistic folk outlaws like Railroad Bill and Stagger Lee (precursors to modern-day hip-hop gangstas) could be seen as noncomic tricksters, ready to assert their freedom and defiance by any means necessary. The line between "art" and "life" had never been so malleable and shifting. Storytellers, songsters, and, eventually, blues singers handed down the lore, as had the griots and shamans of old.

Few blues artists have worn the mantle of Trickster Incarnate with more panache than Bobby Rush.[2] Born Emmett Ellis Jr. in the country outside

Homer, Louisiana, in 1933 (although other dates have also been given), he calls what he does "folk funk." He peppers his fables of lust, infidelity, and romantic mishaps with folksy aphorisms—"A man can give it, but he sure can't take it"; "One monkey don't stop no show"—laid over funk-dripping rhythmic and melodic lines.

In performance, Bobby's persona is unremittingly transgressive. He stalks the stage with his face contorted into a leer of raw lechery as scantily clad dancing girls writhe and gyrate on either side of him; on cue, he'll bend down to the most luscious booty on the bandstand and exult, "Look at it! It moves like it got sense!" as the band tears off a series of staccato runs and the dancer obligingly shakes her derriere in his face. When he's not extolling the ecstasies of sexual one-upmanship ("If you wanna be a hoochie mama, then I can be a hoochie man"), he's romping through scenarios of erotic misadventure in which men and women alike seem primarily bent on getting what they can behind each other's backs, or even in front of each other's eyes ("She made me hold the flashlight while she made love to another man"), before the inevitable payback in which the philanderer is either caught in the wrong ("A married man come home to his wife with lipstick on his collar") or gets witheringly cut down to size ("Your love is like a wet match / You can't light no fire with that").

Bobby, who's famous for appearing on stage wearing at least two or three different outfits per performance, has said that his penchant for costume changes dates back to a late 1950s gig where he emceed in a fake moustache and tramp costume, disappeared for about thirty seconds, and rematerialized as the star of the show. Not only did he have the audience fooled, he insists that he managed to draw two paychecks from the club owner as well. "I was two-guys-in-one," he told *Juke Blues* in 1996. "He never knew it was the same guy."[3]

But it's not just the clothes. Bobby on stage is fluidity in motion—at any second he may or may not be the character he was just an eye-blink before. He'll dart from one side of the bandstand to the other, mugging and rolling his eyes as he ogles his dancing girls, both inhabiting and burlesquing the persona of the incorrigible roué who can't quit even though he knows he'll get caught. Then he'll play the role of Signifier, teasing and provoking his audience. Sometimes, as he told *Living Blues* magazine in 2003, he'll even intentionally stir up the passions of a particular couple he's identified as having relationship problems, shifting their attention from his own studly persona to the luscious sensuality of his dancers then back again, never allowing the energy to remain focused long enough to become dangerous, until the tension is gone and everyone can "leave there with joy in their

Figure 12. Bobby Rush's revue, including (left to right) dancer Jazzii, bassist Terrance Grayson, dancer Mizz Lowe, and Bobby Rush (on harmonica), Club Ebony, Indianola, Mississippi, August 2004. Photo by Gene Tomko.

mind."[4] He's the *heyoka,* the ritual clown, aping our quirks and foibles to diffuse our anger and keep peace. Then he'll shift identities again and become a tough-talking street poet who throws down challenges to a would-be rival—"I ain't studdin' ya!"—even as his sly grin and quick-darting eyes playfully acknowledge the inevitability of defeat.

Most of his critics miss the point, but it's this defeat that represents the core of Bobby's act. Despite their unabashed carnality, his routines are, at their heart, morality tales. Like the Signifying Monkey, who gets roundly trounced for his hubris in the end, Bobby's philandering character inevitably gets his comeuppance, whether at the hands of a cuckolding buddy ("my best friend Paul") or his own long-suffering woman ("She said, 'What's good for the goose is good for the gander, too'"). "A man can give it, but he sure can't take it," he concludes, reminding us again that in the world outside this ritual, actions have consequences.

It's one thing, though, for the trickster to get out-tricked by a rival in ritual combat, on stage, or in song. It's quite another for his very persona to be misunderstood by people who lack the cultural frame of reference to understand what he's about. At least since the days of minstrelsy, black performing artists have found their tricksters' masks cruelly misrepresented by whites. As Mel Watkins documents in *On the Real Side,* his 1994 history of African American humor, when comic characters such as Amos 'n' Andy or gifted performers like Hattie McDaniel and Stepin Fetchit were presented to white audiences outside indigenous African American cultural contexts, they became reduced to "coon entertainers," perpetuating racist stereotypes.[5]

Bobby Rush, with his hipster's wit and funk-propelled rhythmic impetus, probably doesn't have to worry about being typecast as a modern-day Fetchit; he has sometimes found, however, that his act can garner a very different reaction from white audiences. When he first appeared in Europe in the 1990s, he was almost booed off the stage (subsequent Continental appearances have gone more smoothly); in the United States, as well, there have been complaints about his act and lyrics among white intellectuals, critics, and even some musicians.[6]

Certainly it might be argued that using "girls" as "decoration pieces," as Bobby has sometimes put it, represents a less than enlightened attitude toward women in showmanship (if not in life itself), even though one seldom hears a woman performer like Madonna castigated for using men in pretty much the same way. And maybe Bobby will compromise a little, at least to the extent of allowing his dancers to face the audience as much as they showcase their booties or even giving them a few spoken lines of their own—perhaps during his "Henpecked by the Right Hen" routine, where he plays an aging womanizer who leers foolishly at the "young hen" before finally admitting that the older woman is more appropriate—and more pleasing—for him.[7]

But such compromises probably won't address the core issue: it's not the particulars of the Bobby Rush show that make some whites uneasy as much as the tradition he works in. To truly appreciate what Bobby does, his newfound audience needs to understand something that most of his longtime admirers seem to have no problem grasping: the liberating social function of the trickster—Lord of Misrule—is *ritual* in nature. In his trickster role, Bobby opens the portal to a freer way of being, just as Eleggua opened the portal to the spirit world as Guardian of the Crossroads. But once the ritual is over, that portal is reclosed.

Human beings and human society need an outlet, a place of illumination and release, where the boundaries of empirical reality and moral constraints can be transcended, even if only for a time. Allowing access to this is, in part, the trickster's role. But to become truly empowered by this kind of liberating spirit, people need to maintain a solid foundation of morality and faith—newly defined, perhaps, based on humanistic, life-affirming principles—as well as the ritual abandon of the bacchanal. This is one of the most important, as well as one of the most misunderstood, legacies of the blues performance tradition, and Bobby Rush embodies it.

• • •

"My problem," says Bobby Rush, the intensity of his gaze belying his genial tone and demeanor, "is knowing what I know. God has given me a gift, and it's a dangerous person that know what I know."

We're talking in the lobby of a motel in the southern suburbs of Chicago. Bobby is in town to lend his support to a CD release party on behalf of a longtime friend who's embarked on a quixotic plan to start his own soul-blues label. Bobby is not on the label, he's not booked on the show, and in fact his precise self-interest in all this isn't entirely clear ("I don't know what this gentleman is gonna do with the record company; I'm hoping well, because he is a friend of mine"). Right now, though, he's reminiscing about his own fifty-plus-year career as an entertainer, relating tales from the old days that segue into his philosophies on life, the music business, racial equality, and both the present and the future of the blues. Laced with aphorisms and vignettes reflecting the same "folk" sensibility that characterizes his music, Bobby's conversation reveals him to be a thoughtful, somewhat world-wounded but still combative and confident man. To hear him tell it, the trickster role isn't simply something he uses to win over audiences; as a black man, it's something he's had to master in order to survive, almost from the beginning.

"I could never display what I know," he explains, "when I was twenty-five or thirty years old. That didn't mean I didn't know it. But now I'm an old man; I can get away with saying it. I knew it all the time, but I couldn't get away doing it and saying this."

I don't mind you calling me, not [just] a blues singer, but a black blues singer. I am a blues singer. I am a black man. I am a black blues singer. I'm one of the few, one of the very few, who'll claim my name like that, as a black man. Because when you say "blues singers" or "soul singers," you're saying that you're really labeling them as a nationality, not just as singers. And nobody wanna get put in the trap. They're ashamed of who they are. I blame themselves, and I also blame the media for their approach; they know the questions to ask and the way to ask, to get people to feel bad about the name they carry, who they say they are.

Yeah, [the media] love the blues, but it ain't always been the white media who love the ones who created the blues. So, sure they love the blues. Oh, people love B. B. King. But fifty years ago, I don't think they was in love with B. B. King; they just didn't have a white guy at the time who could do what B. B. King was doing. So they learned to love where it come from, and then he got old enough, and so has Bobby Rush, so now [we're] not a threat. They figure we won't live long enough to make a difference, and the "real" guy, the white guy can stand up and say, "I'm the real deal," and we'll be dead and gone before we can tell 'em who the real deal is. And it's in the media's hands to tell the story.

Bobby Rush's own story can be tricky to pin down; various specifics— dates, recording sessions, associations with famous names—have evolved somewhat serendipitously through repeated tellings over the years. True again to his "folk" persona, Bobby spins parable-like tales that often aim for truths both higher and more metaphoric than the details, so beloved of fact-checkers, that may precede them.

His initial decision to change his identity, though, had more to do with a son's devotion than a trickster's guile. His father, Emmett Ellis Sr., was a preacher. "My daddy influenced me more than anybody or anything that I ever done. Had he told me not to sing the blues, it would have damaged me because I wouldn't've did it. That's how much love and respect I had for what my daddy said." So in the late 1940s or early '50s, the aspiring young bluesman made up a new name "because of respect for my father, for what he done biblically, and the love I had for my father and the friend that I had in my dad."

The combination of wit, opportunism, and calculated self-interest he summoned to create the name "Bobby Rush" was indicative of almost everything he would do professionally from then on. "I kept playing with the name—Emmett Eisenhower, Emmett Lincoln, Roosevelt, Truman— then I said, 'well, Bob Hope. Nobody call him Bob, nobody call him Hope. Everybody call him Bob Hope.' I said, 'that's it.' If you notice, nobody call me Bobby, nobody call me Rush. Everybody call me Bobby Rush. That was it. That was the name."

Precisely when the renamed Bobby Rush moved north and began to hustle his way into the Chicago blues scene has been lost to history; earlier accounts suggested 1956, but he now insists it was several years before that. He also maintains that he encountered racial hostility of the type that many northern whites like to deny existed in their cities during that time.

"It makes me more angry now than it did then," he asserts. "At that time, see, that was common to me as a black man. Even up North. Oh, yeah. Oh, God, yeah. Even up North."

> I believe it was a place called Apex, in [suburban] Robbins, Illinois.[8] About 1952. Black ladies would come there on a Wednesday and a Thursday; white guys would come to mingle and deal with the black ladies. We played in this place on weekends. All-white audience. They wanted to hear the black music, but they didn't wan' to see our face. They had a curtain. Once a night I could take a bow; when they opened the curtain, they said, "Ladies and gentlemen, you've been [entertained] by Bobby Rush," and they open it up, I take a bow, and—foo! They close it up. Just like that.

Things weren't much better in Chicago itself. The Rush Street district on the North Side was then known for its jazz clubs. Sometime in the mid-1950s, Bobby Rush auditioned at a nightclub there called Bourbon Street, a Mob-connected establishment that featured, at the time, two different bands playing alternating one-hour sets behind what Bobby describes as "four go-go girls" who were the main attraction. He passed the audition, but with an all-white band he'd assembled for the occasion. Not thinking, he says, he brought his usual sidemen to play the gig:

> There was only one [dressing] room at first. They said, "Well, we got to get another dressing room for you-all, you-all can't stay in here with the white band." So they went, they got this cloakroom, and they put us in that, but they put a chain on the door and locked the door; locked us in there. So we had to stay on this one side; when we wanted to go to the bathroom, it was three knocks. Sandwich was five knocks; we had a knock for everything we wanted to do. They'd bring us out one at a time. We couldn't come inside of the club; we just played [on the stage] in the back of it.

Eventually, he says, the proprietor took a liking to him, and his accommodations improved. The racial atmosphere, though, remained tense. "I could see the concern, with his customers. He said, 'Well, Bobby Rush, you know, it's okay by me, . . . ' but he's concerned about, 'the people who come in, spending money, may not see it the way I see it.' I understood why."

Bobby also maintains that he spun off a variation of his quick-change gimmick to collect several paychecks at once during his tenure at Bourbon Street. "I had my steady job, and then I had an hour off every other hour. My band would play, sometimes, fifteen minutes, so that give me an hour and fifteen minutes to get back. I could go do another show right quick, make me thirty-five dollars.

"Walton's Corner, Phyllis's, the Zanzibar, Theresa's—every place there was a joint, Bobby Rush played in. I was this flashy guy who comes in, where the other [performer] was in the blue jeans. I would never wear the same suit. I was doing about thirty-five to forty-five dollars a night in each one of these places. I wasn't making it in one club; I was making three clubs [a night]. I was making more money than Howlin' Wolf and Muddy Waters."

Bobby says he was so successful with this hustle that he didn't seek out a recording career as early as he might have (his first releases were on obscure local labels like Jerry-O and Palos in the early and mid-1960s). He did, however, manage to con Chess Records into letting him cut some demos without a contract:

> I went into Chess, and I told them that I would love to record for the company, but I had six to eight more months, whatever I told them then, on my contract with this Jewish guy. Apparently I convinced 'em that he was like an Al Capone-ish kind of a guy, bad guy, and as soon as my contract was up, I was going to record for them. But the meantime I could record right now, to get a few tracks down. So we went in, at night and between times, we got a few tracks down, and he said, "What is this guy's name?" I said, "His name is Emmett Ellis, and when I get through with this contract . . ." But anyway, the contract I never had, and I walked out with my little masters, because they didn't know Emmett Ellis and Bobby Rush was the same guy.

Nonetheless, through his friendships with Howlin' Wolf and other Chess recording artists, Bobby insinuated himself into their circle, and he attended some legitimate sessions at the studio (he eventually released a single, "Sock Boo Ga Loo," on the Chess subsidiary Checker in 1967). He claims he played bass for at least one Howlin' Wolf session that was never released, and which no known discography has acknowledged. Wolf's recalcitrance in the studio was legendary; some of his associates ascribed it to simple stubbornness or even stupidity.[9] But to hear Bobby tell it, at least some of Wolf's obstinacy derived from both personal and racial pride:

> I'll never forget, on this record, Howlin' Wolf was playing, and they said, "Now Wolf, on this song you gotta do a lot of howling, because you're

Howlin' Wolf." And he would say, "Y-e-e-a-a-up . . ." But when Phil and Leonard [Chess] would walk out of the room, he would say [imitates Wolf's raspy growl], "I'm not bustin' my gizzard for these white folks. I do what I wanna do." They would come back in, say "Wolf, you got to howl." They would walk out, he would say, "I'm not howlin'. I howl when I wanna howl." And he would sit back down. I heard Willie [Dixon] say, "Wolf, did you understand what that mean?" He said, "Sure I do." He said, "Well, what you gonna do?" "What I wanna do."

We laughed, and he looked up. "What the hell y'all laughin' about?" So we all got the message—he was serious about it. I'm a young man; it was funny to me for him to say what he said, "bustin' my gizzard." But it was serious with Wolf. He was serious, and he did not do it.

Bobby probably never had to affect that kind of belligerent obstinacy to get his way, but as his career grew in the 1960s and early '70s, he found his own repertoire of tricks expanding. At one point, he recalls, he asked the owner of a record label ("shouldn't probably give the name") for "an unbelievable amount of money, at the time, for a black man to ask for. The guy laughed at me. He said, 'Who do you think you are?' I said, 'Well, I'm just trying to get what's due me.'"

The owner ("he used the n-word") then threw down a challenge that he most likely didn't expect Bobby to accept: if Bobby could sell a hundred thousand of his own records, they'd give him almost twice the amount he'd asked for. "I said, 'Okay, write the contract up.' I signed the contract. They went back and laughed at me. Say, 'Here that little boy in here, talkin' 'bout he gonna sell a hundred thousand records . . .'"

So I put my little antenna to work. I called across the country. I got in my car, and I drove to all them mom-and-pops. Set relationships as a man, as a black man, to black record shops. "Here's what I need you to do. I need you to get a thousand records, five hundred records . . ." [They] said, "We'll return 'em." I said, "Oh, some of 'em are returned, some not returned. Don't make no difference." I told people what I was doing. They say, "Oh, is that what you're doing? Well, it's time for us to do something like this." I "sold" two hundred thousand records—on paper.

When the returns come back, I had my money and gone.

Bobby says that he first hired a dancing girl in the mid-1950s, when he decided to update a theme that some African American entertainers had used in earlier eras: featuring scantily clad "jungle" dancers, often to entertain exotica-seeking white tourists (Josephine Baker refined the concept somewhat and conquered Paris with it in 1925). He'd seen acts like that in his younger days, but characteristically he wanted to put his own spin on the idea. "The girl that I had saw with a snake dance was a girl that looked like, from Tarzan's jungle. But I wanted this girl dressed up. Put on some red high-heeled shoes, some shorts, look like a shake dancer. And half the people'd be looking at the snake, and half the men would be looking at the girl. So I said, 'There it is. Drop the snake, keep the girl.'"

For all of his enterprising nature, though, Bobby Rush didn't hit the national map until the early 1970s. "Chicken Heads," his first chart hit, found its way onto wax through yet another bit of Rushian subterfuge. He first brought the song to his friend Calvin Carter, who had been the head of A & R (Artist and Repertoire) at Vee-Jay records before Vee-Jay folded in 1966. In the early '70s, Carter was running an independent production company along with Leo Austell, another longtime Chicago record industry veteran. As Bobby remembers it: "I said, 'Calvin, I got a song.' 'What's the name of it?' I said, 'Chick Head' [i.e., a "chick" giving

Figure 13. "Not only can it talk, it can sing, too!" Bobby Rush and Mizz Lowe send out a booty call to the 2007 Chicago Blues Festival. Photo by Paul Natkin/Photo Reserve, Inc.

him head]. I was way ahead of what the rappers do. He said, 'Chick Head'? And he laughed."

Carter's partner was a tougher sell.

> Leo Austell [was] a Jehovah's Witness preacher. I taken my guitar [he hums the well-known introductory riff and sings]: "Daddy told me on his dyin' bed / give up your heart, but don't lose your head." He said, "What's the name of it?" I said, "Chick Head." He said, "What?" I said—and I caught it. I said, "Chicken Head." He said, "Oh, yeah. You eat chicken heads down South, don't you?" Right away, I caught, him bein' a preacher, he didn't like "Chick Head." Had nothing to do with a chicken. But he said, "Yeah, that's a good record.".
>
> He said, "What's the B [side]?" I said, "I got another song." He said, "What's the name of it?" I said, "Mary Jane." He said, "Oh, yeah, I had a girl called Mary Jane." And I wasn't talkin' about a lady at all. I was talkin' about some reefer. I said, "Oh, wow! I can sing anything to these guys. They don't even know what I'm talking about. I got me an easy pickin' here. Like a bird's nest on the ground."

"Chicken Heads" backed with "Mary Jane" was issued on the Galaxy label, and it became Bobby's first chart hit, peaking at No. 34 in 1971. Within a year or so, Carter and Austell expanded their operation to include a label called On Top; they released a few more of Bobby's singles on it, including the funk-dripping punfest, "Bow-Legged Woman, Knock-Kneed Man" ("Chicken in the car, and the car won't go / that's the way you spell Chi-Ca-Go"). These caught the attention of Stan Lewis, proprietor of the Jewel label in Shreveport, Louisiana; Lewis signed Bobby in about 1973 and reissued "Bow-Legged Woman," which became a regional hit but still didn't make the national charts. While at Jewel, Bobby also recorded his faux-Creole patois workout "Niki Hoeky," which lubricated his streetwise funk strut with an insinuating swamp-mud greasiness.

It wasn't until 1979, though, that he charted again, with "I Wanna Do the Do" on Philadelphia International, which topped out at No. 75 during its five-week run. After his brief tenure at PI (he credits Kenny Gamble and Leon Huff, who produced *Rush Hour,* his 1979 LP on the label, with helping him grow as a songwriter), Bobby moved to James Bennett's LaJam imprint in Jackson, Mississippi. Several of his LaJam sides garnered regional success (spurring him to move to Jackson from Chicago), but the most significant was the title track from his 1983 LP *Sue,* an intricately woven tale of a young man's sexual coming of age at the hands (and tongue) of a kinky country girl ("She sat on the low stool, and I sat on the high stool"). Today, "Sue" is probably Bobby's best-known song, even more popular than "Chicken Heads." The introductory riff is instantly recognizable, and the story line, as ribald as it is, is all the more effective for its avoidance of outright salaciousness; Bobby generates more erotic heat via insinuation than a dozen X-rated, ho'-dissing gangstas could with a barrage of f-bombs.

Nonetheless, and even though LaJam released an edited version of "Sue" as a single, it never saw national chart action, and it's doubtful whether it landed him many gigs outside the chitlin' circuit. In fact, all of Bobby's "hits" since "I Wanna Do the Do" have been regional (primarily in the South and Southwest, along with the usual outposts in midwestern industrial areas like Chicago and Detroit), and his performing career has consisted mostly of endless strings of one-nighters—as many as three hundred a year at his most active, now between one hundred fifty and two hundred fifty. He plays venues ranging from auditoriums and civic centers to the kind of backstreet gin mills and jukes that many performers of his stature wouldn't deign to appear in. And although he likes to claim righteousness about being paid his full worth ("I think by next year my price will be up to twelve, fifteen thousand dollars a night, and I got about twelve or fourteen dates I can get about twenty, twenty-five"), necessity often demands settling for far less than that.

It's the kind of grind that has worn down many over the years. But Bobby maintains he still feels "blessed" to be able to do what he loves for a living ("The last time I was there in Chicago, it rained, rained, rained, but we couldn't put the people in the house, there were so many people. Oh, I'm so thankful"). He also stresses his determination to give some of his good fortune back to his community, emphasizing that not all of his colleagues feel the same obligation:

> The people who think it's easy are the people who have that attitude, like, "get everything out of it." I did the Blues in the Schools, I did the jail ministry for about fifteen years off and on. I ministered to the people in jail, who unfortunately sometimes are there for no reason. Some are there for a reason, but I [still] try to give them hope and let them know that through a mistake, you can learn. When a man learn from a mistake, that's a stepping stone.

(In 2000, the state legislature of Mississippi passed Senate Resolution 43, commending "Mr. Bobby Rush" for his "career and humanitarianism," citing his work for sickle-cell anemia research as well his participation in Blues in the Schools programs and the prison ministry in Jackson.)[10]

What he doesn't feel good about, though, is the state of the music itself.

Part of his discontent has to do with the overall depression the recording industry has suffered in recent years. "In the record business, it's gone," he says, his eyes taking on an even steelier glint than usual.

> That goes for me, everybody else. In the record business, it's gone. And you only can perform when people know you from records. So you produce yourself, you record yourself, but you still got to have a name. Like me. Ain't nobody getting on record, but one who got a little name. I had someone tell me today, said, "Well, if I was you, I'd get somebody else to do this stuff [i.e., promotion, publicity, etc.]." But what they don't know is, ain't nobody to do it but you. [Bobby has been producing and releasing his material on his own Deep Rush label since the early 2000s.] Guys going around, cutting a record, looking for a record deal—ain't no deal. Deal is gone. The "deal" days is gone. Labels—God bless 'em. They're labels, but they ain't no labels. They do all they can do, but come on! Because ain't nobody buying records.

Performing opportunities are looking bleaker, as well. Even the southern circuit, where multiact revues still pack large venues on a regular basis, looks to Bobby more like a Potemkin blues village than a thriving musical environment.

> Yeah, they sell out because—a one-eyed man is hell in a blind house. No competition. The promoter's smart enough to know that if you get twelve acts, they have no competition, because who they gonna hire? They ain't got but twelve in Mississippi, so he got 'em all. It's about the dollar. Everything about the dollar. Everything about the money.

Paradoxically, though, he believes the music will improve as the competition gets fiercer to win whatever ears (and dollars) are still available. "I think it's gonna get better," he insists. "Because the less records that sell, more people gonna dive into the real music. A cat will scratch if you back him up against the wall. That's where the music gonna come. Came out in the Muddy Waters [era]—that's all he had, that's all he had to offer, and it was soulful."

But that's the long view. For the time being, the man who once slipped a coded reference to oral sex past a Jehovah's Witness in the recording studio also professes to be disenchanted with the unsavory direction the blues—or, if you prefer, southern soul ("'Southern soul,' that's a short-lived name, here today and gone tomorrow")—has been taking in recent years. Songwriters and performers seem increasingly willing to opt for cheap-seats pandering over the craftsmanship Bobby considers his hallmark; the result, he says, can be a kind of musical guilt by association.

If you run with a thief, and if the thief get caught, whether you do any-thing or not you're with the thief and get counted as what the thief did. Someone say, well, he's just another blues singer like some of the rest of the guys who've been doing it and maybe don't mean good about the blues or the people who sing it. They put me in the same category and throw me in the same box as the rest of 'em.

I always had a story. I ain't never [just] talked about "gettin' it from the back" or "lickin' it." I'm writing this song now. I'm talking about this woman that I know, supposed to be my woman, and I asked her, I said, "Baby, don't you think your dress is too short?" And I said, "When you went to church, and I noticed . . . the preacher couldn't hardly teach his text for lookin' at your under-yonder." See, "under-yonder" means look-ing beyond what he really see, whatever he saw that he thought he could see more. Now I said it like that because he understands, because faith is the substance of things unseen. That's a biblical statement in there. That's kinda deep! The old saying, what you don't know won't hurt you, but what you *think* can kill you.

As he warms to his topic, Bobby gives other examples of how deeply rooted his "funk-folk" really is:

I'm writing [another song] now about, I came home, and I could tell something was wrong because I saw the look on my wife's face, made me think that I surprised her when I came home. When I went into the bedroom, the bed's tore up, the pillows are on the floor like she had been in a pillow fight. And when I asked about it, that's when she got mad, and she started trippin'. That's what made me believe somebody's dippin' a dipper in my dippin's.

I'm talkin' 'bout what I believe. I ain't accusin' her, you follow me? What about when I walked in the kitchen; what about all these dirty dishes? And then I looked in my bar, there's a glass, two of 'em, they're still full, and a candle lit. Now what have you done, or what you plan to do? Now, it look like somebody been sitting at my table, eating the bread, in the cookie jar, and sleeping in my bed; I see ashes in my ashtray; I don't smoke. I seen footprints when I came in the house, leadin' to my back door.

In other words, I'm telling her in a way where a lady [in the audience] can say, "My husband think that, too, but you know what I'm gonna do tonight? I'm gonna get him right; I'm gonna tell him, 'Baby . . .'" See, re-ally I didn't accuse her; I was leaving her the room. "I'm thinkin' this, I believe that." All she got to do—"Baby, just pat me on the head and say it ain't true. Lie to me!"[11]

I'm writing about situations you can turn your head to. I know that nothing never slip up on a man. Because in the Old Testament you had to be taught right and wrong. But since the Resurrection, you don't have to be taught. It's called conscience. Any man know when he treatin' another man like he shouldn't be treated.

"Under-yonder," of course, is a play on "over yonder," the well-known metaphor for Heaven from the spiritual/gospel tradition; Bobby also cadged the "Dipper" allusion almost word-for-word from Cicero Blake's mid-1970s hit "Dip My Dipper." But there's a lot more going on here than irreverent wordplay. Bobby's references to "the substance of things unseen" and the Old Testament aren't just a bluesman's bon-mot attempts at profundity; they represent the core of what he is invoking with his parables in song, and they show that he's fully aware of its significance.

One of the most deeply held articles of faith in Africanist philosophical tradition is that only through personal experience can truth be ascertained. This tenet, rooted in pre-diasporic spiritualist beliefs and practices, was later adapted to the Pentecostalist notion that salvation is attained through an individual's one-on-one encounter with the divine, via the visitation of the Holy Spirit. "Things unseen" are made manifest, not by text or talk, but by witnessing and encountering them in their revealed form.[12] The preacher in Bobby's "under-yonder" story is conscious of "things unseen," but he won't be satisfied (or, by analogy, saved) until he experiences them firsthand.

In African American culture, this core belief is evidenced in everyday vernacular—"I'm telling you what I *know*, not what I've heard"; "These eyes don't lie"; the ubiquitous "can I get a witness?"—and signified upon in folklore and humor (as in the story of the man caught in *flagrante delicto*, who demands of his accuser, "Who you gonna believe—me or your lying eyes?"). Countless blues and R & B songs have played on it; the late Ronnie Lovejoy's "Sho Wasn't Me," popularized by Tyrone Davis in the early 2000s, may be the best-known recent one.

Having established this context, Bobby's second narrative exemplifies his "folk funk" technique at its most subversively rootsy and profound. His protagonist is a witness, confronted with evidence his eyes cannot deny. As he makes his pilgrimage through the house, he's experiencing revelations every step along the way. But this is not the odyssey of the spirit; this is the carnal, upside-down, backward world of the *heyoka*, where truth is both burlesqued and revealed through its opposite ("Baby, just pat me on the head and say it ain't true. Lie to me!"). In the irony-laden, signifying world of the blues trickster, a lie, not the truth, may set you free.

Contextual understanding such as this is felt intuitively rather than discussed or, probably, even thought about consciously by most of Bobby's core audience. The laughter and delight that erupt during his act in a nightclub, where almost everyone knows the routines word for word, are akin to what goes on at a family reunion: the old jokes and stories are trotted out and celebrated as shared heritage, not merely entertainment. As much as anything having to do with dance moves or physicality ("If you know the history of African people," he says, "and black people as a whole, we dance, we play ball, we run, we jump, we box; those are some of the traits of black people"[13]), this is what Bobby is getting at when he insists that he does a "black show," and that any attempt to modify or censor his act is an affront to his identity as well as his art. "If you're a black man," he maintains, "you're not, sometimes, treated as fair, you're just part of—There's something that comes with being black. It's part of life. You're a lower-class citizen to some people."

He gives little credence to well-meaning whites, musicians and otherwise, who suggest that this kind of racialist identity-mongering is an artifact of the past. Although he admires some white blues artists, such as Eric Clapton and Bonnie Raitt, whom he sees as giving credit to their music's origins and progenitors, he insists that the music must retain its cultural identity to be understood and that liberal bromides such as "music has no color" are disingenuous at best.

"That's a way of copping out from telling the truth for what it is," he maintains. "Music don't have no color? It does. It does. Or, music don't have no color, but the people who sing it and think about it, they have colors, or races, in mind, about how to separate who sings what. Because if it's a black band, where they may be getting fifty dollars a night for four guys, you pay the white boy, same thing I do, you pay him three times as much money."

If more evidence were needed that "color," or at least ethnicity, is inextricably bound with blues expression, he cites the mannered verbal blackface many white blues musicians seem to feel compelled to adopt in the name of "authenticity"—an affectation that Bobby, for all of his own masking and identity shifts, finds deeply offensive.

> The worst thing that ever happened to me, personally, when I hear older black people singing, "I don't like the way you do dis and dat"—not "this" and "that," "dis" and "dat," usually because they weren't educated to say it; then we got white guys, very educated white guys, sing the song as such. And that bothers me. They just want to sound like the black guy was sounding. A white guy trying to say it just like the black guy was saying it. What [the original black singer] was saying lost all its meaning and guts.
>
> There is color; that's a cop-out. Because there is a difference. Nobody wants to keep on saying about black and white issues, but it do, it do appear in a lot of angles, and it's happening. I'm not talking about you're supposed to dive, wallow in it, but it's the truth.

Figure 14. "This is all about a joke . . . and they leave there with joy in their mind."
Bobby Rush and Mizz Lowe take a bow at the 2007 Chicago Blues Festival. Photo
by Paul Natkin/Photo Reserve, Inc.

His response, predictably, has been to dig more deeply into his armamentarium of trickster's ruses ("It's nothing wrong with picking cotton if
you own the field that you pick it out of"). Although he insists that "the
public ain't never said I was raunchy. You know who said I was raunchy?
People like yourself—the people who write about it," at times his act has
set off definite ripples of culture shock among white "crossover" audiences
and listeners. It's not just political correctness on their part; some have
shown him condescension or even outright disrespect, which he's parried
appropriately: "White guy look at me, big ol' smile on his face, say, 'Hey
Bobby Rush, where the booty girls at?' I tell 'em, 'At your house.' And
what I'm [really] saying is, 'That's your mama, that's your sister who's the
booty girl.'"

Usually, of course, his signifying goes well over the questioner's head.

The dancers can also cause other problems, especially among jittery white promoters. In one instance, Bobby recalls, a promoter told him, "I want you to work this show for me, but I want to ask you something. Can you work without the girls?"

> Study it! This is what she says. This is how I understood where she was coming from, while she's telling me. I said, "Sure I can." I signed the contract. I had four girls with me at that time. When I got to Florida, I had ten. She said, "Oh, God, I thought you could work without the girls." "I said I *can*—I didn't say I *would*." 'Cause I knew what she was getting at. Now she said, "This is a family-orientated show." She underestimated me. When I got up there, the girls had the gowns on, they didn't turn around, and I [even] did some gospel. She said, "Oh, I didn't know you could do that." I said, "Because you underestimated me. You underestimated my intelligence."

The gamesmanship has gotten even more complex as the money has gotten tighter. One of the ways Bobby has kept active during the recent economic slump has been to strip down his show. Sometimes he performs solo, accompanying himself on guitar and harmonica, which allows his storytelling gifts to shine even more brightly than usual. This means, though, that it can be hard to predict which show he's going to bring in unless the contract is very specific—a specificity he seems to manage to avoid quite often. In fact, his tactics in these cases, as well his pride in using them, could stand as emblematic of how he's managed to maintain his career through the years in the face of unpredictable record sales, shady promoters, fluctuating public tastes, shifting commercial trends, economic uncertainty—often, it seems, in the face of logic itself and with few apparent resources other than the sweat of his brow and the depth of his guile.

"I went to work last year," he relates. "I did my acoustic thing. The man, he loved it, [but he] said, 'I thought you were bringing the band.' I said, 'I didn't tell you about bringing no band. You hired Bobby Rush.' 'I though the girls gonna be on this show.' I said, 'I didn't tell nobody they would or they wouldn't. I decided I wouldn't use 'em tonight.' I didn't tell him I wasn't gonna bring nobody. I didn't tell him I was gonna come with the acoustic. I didn't tell him I wasn't.

"I'm still in control. I had my money."

Part III

"Now Playing Love Games"

Voices from the New Generation

5

Willie Clayton

Last Man Standing

I am for the young, as well as the old
I am rhythm and blues . . . here to soothe your soul
You got hip-hop and rap all over the earth
But I am rhythm and blues, I was here first
—Robert Jones, Willie Clayton, and Todd Vaughn,
"I Am Rhythm and Blues," 2012

"I ain't tellin' you what I *think*; I'm tellin' you what I *know*."

When Willie Clayton wraps his honey-and-molasses croon around a ballad like "Simply Beautiful" or "I Love Me Some You," he can melt hearts in the most cavernous auditorium or civic center. Right now, though, he's in preaching mode.[1] Fired by the same determination to stake his claim—and, above all, to *win*—that has propelled him through the years from a restless small-town Mississippi childhood through the vicissitudes of midlevel R & B semiobscurity into the forefront of contemporary soul-blues stardom, he tightens his voice into a hoarse bark and builds to a shout as he reaffirms his conviction that he, and he alone, is qualified to decide how he should be categorized.

"People talk about, 'Well, what are you?'" he continues. "'Are you a blues singer?' I tell 'em simply one thing: 'I'm a singer.' There is no title for a singer. I'm a singer. I can sing whatever. I'm a singer."

Not to discredit anyone [who] want to be called "Southern Soul"; that's them. [But] I'm not that. Never have been, never will be. I'm old school, bro. I'm not tootin' my own horn, but the great singers—the Johnnie Taylors, Tyrone Davis, them guys, I miss 'em. Because you don't hear that type of good singing no more. Marvin Sease—Marvin Sease was a *soul* singer. J. Blackfoot, cats like that—we're not "southern soul." You think about it. There's no "southern soul" category in the Academy [i.e., the National Academy of Recording Arts and Sciences, which sponsors the Grammys]; so why would I want to be called something that don't even really exist in the Academy?

"I'd rather be called blues," he adds, perhaps retreating a bit from his initial declaration. His main point, in any case, is clear: "I'm not southern soul."

What it really should be labeled as—if it's gonna be labeled as anything— it's soul-blues. That's what it is. Blues—you gotta really have soul to sing blues, too, now. Can the southern soul singers really sing blues? So once again, don't get me wrong; it's not to discredit anyone that wanna be called southern soul. [But] listen to the production, and listen to the vocals. Then you go find me some Johnnie Taylor . . . some Tyrone Davis, J. Blackfoot, some Marvin Sease, some Otis Clay, even some Shirley Brown, Denise LaSalle—note, now, I didn't put myself in it—and tell me: what artist that call themself southern soul can sing like that?

His baby-faced countenance, his supple voice with its mellifluous upper range, and his willingness to incorporate modernist R & B and hip-hop influences in his studio production might seem to belie his "old school" claims, but Willie has mastered the art of looking both fondly back and bravely forward at the same time, simultaneously avoiding the twin traps of trendiness and nostalgia. At fifty-seven, he's still relatively young by the standards of the genre he claims to disdain but which nonetheless embraces him as one of its own; although he's been a professional for over forty years, he didn't chart until 1984, and it wasn't until the early 1990s, when he hooked up with Johnny Vincent's Ace label, that he become a household name on the southern soul-blues circuit.

Billboard's national R & B singles charts list only six moderate hits for Willie in addition to that 1984 debut, none reaching higher than No. 52. Yet quite a few of his latter-day releases have become soul-blues standards. In fact, although there's no official tally to document it, he's probably had as many radio and club hits as any soul-blues artist since the genre emerged in the early 1980s, even though he didn't really get on the bandwagon until about a decade later. His flamboyant, often cocky stage demeanor makes him among the most captivating (and sometimes incendiary) figures on the circuit. He is, in short, the closest thing soul-blues has to a bona fide "superstar," now that both Johnnie Taylor and Marvin Sease have passed away.

To hear Willie tell it, his success was virtually ordained from the start. Born in 1955 by midwife in an unmapped hamlet called Fansonia outside of Indianola, Mississippi (there is still a Fansonia Plantation Road a few miles northeast of town), he moved with his family to the nearby town of Sunflower when he was young. His father, L. C. Clayton, did farmwork; his mother, Rosie Clayton, labored as a domestic in "rich white folks' houses." Willie, though, became focused on music almost as soon as he was old enough to know what it was.

"The story goes like this," he asserts. "From the time I was a little baby, I was singing. So it has never been a doubt in my mind what I wanted to

Figure 15. Willie Clayton, 2007 Chicago Blues Festival. Photo by Paul Natkin/ Photo Reserve.

do. With no formal vocal training, you know it's got to be a God-gifted talent in order for me to be able to do what I do with my voice. I been wanting to do this since I was five, six years old; this is all I've done all my life."

Willie remembers that his mother used to sing in the kitchen while she was cooking, and his father both sang and played harmonica ("At one point I started messing with the harmonica; I left it alone, but I wish I had kept it up"). His real musical education, though, occurred in "a little tavern, which down South was called a café," that his parents operated. He'd listen to the jukebox ("Back then, the jukebox wasn't called a jukebox, they were called Seabirds [i.e., Seeburgs]"), and when his older brother, L. C. Jr., began to manage a local soul band, they'd rehearse there. Willie smelled opportunity almost immediately.

"I would go and watch them through the window, practicing. I would often tell my older brother, older sisters, 'I can sing.' One time they was playing at my mom's café. The drummer didn't show up, so they said, 'Come on, let us see can you sing.' I not only showed 'em I could sing, I could play drums, too, and they didn't even know it. So I did 'em both, and the rest is history."

It didn't take long for the prodigy to expand his reputation. "I remember my older sisters, my older brother, used to sneak me out of the window when my mother and father would go to sleep, braggin' about this little brother they had that could sing. They would sneak me to Ruleville, Mississippi, all the different little towns. [I was] 'bout seven years old, eight years old. They would get me back so I wouldn't be too tired for school."

> You know, it's funny that certain things, God bless you not to be able to forget. I'm glad for those times, because I honestly feel like that's what really prepared me for later in life. I remember my first pay I made—fifty cents. And the most I ever made was five dollars. I was about eight years old; I don't remember the name of the place, but I was a little shorty; I was a kid. In Ruleville, Mississippi. I made five dollars—my first official gig. They always say you are truly a professional when you get paid; I don't care whether it's a quarter, nickel, or what; you get paid, you are considered as a professional. So that was my first professional gig—I got paid.

Child stars have long been a mainstay in black pop music (Sugar Chile Robinson, Frankie Lyman, Little Esther Phillips, Little Willie John, and, of course, Michael Jackson are only a few of the better known); young Willie Clayton found himself in demand early on. Within a few years, he was traveling the local circuit with a ten-piece big band under the directorship of a Mississippi Valley State College grad and local music teacher named Leon Wright. "I was this little kid singing with all these grown guys," he affirms. "Everyone in this band, they all had college degrees. We used to play the college circuit quite a bit, and we'd play clubs like the VFW in Greenville; we'd play Indianola. We was the hot thing; people was coming to see this little singing sensation in front of a big band."

He also worked with other, bigger chitlin' circuit names. Texas-based vocalist Ernie Johnson (who is still a soul-blues mainstay) hired him as a drummer and occasional singer on his show ("Ernie was more of a big brother to me," Willie remembers fondly, "watching over my little butt out there"); when famed guitarist Jimmy Liggins brought Johnson onto his own tour, he was duly impressed by the talented youngster in Ernie's band. He recorded a single on Willie, "That's the Way Daddy Did" and "Falling in Love," and issued it on his Duplex imprint. The disc didn't go anywhere, but its very existence was more evidence—if any were needed—that Mississippi was not big enough to contain the talent and ambition of Willie Clayton. In 1969, at "fourteen, going on fifteen years old," he hit what he already knew would be his road of destiny.

"It wasn't happening in the South the way that it should," he attests. "Plus, there was no opportunity for a young black man in Mississippi back then—his chances was very, very slim, without getting throwed in the river. I love my Mississippi roots, but I had to go where I could survive."

> For a young black singer or musician, it was no different than [any] black man trying to get from down South to get North—where'd they migrate to? To Chicago, where the opportunities was at. They might go to Chicago, Detroit. . . . Where did Little Milton end up at? Chicago. Where did Tyrone Davis end up at? Chicago. Where did Jerry Butler end up at, and [he's] still there? Chicago. Where did Willie Clayton end up at? Chicago. And it just goes on and on—Muddy Waters, Jimmy Reed, Little Milton Campbell, Otis Clay, Denise [LaSalle] . . . there you have it. It was the way out.

Although he still had to go to school in Chicago, at least for a while ("Man, that been so long ago, I don't even remember the name of the school. All I know, it was a private school"), he kept his mind focused on what by now felt more like a calling than a dream. "I did what was more important to me at the time," he says, explaining why he left high school as a senior. "Kept it moving." His sisters, Ethel and Jeanette, the same ones who'd spirited him out of the house to perform in Sunflower, were already living in Chicago. Once again, they lent their baby brother a hand.

"My older sisters asked me, was I scared? Did I feel I was ready? I'm like, 'Yeah!' So we went to the Burning Spear, 5525 [actually 5521–23] South State Street. Pervis Spann the Blues Man was running the Burning Spear at the time; I think him and E. Rodney Jones. That was 1971—so how long ago was that? That's a long time, brother."

Spann was—and is—an icon in Chicago black music. One of the legendary "Good Guys" on radio station WVON, he was still hosting his famous all-night *Blues Man Show,* which helped keep the blues alive in Chicago's black community long after the music faded from popularity elsewhere, when Willie arrived in town. He was also one of the city's most successful—and, in some quarters, notorious—promoters ("I had all the entertainment, black-wise, in my hand," he said. "The white folks wouldn't fool with no black entertainment . . . they just left it to me"[2]), renowned for his multiact extravaganzas at venues like the International Amphitheatre on the South Side and the Arie Crown Theater near the Loop downtown.

Along with revues featuring both local and nationally known performers, Spann instituted talent shows that launched several important careers (he's credited with being one of the first to recognize Michael Jackson's genius); he eventually expanded into artist representation as well; his roster at one point included B. B. King. In the mid-1960s, he and fellow WVON personality E. Rodney Jones opened the Burning Spear (formerly Club DeLisa), which rapidly became one of the Midwest's hot spots for soul music and R & B as well as the occasional old-school blues act like King or Bobby "Blue" Bland.[3]

By his own account, Willie Clayton was awestruck by neither Spann's presence nor his reputation when he and his sisters arrived at the Burning Spear that fateful night in 1971: "My sister told 'em, say, 'We got our little brother; he can sing. You let him audition.'"

> Pervis Spann looked at me, said, "So, little boy, you think you want to do this?" I said, "Yes, sir." Back then at the Burning Spear, they would bring acts in like the Stylistics, the Enchantments, the Dramatics, whoever was hot, they would bring 'em in for five or seven straight days. Pervis Spann had a nephew named Earl English from Battle Creek, Michigan, and he was the opening act. I said, "Man, I've never heard your nephew sing, but I'll blow him clean off the stage." He was like, "Okay." I said, "Better than that, I'll steal the show from the Stylistics!" So he told my sister, bring me back up there that Friday. Buddy, I hit the stage singing "Stand by Me," and I stole the show, true enough. And he fired his nephew. I ended up with the job.

Spann recognized a winning hand when he saw one. Before long, he was managing Willie; he put him on shows opening for Al Green, among others ("anybody that was doing anything worthwhile, I was with 'em"), and he hustled his name around the industry. Willie knew he'd latched onto a good thing, too. "Pervis was over there at 'VON," he remembers. "Those guys, they was it. If you wanted a record to really break, your record had to get broken out of Chicago. And if 'VON didn't play it, nobody was interested in playing it.

"I did all the major stuff; I didn't play any small places. Smallest club I performed in was the Burning Spear, and at the time the Burning Spear was the hottest thing on the scene. I did the Auditorium [Theatre]; I did the Opera House; I did the McVickers Theatre downtown; I did the International Amphitheatre."

As was his wont, Spann parlayed his clout and charisma into a rare opportunity for his budding young star. "Pervis Spann knew Willie Mitchell," Willie recalls. "Over there at 'VON, they broke the Al Green records out of Chicago. This business, it's all about who you know or who know you. Back then, and even to this day. So quite naturally, I'm sure that's probably one reason why Willie Mitchell said, 'Okay, Spann—let's see what he got.'"

Willie Mitchell, long respected as one of soul music's most brilliant and influential producers, was by now also vice president of Hi Records, the label that had brought Green and Ann Peebles, among others, into prominence. Hi was a heady place for a virtual unknown like Willie Clayton to land, but by the time he arrived there, the mood at the erstwhile Memphis hit factory was beginning to darken. Green, Hi's biggest star, was beset with existential and spiritual uncertainties, wrestling with the age-old contradiction between Saturday night and Sunday morning, wracked with guilt for not having dedicated his life and voice to the Lord. Although Hi had other dependable artists in its stable, Green was its top draw and main moneymaker; losing him would (and, in the end, did) plunge the entire operation into crisis.

Meanwhile, even though Hi was still generating plenty of hits and as gifted a producer as Willie Mitchell was, he'd begun to come under some criticism. That boxy Hi beat, seasoned by Latin-tinged rhythmic textures, leavened by organ swirls, and prodded by Mitchell's trademark "lazy" horn lines, had been a breath of fresh air when artists like Green and Peebles rode it to stardom in the late 1960s and early '70s; within a few years, though, deejays and some critics were complaining that everything coming out of Mitchell's Royal Studio sounded the same (a charge that's been leveled, at one time or another, at virtually every label or studio with an identifiable "house" sound). In response, Mitchell established the Pawn subsidiary in 1974, apparently hoping that a new imprint and a few fresh voices might bring some diversity to the proceedings.[4]

Whether the plan succeeded is a matter of debate; some of Willie Clayton's Pawn sides sound so close to what had become Hi boilerplate that it's still something of a shock to hear a voice other than Al Green's come in after the intro. But the songs were, for the most part, well crafted—most were written by Hi's in-house team, although a few were credited or co-credited to Pervis Spann himself—and Willie's voice, although it had yet to attain the subtleties of nuance and emotion that would distinguish his later outings, was shot through with confident power. In places, it sounded as if producer Mitchell was trying to answer his critics by adapting to the era's rock-tinged, hard-funk/postfunk aesthetic: he occasionally double-tracked his singer's voice and immersed it in a dense sonic miasma; on some songs he also toughened the trademark Hi lope with a metallic-sounding harshness that presaged both disco and the trigger-drums and synthesized beats that would come to define R & B in subsequent decades.

The Hi Willie Clayton sides, in other words, sounded mostly like what they were: admirable freshman efforts from a gifted young singer still finding his voice, produced by a legendary craftsman who was beginning to see the soul aesthetic he'd helped create give way to a newer, less subtle pop landscape. None made much of an impact, and by 1976 Willie was once more on his own. It would be at least eight years before he would again record anything of significance. He doesn't talk much about those years, but he insists that he remained undaunted. "Later on," he says, "I would run into Willie Mitchell; Willie would say, 'You didn't stop—[you did] what you said you was gonna do.' I told him, any and everybody, all my life, I said, 'Man, listen: don't ever count me out.'"

In about 1980, he formed his own Sky Hero label and released a few sides; he also recorded for Kirstee, which he co-owned with his manager Luther Terry. Finally, in early 1984, he released "Tell Me" on Compleat, a short-lived but influential Nashville-based imprint with an eclectic lineup that included everyone from country singers such as Vern Gosdin and rockers like Bachman-Turner Overdrive through mainstream R & B and soul artists (the Tams, Joe Simon, Willie himself) to the pioneering hip-hop act Autumn. "Tell Me" debuted in March and made it to No. 78 on the national charts, good enough to convince Compleat to issue a follow-up, "What a Way to Put It," later that year. Both were produced by General Crook, a veteran vocalist, songwriter, and producer whose own recordings on the Down to Earth and Wand labels had achieved modest success in the 1970s.

Crook seems to have had a savvier vision for what would bring out the best in Willie Clayton than Mitchell had had. His lyrics were knowing and worldly, presaging the adult themes that would eventually characterize the best soul-blues; the sound was resonant, with strings both enveloping Willie's voice and providing it buoyant support. That voice had matured, as well; it was deeper and fuller, and Willie sounded more at ease than he had at Hi, as if he could let his feelings flow instead of forcing them. His upper range segued into a confident falsetto, and the challenging melodic lines seemed to inspire rather than daunt him. Even though the mix was a bit murky in places, one could hear a new, mature Willie Clayton vocal identity being forged: full-bodied with a tinge of grit, charged with a churchy fervor, and laced with romantic longing.

The songs themselves, though, sounded oddly undefined: were these pop baubles or retro deep-soul testimonials? It may have been this lack of an identifiable niche, as much as anything, that prevented the records from charting higher than they did ("What a Way to Put It" topped out at No. 84). For his part, though, Willie felt as if he was finally glimpsing the beginnings of the success he'd been pursuing—and believing in—since childhood.

"Oh, yeah," he enthuses. "The venues changed—the money changed too, you know? I wound up doing some bigger venues and better things, and I got a chance to perform in some major markets—New York, Miami, places like that."

> ["Tell Me"] was a national hit. It was not only a national hit, it was international. I became one of the all-time favorites over in London, England, over in Japan. . . . I remember in '88, I was over in London, England, performing at the London Astoria, and I went to do two weeks, I ended up being there for two months. I did all of England, I did Switzerland, I did Scotland, I did Wales, I did Germany—I made crazy money. They had a full orchestra for me over there; I took one guitar player with me. They knew music of mine that I'd forgotten all about. I wound up finding out that a 45—"Tell Me" was on a 45—that record over there was selling for like eighteen, twenty pounds. I was like, man! If I'd knew that, I would've brought me a suitcase of these singles over here, man. If you ever really a real, quote-unquote, "star," to them you always a big star.

Meanwhile, though, another fallow period had set in. "What a Way to Put It" was Willie's final hit for Compleat; by the time he went on that European tour, he hadn't charted for at least four years. By his own admission, Willie spent much of his time after leaving Compleat "trying to find my way back, debating what I was going to do." Not that he was totally inactive, he's quick to add: "Oh, yeah—I put out some singles; in 1985, I had a hot single that I put out on my own label [Big City]. That's the first time that I really put a record out on my own label that really went and got some national exposure."

That record, "Happy,"[5] was a frothy celebration of romantic love, something of a throwback to earlier-era pop romanticism. Along with "Your Sweetness" (in 1987) and a few of his other Kirstee releases, it garnered enough attention to keep Willie gigging along the circuit from northern outposts like Chicago and Detroit through the Deep South. Willie also released an LP called *Forever* on the British Timeless label in 1988, which consisted primarily of material he had recorded for Kirstee. His voice seemed grainier and more expressive now (if still disarmingly boyish), and the overall production was tougher and more adventurous than it had been at Compleat, with hints of a George Benson–like jazz-funk fusion in places and greater sonic and textural depth. The standout track was the ebullient "Your Sweetness," on which Willie's muscular vocals smoothly negotiated a challenging melody line as his studio backing conjured up an aura of urbane romanticism.

Having an LP on a British aficionados' imprint along with a handful of regional hits that kept him scuffling on the chitlin' circuit, though, was not the stardom he'd envisioned for himself. Probably for that reason, despite Willie's growing disenchantment with the mainstream music industry ("I said, 'Man, I don't know if I even want to be with a record label'"), the seduction was hard to resist. "We [wound] up doing a deal direct with Polydor," Willie remembers, "and they put me with a producer out of White Plains, New York—biggest mistake that ever took place."

> I started putting down some tracks; it was supposed to been a split deal because we were actually fronting the money, my manager and myself. It ended up, this quote-unquote "producer" took all the credit and just took all the money. So at that point I had a bitter taste in my mouth. So, '88, before I came back to the States, I could've did a deal while I was over in England with Virgin Records, but my manager, I called him from over there, and he said, "Man, we got this situation on the table, and we don't ever want to be people that our word is no good." That's how that ended up. So after I finished with the Polydor deal, after I got out of that, I said, "No more. From here on, I'm on my own."

The records themselves, co-produced by Lionel Job and "Claytoven," were released under the name of Will Clayton. Three of them struggled onto the national charts in 1989, none getting higher than No. 52, which is where "Never Too Late" peaked in the early part of the year. The production had become noticeably more aggressive—but also more forced. The trigger-drum explosions on "Never Too Late" seemed to shoot down, rather than propel, the song's pop-brightened jubilance; the somewhat disingenuously titled "Tell Me" (no relation to Willie's earlier song), which peaked at No. 74, sounded like an attempt to re-create the heady, techno-charged exuberance of a disco dance floor, but the sonic overkill sounded more Wagnerian than funky. The ballad "I Wanna Be Where You Are," with guest vocals by Audrey Wheeler, hit the ceiling at No. 62; pianist Thor Baldursson's romantic grandiosity blended well with the singers' breathy emoting, but once again those drum blasts intruded. Probably most frustrating, though, were Willie's vocals; as strong and on-target as they were, they seemed oddly impersonal, as if in transforming himself from "Willie" to "Will" he'd also changed from a roots-rich soul man into a generic pop-soul crooner.

In retrospect, it seems clear that either "Claytoven," his co-producer, or both were struggling to adapt Willie's deep-soul roots to the demands of a youth-driven pop aesthetic that had been skewed into new shapes, first by disco and then by its high-tech dance-track successors, including, by this time, rap. It also seems clear that it would probably have made more sense for him to jump on the soul-blues bandwagon as soon as it left the barn in the early '80s. He should have immediately recognized Z. Z. Hill and those who followed in his footsteps as kindred spirits. He certainly couldn't have been unaware of the money flowing around the chitlin' circuit as revitalized soul-blues singers began playing to larger audiences again (no doubt some of the gigs he worked after "Happy" broke for him in 1985 were on some of these very shows).

But in fact it took until the early 1990s for Willie to insinuate himself into the southern soul-blues mainstream. A brief stay at Ichiban in 1992 resulted in *Feels Like Love,* an eight-song CD that didn't result in any notable hits but showcased a far more mature singer, supported by production that sounded at least as contemporary as his backing at Polydor but was more complementary to his voice and material. When the trigger drums were used (as on the sprightly pop bauble "Walk Away from You"), they added texture rather than annoyance; on ballads ("Special Lady," "Make Me Yours"), the electronic studio backing deepened the mood rather than getting in the way. Out front, Willie's voice sounded reborn; he was rediscovering the churchy muscularity that he'd hinted at on some of his earlier recordings and which would soon become his calling card.

Being on Ichiban may have raised Willie's profile a bit, but despite the material's quality, it didn't gain him much of a soul-blues foothold. But then, in 1993, he entered into what he still maintains was "just a handshake—a deal together, but there was never no contract" with Johnny Vincent at Ace Records in Jackson, Mississippi. Almost immediately, his fortunes swung upward with the playfully ironic "Three People (Sleeping in My Bed)," which combined bluesy erotic paranoia ("There's three people sleeping in my bed / Me and my woman and the man in her head") with soul's redemptive uplift (Willie tightened his voice into an agonized gospel scream then cooled things down with a jaunty "aw-shucks" chorus). "Three People" was a major soul-blues radio hit, and it's since become a genre classic. It sounded so natural and effortless that one might have wondered why it had taken so long to happen. What had Johnny Vincent done that others had missed? Very likely, he simply had the wisdom to sit back and allow his artist's gifts to shine on their own terms: no gimmicks, no unnecessary control-room intrusion, no pandering to trends—just stay out of the way and let the man be himself.

Whatever it was, the formula worked. In 1994, Ace released Willie's cover of Al Green's "Simply Beautiful," a ballad that laid his gruff croon over an acoustic-guitar-and-strings accompaniment; seldom in southern soul-blues (which still often prided itself on its gutbucket roots) had an artist achieved such an effortless fusion of pop sophistication and naked emotionality. The following year he came out with "Equal Opportunity," penned by Chicago-based songwriter Bob Jones, which updated the cheating-song theme for a new era: over an ironically seductive ballad backing, Willie and guest vocalist Pat Brown sang the story of a two-timing man whose wife finally takes matters into her own hands and has an affair of her own, stopping him in his tracks with the riposte, "Now you call it cheatin', baby, but I call it equal opportunity."

According to Willie's liner notes on his 1995 CD *Ace in the Hole,* his manager fielded over six thousand fan letters in response to "Equal Opportunity"; admirers even organized "Equal Opportunity Clubs" in its honor. That same year, Ichiban dug into its vaults and issued two fresh Willie Clayton CDs, one of which included a spellbinding cover of Lee Fields's underground classic "Meet Me Tonite" (née "Tonight"). (The best of these have been anthologized on *Essential Love Songs,* released in 2002 on former Stax president Al Bell's Bellmark imprint.) "I was riding high, man," Willie confirms today. "From 1993 'til 2000, you couldn't touch me. I was untouchable."

For once, he might be selling himself short. In fact, Willie Clayton has remained pretty much "untouchable" ever since, maintaining his altitude in the upper echelons of the southern soul-blues firmament with scarcely a miscue or a lost opportunity. His recordings since his Ace days have continually both set and raised the bar for soul-blues excellence. As Johnnie Taylor was before him, he is the vocalist to whom virtually all male singers in the field are compared and whom they're invariably accused of imitating, whether deservedly or not, when they tear off an especially expressive or soulful passage. Perhaps even more impressively, he's managed to do it mostly on his own terms. Aside from a mid-2000s stint with Malaco, during which, he insists, he still held the creative reins ("Malaco did not record Willie Clayton. Mr. Couch say, 'Hey, we're not gonna mess with your creativeness. You record it, and you bring it to us.'

Figure 16. Willie Clayton, 2003 Chicago Blues Festival, with vocalists Dee Alexander and Yvonne Gage. Photo by Gene Tomko.

So that's what we did"), since leaving Ace he's appeared on a series of independent labels that he has usually owned, co-owned, or at least had a direct involvement in.

As far as he's concerned, it's all a continuation of the musical mission he's been on since the beginning. The title of his 2005 Malaco debut CD, *The Last Man Standing*,[6] reflects both his self-image and his reputation among aficionados as a singer for whom upholding cherished soul values is a calling as well as a calling card. Despite his Polydor-era concessions to postdisco artifice, he's succeeded primarily by refusing the pose of ironic detachment in favor of emotional honesty: whether on romantic ballads like "I Love Me Some You" or eros-charged workouts like the steaming "Boom Boom Boom" (from 2006's *Gifted,* also on Malaco); whether extolling the virtues of old-school juking ("Party Like We Used to Do," penned by his erstwhile keyboardist Terence Kimble, known today as T. K. Soul) or transforming what could have been a playa's boast into a tender erotic promise ("Love Mechanic"); whether throwing down a challenge to hip-hop–era haters by mashing up spoken-word tracks from rappers Young Bap and the Ying Yang Twins with his own grits-and-molasses croon on such outings as "Fact, No Rumor" and "Monkey See, Monkey Do" (both from 2005's *Changing tha Game*) or paying affectionate tribute to his roots (he has covered standards by Tyrone Davis, Bobby "Blue" Bland, the Manhattans, and others); whether revisiting the perennial soul-bluesman's pose as a lovable rogue (the Z. Z. Hill–like "How Do You Love Two"), pleading his case for steadfast romantic values ("Unconditionally," "Old Fashioned Girl"), or celebrating love's soul-rejuvenating power (the various versions of "Happy"/"Happy Time" he's released over the years), he unfailingly invokes the spirit of the giants he acknowledges as his role models (Tyrone Davis, Al Green, Johnnie Taylor), even as he refuses to admit having patterned himself after any of them ("I didn't want to sound like anybody").

At the same time, his production has developed into what is probably the most deeply textured in southern soul-blues. "It's like this," he explains. "If my 1972 car is not running that good, get out of it and get into the new age type car. I look at music pretty much the same way: Where's the music going? How can my music be relevant today, just like it was in 1973 or 1984 when I came with 'Tell Me'? When they [i.e., radio programmers] tell you that line that 'it don't fit our format,' what they mean is, the production is too poor. So what I did, I went out and got some young producers. I used some of the same producers that the hip-hoppers use."

But alongside the programmed tracks and synthesizers, he flavors his songs with acoustic guitar lines, natural-sounding percussion fillips, and other throwback reminders of soul music's origins. His vocals convey the timeless soul balance between sensuality and spirit; even when he embarks on one of his rare sojourns into raw carnality (e.g., "Tongue Bath" or his take on Marvin Sease's "Candy Licker"), he manages to sound more like a man bent on fulfilling his lady's desires than a braying stud. The title of another of his CDs, 2009's *Love, Romance, & Respect,* invokes sentiments not often heard in contemporary R & B, let alone soul-blues, but it's true to both his self-proclaimed "old-school" stance and the values he says he was raised with and tries to honor in his music and his life.

"When your foundation is laid," he says, again ascending into a preacher's tone and cadence, "the house will always stand. A tornado can come through, a hurricane can come through, blow the whole house away, but the foundation's still standing. My foundation was laid from a child. Mama didn't go wrong when [she] told the baby boy, 'Don't forget that God made it all possible; don't forget that if you ask in the name of Jesus, then God will grant it in grace.' I did a gospel CD [*God Has a Plan* on Avanti in 1998]. I didn't do it to get money from it; I did it for my own salvation."

> I don't come to preach, but . . . no one knows how God want me to get His message out there. No matter where I go, whether it be a club, whether it be an auditorium, God is with me everywhere I go. When I perform, I praise Him; when I'm home, I praise Him. . . . Look at it like this, and this is not to convince anyone, but if you know the story of David, then you know mine. David was a man after God's heart. God created all things, then who created this secular music? I'm not hurtin' nobody; I'm not singing about how I'm gon' shoot somebody; I'm not singin' about how you go beat up on your woman. I sing about relationships: "I Love Me Some You," "Unconditionally," [even] "Three People Sleeping in My Bed"—those are relationship songs.
>
> I continually steer my life, trying to develop my vocal skills, my production, to wherever this music is going. I'm still relevant, and the music is very, very much alive that I'm doing. Listen to "Love and Happiness" by Al Green, which was recorded in 1973,[7] you can appreciate it today like you did then. You can listen to Frankie Beverly and Maze, "Southern Girl," music like that, you can appreciate it today like you did back then. You don't get no major radio in Chicago or New York or Atlanta playing southern soul, but they still play Marvin Gaye every day, they still play Frankie Beverly every day, they still play some Johnnie Taylor, some Tyrone, [and] I've had major airplay in Chicago, major airplay on both of the stations in Detroit; Milwaukee; St. Louis; Kansas City; Los Angeles, California; Rochester, New York; Buffalo, New York; Sirius XM, because I've been cutting [with] that caliber of production and those caliber type songs.

When we finish this next CD [in 2012], the title of the CD is gonna be *I Am Rhythm and Blues.* Where does "I Am" come from? The Bible. I didn't make this up on my own; God in Heaven gave me this [title]. I called [Chicago songwriter] Bob Jones and I said, "Bob, look at what God gave me. You wanna be a part of this?" Listen to the lyric:

"I been all over the world, payin' dues / I've got the right to rhythm and blues / Come on, people, let's have a ball / I am rhythm and blues, and I'm still standing tall."

6

Sweet Angel
Lessons in Life

September 26, 2009: Sweet Angel is hosting a combined birthday party for herself and her husband, Mike
Dobbins, at the Whitehaven Celebration Complex on
Elvis Presley Boulevard in Memphis, Tennessee. The
wall behind her on stage is draped with silver tinsel;
as she sings and banters with her audience she strides,
gyrates, and shimmies back and forth across the stage,
her legs ample and sexy in full-length fishnet stock-
ings. Lithe, occasionally provocative, and almost constantly in motion, she radiates sensuality like a diva in
the great blues and soul tradition, updated for a more
explicit age.

Thus far she's led her listeners through a carefully
choreographed emotional journey. They've navigated
through highs and lows, moments of victory, womanly
solidarity ("I know somebody out there tonight been
there. . . . Somebody goin' through it right now"), defeat, and renewal—from the ribald dance-floor exuberance of "Butt Up!" and the double-entendre silliness of "The Tongue Don't Need No Viagra" through
the gently swaying, playfully ironic "I'd Rather Have a
Cheating Man" to a ramped-up but careworn version

of "I Must Be Crazy," the Mike Dobbins–penned country-soul ballad that appeared on her debut CD, *Another Man's Meat on My Plate*, in 2007.

It's been, more or less, a typical southern soul-blues evening: musical tales of infidelity, cuckoldry, sexual one-upwomanship, and erotic satisfaction interspersed with moments of intimacy (she silenced the room with her spoken testimonial in the middle of "I Must Be Crazy"). Now, though, she murmurs a seemingly oblique reference to "my pet—and I know that's what y'all came to see, right?" as the band lurches into a minor key, triplet-heavy 6/8 grind. The song is recognizable as the title tune from her 2007 CD. Ostensibly, it's just another tale about a take-no-mess woman putting a no-good man in his place. But this crowd knows Sweet Angel. They know her show. The air is charged with anticipation.

Angel turns her back to the audience and confers briefly with an assistant standing in the wings. When she turns around again, she's clutching a floppy, foot-long black dildo. The room erupts into shouts and applause as she slinks back across the stage, waving the dildo like a semaphore over her head, up and down in front of her body, and in circles. Occasionally she dangles it between her legs or aims it outward like a gun; at one point she caresses her face with it and moves it teasingly toward her lips. All the while she's singing—"Stop! Wait! I've got another man's meat on my plate!"—and eventually she improvises some new lines appropriate to the occasion and the prop: "See, ladies, this kinda meat, you don't have to worry about it running the street / and when you call on him, you gon' come!" At the routine's climax, she straightens, thrusts her hand into the air, throws her head back, and lowers the dildo to her mouth—a living icon of transgression and triumph: Lady Libertine.

Over the next half hour or so, she'll growl out the blues ("Bold Bitch," modeled on Koko Taylor's "I'm a Woman"), romp through irreverent slice-of-life vignettes ("Good girls do bad things / That's how the preacher got his wife and the choir can sing"), and boot out a solo on her alto sax, demonstrating a tubular, occasionally quavery timbre and a lively improvisational imagination. Her final number, though, is both more serious and more ambitious: a personalized reworking of Prince's "Purple Rain." She delivers the lyrics in an intimate yet full-bodied croon, transforming what was originally a cry of agonized transcendence into a rueful ballad. Her sax solo caresses the theme instead of launching it into hyperdrive the way Prince's instrumentation did. She concludes by strolling through the crowd with her horn, blowing chorus after chorus until she's flushed with exhaustion, accepting a few hugs along the way, reaffirming both her dedication and her bond with the audience.

Figure 17. "I'm going to come and bring it." Sweet Angel, Tommy Johnson Blues Festival, Terry, Mississippi, August 18, 2010. Photo by Jeff Rose.

Once again, she's enveloped the room in a web of celebratory intimacy. "Lady Libertine" seems almost forgotten.[1]

• • •

"The King of Pop, he grabbed his crotch all the time. Was that vulgar, or—? And now they got three-year-olds doing the same thing."[2]

Sweet Angel glances over at Mike Dobbins, seated beside her in a cluttered back room at the Ecko recording studio in Memphis. She's dressed in a casual blouse and slacks, her platinum blonde hair is closely cropped, and she speaks in the measured cadences of a banker or a real estate broker, both of which she's been at various times in her life. Right now, though, she's abrim with excitement about her newfound calling as an entertainer. Angel has been active in southern soul-blues since 2007, not long after she took the plunge and swapped "working in corporate America" for trying to succeed in the more exotic but less dependable world of show business. Her latest Ecko CD, *A Girl Like Me (Lessons in Life)* (2010), has just been released; she's working quite a bit these days, albeit not always in the most prestigious nightspots ("I will be going to Meridian, Mississippi; Terry, Mississippi. Yeah, it's festival time. I was just in Pine Bluff. El Dorado, Arkansas—it looks like Arkansas is loving me"). This afternoon, though, both she and Mike have a few thoughts for naysayers who'd fault her stage routine for being too explicit or somehow giving southern soul a bad name. Mike chimes in: "The thing that I don't understand, you know—the guys on stage that swing the mic in front of them, and holding it like this, and then they're grabbing their crotch and licking their tongue out while they're grabbing their crotch, and nothing is said. But when a woman comes out, like Sweet Angel, Ms. Jody, or whoever comes out and do something, then you got all this negative talk."

> "I'm not the first one that has done that," Angel continues. "In fact, I've got the video: Marvin Sease brought 'interesting' things to the stage."
>
> MIKE: "On that song 'Sit Down on It' . . ."
>
> ANGEL: "'Sit down on it and ride it like a pony.' He [brought] it out on a saddle."
>
> MIKE: "They rode a saddle out on a cart or something, and they got the saddle sitting there with a dildo sticking up, and they [would] just bring it out there and let it stay there during the whole song: 'Do you want to ride it?'"[3]
>
> ANGEL: "I'm not the raunchiest person out there. They get vulgar and they get nasty. And just because I pull the dildo up, that doesn't—

I'm not going to be doing anything else with it but just flashing it. You can't please everybody, but all I want to do is get the name recognized, and each time, it grows and grows and grows. You're going to get classified, no matter what, because people are going to converse."

Conversations like this, though, aren't exactly what the teenaged Clifetta Colbert had in mind when she took up the clarinet in junior high school. Her mother, Lucy Mae Colbert, was an avid blues fan who'd owned a couple of cafés, the Town Talk and the Mocombo Grill, in southern Memphis. By the time Clifetta was born in 1964, her mother had retired from the club business, but the music was still dear to her heart: "She would turn WDIA on every Saturday morning while she was doing her housework, and that's what we would listen to constantly. She was just a connoisseur of blues music."

Clifetta's father, Robert Colbert Sr., served as a deacon at St. Peter Missionary Baptist Church on Pillow Street. He was also, she remembers, the church's "lead singer." But as inspirational as his singing was, and as much as Clifetta loved both gospel and the blues singers she heard on the radio, she had no desire to emulate any of them. "I was a little bit too shy," says the woman whose name is now virtually synonymous with "brazen" among a lot of her fans. "I never really took to the singing part."

She did, however, participate in the Orff music program at Lincoln Elementary School, where she sang in the children's chorus and played xylophone. A few years later, having matriculated into Lincoln Junior High, she found herself enamored by the sweet, woody tonalities of the clarinet. Playing clarinet in the school band wasn't as threatening as singing in front of a crowd ("I could always play my horn and close my eyes"), and it even earned her some prestige. When she was in the eighth grade, she made fourth-chair clarinet in a citywide band competition, which gave her the opportunity to garner a spot in the All-West Tennessee Band and participate in a gala concert at Union University in Jackson, Tennessee.

Even then, though, tucked safely away in the reed section ("up in Jackson I was like seventh or eighth chair"), she had a hunger for flamboyance. "The clarinet," she says, "was just not a fancy instrument; it didn't appeal as much to me. I moved on to the saxophone. That shiny horn, you know? It glistened like gold—I wanted to have one! We had a marching band [in high school], and I would love to be on the end and I loved to dance, and I liked to have that big tenor [she eventually switched to the smaller alto]. I would play at weddings periodically, and I would play for my church. I did that for a couple of years."

After graduating from high school in 1982, Clifetta pursued a conventional career path ("I have sold real estate and [worked] in mortgage banking, actually overseeing foreclosures"), cultivating the soft-spoken yet forceful demeanor that still marks her everyday conversation. But then, in 2004, she met Mac "Mike" Dobbins, a retired truck driver who had deejayed and promoted events at various Memphis clubs. The two began dating, and before long they were planning a future together. In 2006, he opened Mike's Place, a club on Florida Street south of downtown. "He trained me how to deejay," she remembers. "I was the disc jockey at Mike's Place." The statuesque, platinum-haired Clifetta was an immediate hit, and pretty soon she began to expand her repertoire.

> I was spinning the records as the DJ, and on karaoke night, you know, everybody would be a little bit shy about getting up. So there always had to be somebody, a "fall guy" to get up and start the process. And that was me. "Sweet Angel" was actually my DJ handle. It just came about. [Mike] said, "Oh! Sweet Angel!" It just happened. But that's who I am—sweet, and I'm an angel. Some people say otherwise, though! But that's the funny part; it's a play on words. When they hear the name Sweet Angel, they don't think I'm going to come and bring it.

After so many years of considering herself too "shy" to make music without the reassuring presence of a horn or other musicians around her, singing for the club-goers at Mike's was an unexpected inspiration. "It's just something about the stage," she admits. "Once you have the desire, it hits you that you want to do something; you want to perform. It's just something that you know.

"Once the club opened in 2006, I retired from corporate America. We were handling the club pretty much full time; we were a pretty much seven-day-a-week facility where we did not close. It was Sunday through Monday through Sunday."

Meanwhile, behind the scenes, the couple began planning even bolder moves for the newly nicknamed chanteuse. Mike, who'd once aspired to a singing career of his own, had some experience in songwriting. One of his tunes, a ballad called "I Must Be Crazy," was originally styled as a country weeper—he'd thought about pitching it to Randy Travis—but as soon as Angel heard it, she began to think about recasting it in her own image.

"I wasn't thinking of a genre," she maintains. "I did not come into this business thinking it was 'southern soul.' That was new to me. I was probably thinking of more R & B. I love pure, good soul music and R & B, and I love the blues. So [the] music that I prefer will incorporate all of that."

With this in mind, she began to turn Mike's country song around in her head: "He told me how he wanted it to go, but when I listened to it, sitting there trying to think of how I would sing it, I kind of changed the arrangement." The result, as it ended up on her breakout CD, was an understated but vivid vignette of heartbreak, fueled by churchy intensity but with a sensuous flow that bespoke both erotic desire and eventual worldly triumph.

By now, the couple was determined to take Sweet Angel as far in music as she could go. Mike knew Larry Chambers, promotions director at Ecko Records, from his days working as a club DJ. That made it easy to book some time at the Ecko studios in early 2007. "'I Must Be Crazy,'" Angel remembers, "was the first song I recorded. I heard my first recording laid out—you know, you get that fever. You get that fever and say, 'Oh, okay, I can do it. I can do this. I really can.'"

> Once you get the fever, we started thinking of other things. "Another Man's Meat on My Plate" was just a matter of, we were sitting down to eat dinner, and he had my piece of meat on his plate, and that's how it all derived. And "Right Street, Wrong Way" is one where we were coming in, getting ready to pull into our drive. And a lady was on the street, and she said, "Can you tell me where 'whatever street' is?" He said, "Well, you're on the right street, but you're going the wrong way." I'm sure all writers are like that, where you hear something catchy, and it sticks with you, and you say, "That's a song."

It took about two studio sessions to compile enough material for a CD, which Angel and Mike issued on their Mac label in 2007. The only song on the disc they didn't write was a bouncy, jazz-lite pop-soul confection called "Easy Loving You" by Morris J. Williams, an Ecko session musician and vocalist whose career in soul and R & B extends back to the 1960s. The front cover photo portrayed Sweet Angel as a demure seductress wearing a lacy black negligee, her expression enigmatic, neither coy nor stolid.

The material itself showcased her timbral strength and emotional depth as she summoned feelings ranging from desolation through sexual fervor to salvation-bound optimism often over the course of a single song. Angel's tendency to slide over, under, and around a melody line brought sly irony to "I Must Be Crazy," a tale of womanly vulnerability that gained further power from her church-honed ability to invoke deep feeling without bathos. She rescued the minor-key title tune, with its obvious nods to Screamin' Jay Hawkins's "I Put a Spell on You," from parody by delivering it in a steady midrange, neither cat-scratch fierce or hoochie-mama hot.

"Easy Loving You," with its urban-contemporary sheen, allowed her to showcase her voice at its jazziest and most supple. The 6/8 ballad "Right Street, Wrong Way," on the other hand, pushed her chops to their limit (her phrasing sounded tentative in places, and occasionally she lost focus on extended lines); the lyrics, though, showed admirable depth, as the singer rued both her indiscretions and their inevitability ("I got caught cheating on my man / my husband was the best thing that I ever had . . . Y'see, my husband worked all the time / so he was hardly around when my love came down"). The harshly percussive "I Got Love for You," while again challenging her still-developing vocal prowess, showed that she had an ear for contemporary R & B as well as boilerplate southern soul-blues. All told, it was an impressive debut from a vocalist who'd never even considered herself one until not long before she entered a recording studio for the first time in her life.

Meanwhile, it was time for more strategizing: if Sweet Angel, this character that Mike and Clifetta had created to entertain patrons at his club, was going to take her show on the road, she'd have to decide how she wanted to present herself. Once again, the trusty sax proved an important ally; there weren't a lot of women instrumentalists around, especially woodwind players. First, though, she'd have to shed a few more old inhibitions.

> It was a challenge for me to think, okay, I've got to go out there and sing, and I've got to go out there and play my horn. I said, "Mike, that's a lot." He said, "But it takes that if you really want to be somebody special in this business. It's a lot of people singing. You have to have something that really sets you off from the other ones." So now it's just part of what I do. And I'm like, you don't take my horn, you know? Even if I'm just doing maybe one song, that one song has got to be something that I'm going to sing and play my horn on. I can't say that I'm one of the best female saxophonists around, but what I'm going to do, I'm going to deliver that to you.

As things turned out, it didn't take much road work for the very notion of inhibition to become a thing of the past. Initially, Angel says, she would "do the microphone type thing" (brandish it like a phallic symbol) in her act, but that was before she stumbled upon what would become her most notorious trademark. "I think we were somewhere in Mississippi," she says, "and we went into a shop that sold CDs. The guy was selling CDs—'Yeah I got some Sweet Angel'—and he was [also] selling these [dildos]. And we looked up there, and, like, 'Wow! Look at there!' I said, 'I can use that on my show.' And that's how it started."

She's quick to add, though, that despite what some might think, she doesn't consider the dildo routine central to her performance. In fact, it's not even all that dear to her heart:

> It's just one of those—it's a memorable moment. It's being an entertainer. If you're an entertainer, you're going to bring it, whatever delivers and whatever clicks in their mind. You've got to bring something that's different. [But] the thing is, that's not the complete—I mean, if I don't do that, that doesn't take away from my show, because I'm still going to give a good performance, whatever I do. If they book me and they say, "We're going to have kids there, keep it clean," that's what you have to learn how to do—how to cater to what's going on. So if my promoter says don't do this, or we can't have that, then I'm able to deliver you a good show without having to be risqué.

With its strong songwriting and production, *Another Man's Meat on My Plate* was several cuts above the average DIY southern soul project, and according to Angel it made some encouraging noise, at least at first ("We worked it as best we knew how, being very new at it and just getting into it"). Her next disc, *Handle Your Business,* was also recorded at Ecko and released independently. One of the tracks, an instrumental called "No Boundaries," featured her on sax. Not long after it came out, though, Ecko president John Ward decided to sign her and reissue *Handle Your Business* on his label (Ecko eventually picked up *Another Man's Meat* as well). Ward dropped "No Boundaries" and another track entitled "Women's National Anthem" (a remake of James Brown's "It's a Man's Man's Man's World") and replaced them with songs written in-house; he and staff writer Raymond Moore penned "Guilty as Charged" and "I'm Sharing Your Man"; the final track, "You Gotta Make Love," was credited to vocalist-guitarist Gerod Rayborn, along with both Moore and Ward.

Finally having a CD on an established label represented the culmination of a dream for Clifetta, but it was also a little unsettling. The original cover art for *Handle Your Business* had included a shot of her playing sax; Ecko kept the picture, despite dropping "No Boundaries," so buyers expecting to hear a Sweet Angel sax solo were probably going to be disappointed. According to Angel, the different track listings on the different versions of the CD also caused some consternation among marketers and purchasers. She believes, as well, that when Ecko reissued *Another Man's Meat* (again with a couple of new songs added), the resulting confusion—two pairs of identically named but not-quite-identical Sweet Angel CDs competing with one another on two different labels—hurt business, at least initially.

Nonetheless, she was now a legitimate recording artist, and recognition wasn't long in coming. In 2008, the Jus' Blues Music Foundation, an Atlanta-based organization that holds an annual convention and awards ceremony in Memphis, named her the year's Best New Female Southern Soul Artist. Gigs began to get more plentiful as well, first around Memphis and then expanding into other southern states. From the beginning, though, she was aware that the pressure to succeed and top herself on every show and every recording would not relent. Especially on a circuit where the audience has traditionally been mostly female and where sex appeal is at least as strong a selling point as musical prowess, a woman entertainer has to work hard to stay afloat.

"No matter what," she acknowledges, "you still have to keep yourself in people's faces in order for them to realize that, hey, it's another artist. Even though the name is ringing when you've got a hot female out there. I think the gentlemen probably get more opportunities because there are usually four or five men on the show, and [the promoters] swing a woman in there every now and then."

And, of course, establishing and maintaining an appropriate image is essential. *Handle Your Business* had been cast in the same overall mold as Angel's debut CD. Sassy and sexy though most of the songs were, they didn't pander, and the vocalist maintained her dignity as well as her sense of womanly authority. The disc's opening track, "I'm Leaving," was a mistreated wife's declaration of independence; the title song found the singer demanding both fealty and prowess from a wayward lover; "Hard Times Were Good Times" was a vintage deep-soul survival saga set to a contemporary synth backing. But Angel's next Ecko Release, *Bold Bitch!* in 2009, although it finally allowed her to strut her saxophone chops on record, seemed to herald changes—subtle, but noticeable—in the way she was being portrayed. The cover showed her wielding her alto sax, looking as sturdy and uncompromising as ever, now, though, she was clad in a revealing red negligee.

"I got your attention with *Bitch!*" she says. "You know who I am: the girl standing there with the horn, who means business." The songs, though, many from the Ecko team instead of either Clifetta or Mike, hinted at a somewhat different story.

Angel had never been a prude; she'd dropped the occasional f-bomb in her songs, and her shows had become known for their jubilant carnality. But she'd always chosen material that focused mostly on storytelling with a purpose. "I like songs with meaning," she says. "I like songs that have shelf life, that have real passion, that have some history." *Bold Bitch!*, despite its in-your-face title, wasn't entirely devoid of such fare: "Don't Let the Clean-Up Woman Pick Up Your Man" wittily carried on the long-standing "clean-up woman" soap opera kicked off by Betty Wright in 1971; John Ward's "I'm Gonna Give You Good Love" was both a sweetly cooed enticement and a throw-down from a seductress determined to remain in control as well as satisfy; both the title and the lyrics of "I'm Movin' Up," ostensibly about a fed-up woman leaving a relationship, were tinged with broader implications of progress and victory in the tradition of such soul anthems as Aretha Franklin's "Think" (with its chorus of "Freedom! Freedom!") and "Chain of Fools" ("One of these mornings, the chain is gonna break / But up until then, I'm gonna take all I can take"). "Good Girls Do Bad Things" sounded more like a blues-woman's declaration of defiance than a hoochie-mama's strut. And her bluesy alto work on "Blow That Thang Sweet Angel" was both raucous and lively.

But offerings such as "Outside Tail" ("You think you can take my man by spreading your legs") and "The Tongue Don't Need No Viagra" sounded mostly like attempts to get easy laughs, and the stop-time, twelve-bar title song came off as a by-the-numbers attempt to cash in on the tradition of bad-mama proclamations recorded by progenitors such as Koko Taylor. Meanwhile, too many of the disc's other songs relied on unexciting two-chord vamps taken at lugubrious tempos—potentially disastrous in a genre where *groove* is paramount.

Bold Bitch! wasn't a failure by any means. Although precise definitions of commercial southern soul "success" can be vague ("I really don't know what would constitute a 'hit' in terms of sales nowadays," admits John Ward. "Nobody is really selling much more than three thousand copies of anything now"[4]), it moved acceptably by prevailing standards and garnered enough airplay to keep Angel performing on a fairly regular basis. Online critic Daddy B. Nice called it a "gem of a CD," noting that for the most part the lyrics were mild enough to earn mainstream radio play despite the "provocative" song titles ("Butt Up!," for instance, was a standard booty-shaking dance number). He also suggested, however, that Sweet Angel might be a little out of place in the down-home southern soul environment: "The jazz and pop hints that made Dinah Washington a crossover star," he wrote, "are there in Sweet Angel's delivery. It's what gives the songs their power. It's also what makes Sweet Angel's songs sound suspect to the Southern Soul ear. At this point in time she represents the urban diva of Southern Soul from the northern and urban point of Southern Soul's world: Memphis."[5]

It's probably stretching things to compare Angel's bluesy bluntness with Dinah Washington's sophisticated sass, but the Daddy's analysis wasn't far from the mark. "I'm not a typical southern soul type girl," Angel concurs. "My diction is not the same. The deeper, grittier voice, I don't necessarily have that." And, she might have added, despite her dildo gimmick, she presents herself mostly as a "good girl" unafraid to do "bad things" rather than an unmitigated "bitch" (bold or otherwise), whether on stage or off.

As if to reinforce the point, Angel's next Ecko outing was her most honest-sounding, thematically varied, and finely crafted yet. Entitled *A Girl Like Me* and subtitled *Lessons in Life,* it seemed from its very first track (the title tune) to announce a return to a more serious, but no less celebratory, artistic vision—and, possibly, greater creative control. "*A Girl Like Me,*" she points out, was "written [mostly] by Mike and I. I brought in someone to do my tracks for me who could deliver me some of the groove that I like, put a little bass in it, bring me some soul music I can really feel. On this one I deliver you some good soul music, some blues—you know, touch on the blues—some real good laid-out music, not just 'southern soul,' that can be enjoyed by quite a bit of the masses, more of the masses than I think any of my other music has. We really just took [it] from where we've been to where we're going."

The song "A Girl Like Me" was simultaneously a club-friendly dance workout, a tribute to living soul-blues heritage, and a sly challenge to conventional standards of womanly beauty. Its basic riff was adapted from Bobby Rush's "Sue," and the (fictional) story line told of the singer's early infatuation with Rush and her dream of someday being one of his dancers. In the story, Rush initially turns down the twenty-five-year-old aspirant because she's too young; about ten years later she tries again, but now he tells her she's "too little" at 155 pounds. Later, when she's plumped up a bit and become an entertainer herself, he rues his earlier decision.

The rest of the set included fresh takes on standard southern soul themes, enhanced by strong production and with vocals as brawny and full as any Sweet Angel had yet achieved on record. "What I Want What I Need" found the protagonist agonizing over which of her two lovers she should kick to the curb; in the rueful "Last Night Was Your Last Night," she gathered the resolve to say good-bye to a man whom she cared about but who couldn't commit himself to a future. "I've Got to Get Paid," by contrast, was the war cry of a wronged wife wielding divorce like a rapier.

"I Like the Money, But I Don't Like the Job" was a working mom's blues, lightened by a jaunty dance beat.

The true revelations, though, were the ballads. Angel had always been in command of an impressive emotional range, but never had she bared such vulnerability, laced with such hard-eyed determination to prevail. The straightforward love songs—"The Comfort of My Man," "I'm Working on My Job"—were simultaneously tender and forceful. "Mrs. Number Two" was derived from the Soul Children's classic "I'll Be the Other Woman," but Angel toughened the "other woman's" erstwhile plea with some caustic postfeminist signifying and a vitriol-tinged vocal tone. "I'd Rather Be by Myself" was both a declaration of independence and a mature assessment of the emotional minefield negotiated by separating lovers. But the centerpiece was "Don't Be Lonely, Be Loved," which she adapted from a poem her sister Adriana Harrison had written in memory of her husband, Charles Leon Harrison Sr., who died in November 2008. "You said if you left first, you didn't want me sad," Angel sang, her voice ascending into a wail of anguish. "I got a question for ya: now who's gonna love me? . . . Who's gonna keep the promise?"

"Don't Be Lonely" was easily the most heart-baring piece of music Angel had ever committed to disc. "It was kind of difficult," she says, "because, of course, that was my brother-in-law that died. And when you're in love yourself, and you think about—Mike and I met April of 2004, which was the spring, you know? [The lyrics of "Don't Be Lonely" tell us that the couple's love affair began "in the middle of spring."] So it had a lot of moments in there where I couldn't quite get through the song for a couple of weeks prior to recording. I had to kind of get myself geared up to actually do that one."

The artistic success of *A Girl Like Me* was probably due, at least in part, to the ease with which Angel was finally balancing her onstage and recorded personas. That's not always easy, especially in her field: Soul music has traditionally drawn from the call-and-response church tradition to generate much of its emotional heat, and re-creating that kind of spontaneity in a studio can be daunting. Conversely, a nightclub audience or festival crowd, boogie-charged and ready to party, might not want to sit through a testimonial like "Don't Be Lonely, Be Loved," regardless of its redemptive power. This time around, though, Angel found a way to strike an appropriate balance between her two roles.

The title song, in fact, actually arose out of a performance. The original idea had been to adapt Bobby Rush's well-known "Sue" vamp into a novelty tribute—"Bobby Rush, doncha wish you had a girl like me?"—that she could use as a hook.

> I was just looking for my band to give me an intro song, and I said, "I kinda like that Bobby Rush groove, a little funk for me to come in on." We started playing around with it in rehearsal. I think we were going to do Mike's birthday party,[6] and it wasn't really ready at that point, so I said, "Well, we'll do the show, and I'll kind of play around with it on the stage." So they began the little funk groove, and I couldn't really remember where I was supposed to start singing the "Bobby Rush" part.
>
> So I started runnin' my mouth, and I started making up the story on the stage. That's how the whole song started, the whole little story line. Finally, I remembered where I was supposed to come in, and I just started singing. Right then it was videotaped. I started listening to what was videotaped so I could remember it, so we could go ahead and record it like that. And that's how it all came about.

Translating an onstage creation into a successful recording, though, is one thing; adapting a studio work into a performance piece can be more challenging. In the past, ballads have often been the highlights of a soul show; a savvy entertainer, often drawing on skills honed on the gospel highway, might silence the rowdiest audience by firing down the jets and "having church" with an intimate sermon in song, which would often culminate with an ascent into house-wrecking transcendence. Although some southern soul artists can still hold a crowd this way, in many cases the relentlessly good-timey nature of the music and the silliness of some of the lyrics mitigate against it.

Given this, Angel knows she needs to pick her spots carefully when it comes to sharing her more personal material with an audience. Part of the challenge is crafting the kind of show that will allow room for as much emotional variety as possible. She doesn't want to set the wrong tone, the occasional R-rated interlude notwithstanding.

> I've sung things that people have given to me, like "The Tongue Don't Need No Viagra." Sure, I sing it, but there again it's really not a show tune for me, you know what I'm saying? I've performed it, maybe—you don't necessarily want to perform it. Even "Another Man's Meat on My Plate" wasn't technically a raunchy song. It was just a play on words.
>
> So when it comes to whether I have a naughty side, yes, I'm going to do some naughty things, and you're going to get a laugh because I'm an entertainer, and it's all about holding attention. [But] I'm going to deliver to each one of those individuals out there something that is going to touch them, whether it's "A Girl Like Me" [or] "I'd Rather Be by Myself," which is pure soul music.

Figure 18. Lady with a horn: Sweet Angel, Tommy Johnson Blues Festival, Terry, Mississippi, August 18, 2010. Photo by Jeff Rose.

> I line my show up according to where I am. If I know I'm at a festival, "Don't Be Lonely" would not be a song that would be on the festival. If I'm in, maybe a club, or a more personal environment that I can communicate the meaning of the song, I'll perform something of that nature.

It can be a precarious balance to maintain, but Sweet Angel has proved adept at it. She seems equally determined to assert ownership of her recorded musical persona. Not long after the release of *A Girl Like Me,* she decided to leave Ecko. There wasn't any great confrontation—John Ward still insists he has no idea why she didn't renew her contract[7]—but it's clear from Angel's own comments that like many others she feels constrained by the preconceptions, if not the stereotypes, often associated with the "southern soul" or "soul-blues" tag.

"Southern soul has been classified as more comical-like music, to me," she says, adamantly but without rancor. "Soul music had its funny lines, too—[Mel and Tim's] 'Backfield in Motion,' y'know? It's a play on words. But then they started playing with the words too much. The classic R & B [has] that smooth groove that you can lay back, listen to it for a while, for a long time; you never get tired of it. It's just something you can feel. That's why it was called soul music, because it was coming from the soul."

> When I went to Ecko I was very green. [Now] I want to see how it is with other studios, or if there's something that can enhance what I have even more. So, hopefully with me getting my feet wet, and now kind of growing from that, I'll have some good sounds coming. Just reading critics' reports on different people and how their music sounds, I'm trying to avoid some things, you know? Even though a lot of the music is synthesized, there are ways to make it not sound as cookie-cutter as the rest. So I'm shopping for the right producers and sounds that can really back me up. I'd rather either be independent or have a bigger role in developing the artist in me that I want to be.

One of her first moves after leaving Ecko was to release a CD single about as far from stereotyped "comical-like" southern soul as possible: "Purple Rain." She recorded it at 901 Entertainment in Memphis and issued it on Mac. Her version, like most covers of the song, starts off with a note-for-note replication of the original guitar intro (played by Lamar Davis, her erstwhile band guitarist), but the overall production is much less theatrical than Prince's was. So are her vocals: she sings it almost as a lament (appropriate to the lyrics) rather than a declamation. Unfortunately, the mix makes her alto sax sound more like a melodica, but when she reproduces the solo in performance it's usually full-bodied, even robust.

"Purple Rain" was a first step, albeit a risky one given the market's obsession with genre categorizing, toward her goal of proclaiming her independence and widening her base. "A lot of people asked for it," she explains. "'Purple Rain' is one that I actually do on the majority of my shows. And I felt bad that I had not recorded it, so I did go ahead and record that one. I released that one in January [2011]."

She says, though, that she hasn't been actively seeking a new label since leaving Ecko. "It may come sooner than I want," she admits. "I have [already] had people to call me." But for now she's encouraged by her burgeoning reputation and the praise she's been getting, even in markets and among demographics where southern soul-blues remains an unknown (or underappreciated) quantity. In 2010, the Bay Area Blues Society named her "R & B Female Artist of the Year" at its annual West Coast Blues Hall of Fame and Awards Show. "I had no idea that I was even up for an award on the West Coast," she marvels. "I have had people call me, people that I am just shocked will contact me regarding my music and where it's playing. I have not crossed every state in the United States where I want to perform, so my show is still very fresh and very new, and the name is getting popular, so I'm just kind of banking on the music that I have, and the show that I have, to keep riding that wave."

Even when she finally decides on a label, though, attaining the kind of across-the-board popularity she seeks (and which soul music once enjoyed) probably won't be easy. As diverse as festival audiences and some club crowds can be, the market for blues, southern soul-blues, and other so-called roots music continues to be strongly segregated—often by age, social class, geographic location, and self-ascribed cultural identity, as much as by race. Clarksdale, Mississippi's, Ground Zero club, which caters mostly to the blues tourist trade, bills itself as the world headquarters for all things bluesy and southern, but according to Angel, the bookers there demand fealty to a vision of "authenticity" she finds restrictive.

"Even though people at Ground Zero know me," she relates, "and I'd say, 'Well you know, I do have some blues cuts that I do,' they're like, 'No, we don't do any artists that sing your kind of music.'[8] So already you know that you've been stigmatized. That's bad, when you can't even go 'blues.' You can't even go 'blues' because you're classified as 'southern soul.' Then you can't do R & B [i.e., break into the mainstream African American market] because you're classified as 'southern soul.'"

So she's writing new songs and seeking fresh opportunities for collaboration, all the while maintaining the faith that she's convinced has been borne out by the success she's achieved so far (even though she continues to hedge her bets by holding down a day job selling burial insurance at a Memphis funeral home operated by her sister Adriana): "I know that eventually, and I *believe* that eventually I will get a lot more recognition. I want to be on the freeway to wherever I can take this thing. I want to deliver some good music that makes more than just a few people happy."

"I'm not even putting it on my plate," she concludes, perhaps punning on the title of one of her best-known songs, "to say I want to be classified as a southern soul artist. It's just this little grouping that, to me, stretches only so far. I'm technically more R & B, and I love the blues because I grew up on the blues and I feel it. I like songs with real meaning. That's where my heart is."

7

Sir Charles Jones
"Is There Anybody Lonely?"

The houselights have been dimmed at the Lufkin Civic Center in Lufkin, Texas, and people are surging forward from their tables for the appearance of tonight's headliner, Sir Charles Jones. On stage, backlit by the reflection from massive red, white, and blue Budweiser and Bud Light signs, Sir Charles's band has segued from a tension-building, suspended chord into a swaying ballad groove. Now bassist Greg King, tall and easy-moving, his bald head shining under the lights, steps to the microphone: "You all ready?" he roars. "If you're ready, say yeah!" The enthusiasm surges through the crowd as King continues: "Lufkin, Texas! Let's bring him to the stage! The King of Southern Soul! Put your hands together, y'all, for Sir! Charles! Jones!"

Despite the buildup, Sir Charles looks almost nonchalant as he strolls into the spotlight, his loosely hanging white shirt open at the neck. Once center stage, though, he wastes no time in getting the house. "If you're ready to party!" he exhorts the crowd, "Do this!" He pumps his right hand into the air and begins a rhythmic chant: "Put your hands up, if you're ready to party! Put your hands up, if you're ready to party! Put your hands up . . ." After a few repetitions, almost everyone in the Civic Center is moving with him, and it's time to kick-start his show with "Friday," his 2001 ode to the pleasures of weekend juking.

"This one is dedicated," he sings, his taut tenor pitched midway between a croon and a testimonial, "to all the workers who work nine-to-five . . ."

> I did my work this week,
> and baby, I just got paid;
> Gonna go buy me a fresh pair of gators
> with some of this money that I made

As he eases into the song, Sir Charles looks serious and intense, his open, baby-faced stare toughened by aggressive body language as he strides back and forth, occasionally bending down to shake outstretched hands. Now and then he breaks into a grin as he trades winks and smiles with his female admirers.

In the recorded version of "Friday," the story line takes precedence: it's possible for a listener to suspend disbelief and envision the hard-partying workingman singing about his own life. Here, though, the real Sir Charles, rather than the man he's portraying, is the focus of attention. Or, perhaps more accurately, the distinction between storyteller and fictional hero has dissolved: as his fashionably shod everyman drops into a liquor store for some refreshment and then goes on to "step in the club, looking canny and clean," it's as if Sir Charles Jones, in the flesh, is inhabiting and living out the story as it unfolds in his lyrics.

At various points, he or bassist King will spike the proceedings with hoarsely bellowed exhortations—"C'mon! Put your hands up! If you came to party, put your hands up in here!"—but these concessions to show-manship don't violate the fourth wall as much as compel the audience to participate even more fully in the fantasy. Sir Charles's expression remains a seductive meld of boyish ingenuousness and player's cool: wide-eyed and slack-mouthed, yet set with purposeful intensity. He's in nonstop mo-tion—not as flamboyantly athletic as vintage-era Michael Jackson, not as driven or self-punishing as James Brown, but in the same tradition. Here's a man who's come a long way to work hard for the people, to grind it out with dedication and without complaint, just as his song's proletarian hero has been doing on the job all week.

Yet there's also an edge to his enthusiasm that distinguishes it from run-of-the-mill soul showmanship. As he makes eye contact with various women in the front row, his pose and his expression are both pleading and demanding, personifying the tough-tender romantic machismo so beloved on the soul circuit. But it goes beyond seduction; since he first hit the stage, he has seemed both caught up in the moment and impelled to triumph over it, driven by a force beyond ambition, beyond self-confidence or even desire, fueled by something deeper that won't let go, the same kind of thing that goaded Brown (or his erstwhile rival Jackie Wilson) to put his body on the line every show, but not as dark or as obsessive, or maybe simply not as openly acknowledged on either side of the stage lights. The blithe assurance Sir Charles exudes is charged with a palpable urgency, as if it's merely the flipside manifestation of the same hunger that seems to drive him to top every moment—and every response, every shriek of ecstasy from the crowd—with a new, more satisfying one. Like the lover in song who establishes his macho cred by crooning "I ain't too proud to beg" and then proceeds to do just that, Sir Charles Jones transforms neediness, even naked vulnerability, into a badge of manhood.

Whether that paradoxical pose of strutting supplication is calculated or has simply evolved over the years is unclear, but it's almost certain that Charles used it intentionally on his breakthrough 2001 CD, which launched "Friday" and several other of his signature songs. The name of that disc, *Love Machine,* bespoke street-tough machismo; the cover photo portrayed Sir Charles, shirtless and tattooed, with a metal band draped around his neck. His expression was hard-eyed and glowering, with just a hint of a smile softening his lips; he seemed to be seething with both erotic hunger and predatory ferocity—a torrid, somewhat unsettling blend of enticement and conquest. The title song sent pretty much the same message: "I'll make it real good to you," he boasted, as a grinding, synth-heavy track pushed him forward. "Make you go crazy, baby . . . Gotta slow roll it, stroke it with emotion / gotta make it so wet, baby, just like the ocean . . . Cause I'm the Love Machine."

But the following track, "Is There Anybody Lonely?"—which ended up being both the biggest seller off the CD and Charles's most significant crossover R & B hit, at least in the South—conveyed a strikingly different message. If "Love Machine" had portrayed the road-warrior singer as a prowling lothario ("Been around the world, from coast to coast / and now the ladies I love say I'm the host with the most"), "Lonely" presented the inverse of that image: the solitary troubadour, adored by millions but loved by none. "I've been around the world," Charles murmured, "Lookin' for my special someone; I'm singin' this one for myself." He's been alone for a long time, he continued, waking up by himself, cooking his own dinner, washing his own clothes, sometimes crying himself to sleep. It was no less a cliché than the other, but he made his pleading seem genuinely desperate, and his sensitive-guy promises ("She don't have to be a movie star, she don't have to be a fancy girl / Cause I see a woman for what she is inside"), designed to seduce as they undoubtedly were, still sounded more soul-baring than disingenuous. To juxtapose this song against "Love Machine" was to offer up, in less than eight minutes, nothing less than an allegory of salvation: even the baddest player (or most rakish soul-bluesman) must eventually repent and submit himself to the redemptive power of true love.

In performance, though, the aggressiveness of Sir Charles's charisma both intensifies and complicates that allegory. "Is There Anybody Lonely" almost always comes at the end of his show; by this time, Charles has established his cat-and-mouse emotional teasing technique with such prowess that his audience is begging to be played with almost as fervently as they're screaming to be satisfied. As women call out the song's name (along with his), he steps back toward center stage, a smirk of anticipatory satisfaction flickering across his face. "Wave your hands!" he shouts. "You all want me to sing that song?" The shouts get louder, the fervor more intense. "I ain't singin' nothing 'til everybody in the house scream!" The band eases into the opening theme, and the room explodes into frenzy. He starts to sing:

"Is anybody . . ."

He cuts himself off, igniting even higher levels of passion. His teasing continues:

"Oh, shit! Lemme hear it again!"

The noise is almost deafening now.

"Is anybody . . ."

He stops once more, chuckling, as the shrieks continue to intensify. Then, finally, he breaks into the song, beginning with his introductory narration about how far he's traveled and how hard he's worked, "trying to find a queen to step beside this king." He strikes dramatic poses, truncates lines for the audience to complete, and continues to exhort ("How many ladies out there lonely? Is there someone for Sir Charles?") between verses.

To a newcomer, it may all seem hopelessly theatrical, if not self-defeating—who is this guy to keep inserting himself and his ego into what's supposed to be a ballad of longing? But soul music, almost from the beginning, has drawn from the churchman's craft as much as it has from the bluesman's pose of unselfconscious emotionality. In church, the message is not complete—the Spirit hasn't fully arrived, the circle isn't truly unbroken—until the congregants' response has become as intense as the minister's preaching. Sir Charles's interjections and crowd-revving asides aren't terribly different from what that minister does when he interrupts his sermon to goad his congregation—"Are you with me?" "I don't think anybody's with me this morning!"—to deepen, rather than diminish, the truth of what he's trying to convey. Seldom will a man of the cloth be accused of "insincerity" or "inauthenticity" for engaging in this kind of stagecraft (or, perhaps, pulpitcraft), no matter how calculated or well-rehearsed it might be.[1]

Sir Charles has secularized the technique, of course, although most of his audience will still be familiar enough with it to respond appropriately. Some might find it problematic that he's employing it to focus attention on himself rather than the Lord (or even, in many cases, the secular texts of his own songs), but such are the pitfalls of ambition in a field where hiding one's light under a bushel has never guaranteed earthly success or, for that matter, the promise of glory later on. In show business, there may be little choice between egoism and immolation; a man who's traveled the road Sir Charles has endured has seen both alternatives up close—too close, in fact, for him to rest easy. However perilous the soul man's high-way may be, it can't throw up obstacles any more harrowing than those he's already seen and surmounted. Behind his strut, behind his tireless demands and entreaties to be loved—"Are you ready to party with the pretty boy?" "Do y'all wanna be satisfied?" "Can I sing a little bit here, y'all? Say, 'hell, yeah!'" "Yeah, I'm lookin' at you, baby! I ain't scared of it, cause I know what I'm workin' with!"—behind his insistence that he, not any of his elders or contemporaries, is the "undisputed King of Southern Soul," loom the specters of rejection and failure. Thus, perhaps, the need to create and inhabit—24/7 if necessary—the persona, self-made and seemingly inviolable, of Sir Charles Jones, the man who *must* be King.

• • •

Akron, Ohio, isn't commonly thought of as a nexus for blues or gospel, but when Charles Jones Jr. was growing up there in the 1970s, that's the music he was surrounded with at home.[2]

> I was born on April 25, 1973, in Summit County Hospital in Akron. My father was a piano player and a writer and a lead gospel singer, come from a famous group from Akron, Ohio, called the Christian All-Stars.[3] My mom, Blanche Jones, had an old piano inside of the house, and she would notice how I could piece notes together, being about six years old, and she was shocked at how perfect of pitch my ears were. I could actually keep a note and sing to the rhythm of the piano—"Mary Had a Little

Figure 19. "Are you lonely, too?" Sir Charles Jones, Bojangles Coliseum, Charlotte, North Carolina, February 2009. Photo by Gene Tomko.

Lamb," and stuff like that. My father started sitting down and teaching me a few chords, a lot of gospel hymns. The hymns and a lot of the scales and stuff that he taught me on the piano, I really kind of just picked it up by ear, on my own; I played it by ear.

The Joneses were a tight-knit family, at least then, and they made an effort to put God first in their lives. "My mother and father," Charles has recalled, "both were ministers and singers,"[4] although they held down day jobs as well. Around the house, though, they didn't enforce many barriers or prohibitions when it came to music: "My father always had a universal mind toward music. His mind was open to all different variations of music, so he could stay creative, keeping the gospel group up to date on what needed to be sung and needed to be wrote.

"Sittin' in the backyard, my mom and them out there barbecuin', they're cooking greens and chitlins and everything, and they got their Johnnie Taylors and their Tyrone Davises and their Muddy Waters—you go and change that, you liable to get a whippin'!"

Meanwhile, the young man spent his free time "groovin' off the radio, being able to listen at a lot of great, great cats like Barry White, James Brown, I really loved Curtis Mayfield; that's one of my heroes of music, and Roger Troutman [lead vocalist and guitarist of the pioneering hard-funk band Zapp, who died in 1999]. I have loved Stevie Wonder ever since I was a little child. Just being able to listen at those guys, how they would be able to piece sounds together, just really impressed me."

In the early 1980s, things began to change for young Charles, although it would take a few years for the full impact of those changes to really hit home. His parents divorced, and his mother decided to move with her five sons to Birmingham, Alabama. "Her parents got sick," Charles explains, "and we left and came to Birmingham to take care of her parents, I would say, roughly 1984."

She had deep roots there, both familial and otherwise. She was born in Lafayette, Alabama, and raised up in Birmingham. She always worked with the civil rights movement since she was, I'd say, roughly about fourteen years old. My mom marched with Dr. King and did a lot of work through Selma, Alabama, and everything, traveled a lot with Dr. King and helped preach, and cooked a lot of the food and marched on the streets.

It was a lot of things going on in Birmingham. You got the Sixteenth Street Baptist Church where the four little girls were bombed,[5] you got your famous Kelly Ingram Park[6] right across the street; so I really come from a deep family, a family that helped desegregate things down South. Deep, deep, deep Alabama roots.

After arriving in Birmingham, Blanche Jones and her sons settled in Tom Brown Village, a public housing development in the Avondale community in the eastern section of the city a few blocks from Sixteenth Street Baptist and Kelly Ingram Park. Known locally as the Avondale Projects, the low-rise apartment complex has since developed a reputation for drugs and crime, but Charles says that his life there was relatively happy. At least part of the reason was his enthusiasm for music, along with the charisma and flamboyance he was already learning to use to his advantage. "I have good memories of growing up in Avondale Projects," he says. "Everyone used to call me 'Li'l Stevie Wonder' because if I wanted a quarter for some cookies or some candy or something, I could always charm anybody by singing a Stevie Wonder song so good."[7]

But if Charles didn't feel pressured during those years, his mother surely did. Having spent much of her early life fighting for social justice, Blanche Jones was not about to let poverty and de facto segregation deprive her children of the opportunities she'd struggled so hard to win for them. "My mom worked three jobs to save up money so that we could have a house someday," Charles remembers. "I look up to my mom a lot, how strong a person she is; she was always a strong lady. Mom ended up saving enough money to get us out of the projects and get us a house in Ensley [a community on the west side of the Birmingham metropolitan area]."[8]

There he attended Bush Elementary School and, later, Ensley High School. By then, though, the temptations of the streets were sabotaging the aspirations of even well-raised young men like Charles Jones Jr. Gangs like the Black Gangster Disciples, many imported from northern cities like Chicago, had established themselves in southern communities, and the lures they offered—fast money, macho prestige, a warrior-like code of honor—could be almost irresistible. Restless, perhaps searching for a kind of emotional bonding he hadn't known since leaving his father behind in Akron, Charles became caught up in the life. It took another father figure to pull him out.

"I was deep off into gangbanging," he recalls. "A man by the name of Mr. James Merriweather, who was the band teacher of Ensley, helped me turn my life around by helping me learn music and putting a trade in my hand, instead of gangbanging and throwing my life away. Mr. Merriweather did manage to save my life and bring out musical talents inside of me that I never knew I had. My most grandest moment was being able to sing in the jazz band at Ensley and gaining much popularity."[9]

Popularity, though, was one thing; academic commitment, another.

Charles left Ensley High without graduating. He worked at jobs such as cutting grass with one of his brothers ("[he] was keeping me out of trouble") and doing stock work at a Birmingham furniture outlet called Consignment World. But he found himself haunted, perhaps for the first time in his life, by the specter of failure—not just personal failure, but the more harrowing dread of failing his family, especially his mother:

> My mother was deeply upset with me about not graduating. I can remember those talks, with her saying to me, "All I worked for, this is how you repay me. I can't believe it. This is how you repay me." And I can't tell you how bad I felt when she told me that, 'cause it felt like I just really just let my mom down, [and] most of all myself. So I continued to lift furniture, cut grass, thinking to myself a lot about my life. Every day I would think about the good times I had in school, when I was a member of the band, just being able to hang around Mr. Merriweather and the band, and doing all the concert band, jazz, and all the musical instruments I learned how to play. It was the only memory that I had of actually doing something right and positive in my life, [instead of] all the gangbanging and fighting. And I [would] think about how I disgraced my parents, of how hard they worked for me, to keep me away from . . . just the type of life that I was leading; they were trying to get me away from that life.[10]

As it turned out, the job at Consignment World ended up opening the door for him to get back into music. One day during his lunch break, his boss heard him singing a Stevie Wonder song. The man suggested that Charles audition at what he remembers now as "the world-fabulous French Quarters of Birmingham," a nightclub where local artists could develop their chops and maybe earn the opportunity to headline the main show. "It's just like being a star there," Charles enthuses, the thrill still vivid. "Because I had such a wonderful singing voice, I managed to get a nice job singing on the weekends there for seventy-five dollars a night. And everything just started taking off from there."[11]

> I would say, roughly, '93; sang there two years. I gained popularity from there in the city of Birmingham. Everybody else sung what the audience wanted, a lot of the R & B stuff that was maybe on the radio. I was the only one chosen to go out there and sing the older songs, the Bobby Womacks, the Z. Z. Hills, the Donnie Hathaways and stuff like that. People really loved it because I put so much soul in what I did.

Toward the end of his run at the club, Charles had the opportunity to meet Marvin Sease, a soul-blues vocalist known as the "Candy Licker" from the title of his career-defining 1987 hit song. That song, an extended, graphic ode to the joys of cunnilingus ("I wanna lick you till you come"), represented a watershed in the development of contemporary soul-blues: some critics still blame it for helping set the stage for today's seemingly endless outpouring of derivative "lick-it-and-stick-it" raunchfests. But it was a surefire crowd-pleaser (Sease claimed that things sometimes got so hot when he performed it that women actually passed out), and it catapulted its originator to a level of stardom and crossover recognition rare in the southern soul-blues world.

"Candy Licker" typecast Sease forever as an X-rated party man, and many of his subsequent outings (e.g., "Condom on Your Tongue") seemed designed to enhance the image. But he was also in command of more substantial gifts. "I'm Mr. Jody," from 1994, with its fervid opening sermon, was (and is) one of the most effective and influential songs in the soul-blues pantheon of fables about Jody, the mythical trickster–home wrecker. (The prototype was Johnnie Taylor's 1971 "Jody's Got Your Girl and Gone.") Sease's ballads, although often overlooked in favor of his more explicit material, further revealed him as a soul man of depth and vision. He continued to cultivate those gifts until his death in early 2011. His prophetic "Gone On," from 2008, may be less well-known than Johnnie Taylor's "Soul Heaven," but it's an equally moving tribute to departed musical greats.[12]

Sease, in other words, was a perfect mentor for a young singer bent on developing a style and an image that could appeal to a wide range of listeners. "Marvin just taught me everything that I know now about the business," Charles affirms. "I wasn't writing yet; once I got a chance to experience being on the road with Marvin Sease, he started teaching me how to put songs together and how to write what I'm feeling."

Charles stayed with Sease for about five years. Sease encouraged him to get some of his newly written songs recorded; he even offered to help produce them. After laying down twelve tracks to serve as a demo CD, Charles went to Jackson, Mississippi, to audition the disc for Malaco. Malaco had developed a reputation for signing and developing artists with fresh ideas, but this time its brain trust couldn't, or wouldn't, hear what the young man from Birmingham was offering. Charles's worst nightmare was about to flash back and possess him.

"They were looking at me like, 'Man, you crazy? Twenty-six-year-old dude singing the blues? No twenty-six-year-old know 'bout no blues. . . . We're off into the Johnnie Taylors, and this and that.' Tommy Couch Jr. told me that he didn't believe in [my] kind of music because it didn't have the Johnnie Taylor horns; this didn't sound like Z. Z. Hill and Latimore."

It seemed contradictory: was Charles's sound too bluesy for a young man or not bluesy enough? Even then, apparently, he was crossing boundaries and challenging stereotypes. The style he was developing emphasized the sensuous grace of his vocal delivery as well as the erotic passion that smoldered within it, the same rough-cut vulnerability—longing girded with steel—that he now displays on his shows and in most of his best recordings. His backing tracks incorporated sounds commonly associated with hip-hop and neosoul; as Couch Jr. noted, they didn't usually feature horns (real or otherwise), and they were insistent even at their most laid-back. It was a young man's sound, equal parts street-tough and bedroom-soft, intense but devoid, for the most part, of the fervid emotionality usually associated with deep soul. It probably didn't fall into any marketable niche Malaco could identify.

In any case, the effect of the rejection was devastating ("Back then I was homeless, had nothing, and they turned me away, and it hurt my feelings real bad"). But unexpectedly, a Jackson-area disc jockey named Senator Jones (no relation to Charles) was also in the room when Charles auditioned his demo, and he heard the stirrings of something new in the young man's style. A canny industry veteran, Senator Jones was currently the proprietor of the Hep' Me label, based out of his home in Bolton, Mississippi. He also had a close working relationship with Warren Hildebrand, whose Mardi Gras imprint (in New Orleans) was another strong player in southern soul.[13]

"Senator was sitting there looking like, 'Don't these fools know that this is a new genre of music that's just getting ready to blow up?' He didn't say nothing; he kept his mouth closed. When we left out, he called a friend. . . . I went over to his house, and he told me, 'Look, don't get discouraged about what they told [you], because everybody's not gonna hear things that's not meant for them to hear.' And that meant a lot to me."

Senator Jones owned a twenty-two-acre spread in Bolton, a rural community west of Jackson, and he invited Charles to come stay with him as he worked to develop himself. "He took me up under his wing," Charles acknowledges, "and molded me and taught me. . . . I wrote some of the biggest records of my life—'Is There Anybody Lonely?,' 'Friday,' 'Just Can't Let Go,' 'For Better or Worse'—I wrote those kinda records out there up under his guidance and direction. And after that, you know, Senator Jones was a disc jockey on WMPR, 90.1, in Jackson, Mississippi, and he started breaking my records."

"The very first album [released in 2000] was self-entitled, *Sir Charles Jones.* Senator promoted that album on his label, Hep' Me, just to get me a name started, and everybody fell in love with it. By that time, we'd recorded another album called *Love Machine,* and Warren from Mardi Gras picked that album up and promoted it [the following year], and he also picked up the first one. *Love Machine* blew up out of the sky like a tornado."

It was about this time that Sir Charles—or someone—began referring to this new, suave-sounding blend of blues-rooted soul music and contemporary R & B as "southern soul" and himself as its "King." "I'm the founder of southern soul music," he asserts. "Actually, being the founder of southern soul, everybody just started calling me the king of it. It was, like, a trait that came up on me. Everybody just labeled me as the 'King of Southern Soul,' so I started using it."

Denise LaSalle, who takes credit for coining the term *soul-blues,* insists that younger singers like Charles had to come up with a new name for their music because older artists such as herself had a corner on the word *blues* ("Just as we get 'soul-blues' going, here come all these [other] people, they started calling it 'southern soul'").[14] But Charles, who speaks highly of Denise as "a real beautiful-hearted lady" and "one of the people that I most look up to," maintains that the new nomenclature represented not just a marketing gambit but an aesthetic shift.

"I brought a lot of R & B flavor to blues," he says. "You can go to my show and see an eighty-year-old lady and her daughter, or a niece, or her grandchild might be sitting next to her, she might be nineteen or twenty. It started a new trend, brought a lot of the younger generation over to what we do. That's the reason why I said 'southern soul' instead of 'soul-blues.' Just to give it a new flavor, let 'em know it's more youth, too, enjoying the music."

As for being "King," the other major claimant to the crown is probably Willie Clayton. Charles, though, maintains that Clayton was basically considered a blues singer until he, Charles, changed the game, or at least the name of the music.

"Willie came way before I did," he admits, "but he was more considering his music as the genre of blues. One of the guys that wrote [Clayton's 2005 hit "I Love Me Some You"], Vick Allen, is another young southern soul singer. And he wrote that song for Willie Clayton. So it really was southern soul producers and writers writing for him."

(For the record, Malaco's Tommy Couch Jr. says that his label originally launched the sobriquet *southern soul* as a marketing term to mollify merchants and radio disc jockeys who were uneasy trying to sell "blues" to a contemporary audience.[15] Clayton, meanwhile, although he's denied being a blues singer in the past, now embraces the *soul-blues* tag with proprietary zeal.)

The first Sir Charles Jones singles to make significant commercial noise were "Take Care of Mona" and "Better Call Jody" from his eponymous debut disc. "Take Care of Mona" [e.g. "Mama"], a tribute to Blanche Jones and other strong black mothers, featured Charles's voice at its most tender and yearning. "Better Call Jody" was a midtempo workout kicked off by a sermonlike intro that harked back to Marvin Sease's "I'm Mr. Jody"; it showcased Charles's voice at its bluesiest (he sounded even more raw on the disc's closer, the aptly named "Blues Spell"). But rather than hitting in the expected southern U.S. market, "Jody" took off first in the United Kingdom. Charles had never been one to doubt his own abilities, but this international recognition took him by surprise. "I was totally shocked," he admits. "It's a lot of my music being played overseas. I get a lot of fan mail from France, London; a lot of people admire my music over there. I never knew about it; I'm a country boy running through Mississippi, and people overseas is listening at my music!"

Despite the intensity of "Jody" and "Blues Spell," though, *Sir Charles Jones* was primarily an exercise in slow-jam seduction. Charles's voice seethed with barely submerged aggression, implying the kind of hot-blooded prowess that bluesmen have long bragged about, and the lyrics of even his most seemingly innocuous ballads ("Candy Girl") were rife with playful but direct sexual imagery; he could soften effortlessly from a growl to a purr, and on ballads he often seemed to be actually caressing the melody with his voice—now gentle, now rough, flowing gracefully up and down its contours, lingering lovingly at various points along the way. On "Hang On," he dropped the sex-machine-with-a-heart-of-gold pose entirely to assure his struggling lady that she'd survive her travails if she could just hold to her faith in both him and God—a message as old as soul music. It spoke deeply to his audience and played a significant role in heralding Sir Charles Jones as an important new presence on the scene.

Perhaps the most remarkable thing about Charles's early recordings is that they thrust him, virtually fully formed, into the limelight ("*Love Machine* was just full of hits. You know, people could just go ahead, put my album in, and clean up the whole house and don't have to rewind the tape"). Since then, over the course of more than half a dozen CDs and a full-length DVD, his sound has remained pretty much the same, and it's stayed *his* sound; a Sir Charles Jones record is instantly identifiable. At least in his case, it's not a matter of having gotten caught in a rut: Charles's ongoing popularity is largely the result of that same teasing blend of familiarity and surprise—nostalgia intensified by anticipation—that has long been the calling card of successful soul, R & B, and blues artists.

According to Charles, another important reason behind his success has been the artistic freedom he's been granted. "That's the beautiful thing about it," he affirms. "[Some labels have] their own producers; if you want to get a deal with them, their producers have to mess with the music and do everything. Warren always believed in doing promotion and distribution deals and letting [artists] have their own freedom to create. So things will flow the right way. And that was the most beautifulest freedom for any artist to have."

He's enjoyed similar autonomy on the business end. "Mardi Gras don't believe in tying an artist to a long-term contract. If they can't do nothing for your career, they don't believe in holding your career. He'll promote the music, he'll lease your music for a certain amount of time, he'll tell you what he's going to produce and help you with, and if Sony Records wanted to sign you tomorrow, you're free to go."

Nonetheless, after the success of *Love Machine* and "Is There Anybody Lonely?" Charles jumped to the PRG label in 2002 to record the generically titled *Southern Soul* (which he also produced and which enhanced his image as a sensitive yet streetwise Casanova with outings like the Philly-styled ballad "When You Love Someone" and "I'll Never Make a Promise," a pledge of commitment from a reformed player to his baby mama). There ensued what one critic called "an ominous recording silence" and rumors of "contract difficulties" and "record company blues."[16] Finally, in 2006, a new disc, *Thank You for Holding On,* appeared, this time on Charles's own Jumpin imprint. He insists that these side projects were undertaken solely for business reasons: "Independent sales—go independently, get a distribution deal where you get eight to nine dollars a record, you just doubled the amount of money that you [earned] when you was signed up with a label." His performing career, meanwhile, never slackened, and he augmented his own recording activities with guest appearances—as both singer and producer—on various other artists' CDs.

Mardi Gras, still in possession of his catalog, issued a "Best Of" anthology in 2007 entitled *For Your Love* (an earlier compilation, *Sir Charles Jones and Friends,* which included previously unissued tracks by Charles and several other Hep' Me artists, had appeared on Senator Jones's imprint

Figure 20. Sir Charles Jones, Bojangles Coliseum, Charlotte, North Carolina, February 2009. The guitarist is Kenneth "Hollywood" Scott. Photo by Gene Tomko.

in 2004). "I always have kept my relationship strong with Mardi Gras Records," Charles maintains, whether disingenuously or not. "We always kept a beautiful relationship with each other, where if one needs the other, we're always going to work together." And in fact, *My Story,* his first new product for Warren Hildebrand since 2001's *Love Machine,* came out in 2008. The pop-tinged acoustic guitar on "Happy Anniversary" brought a new texture to his sound; ballads like "You Mean the World to Me" and the wracked "My Taboo" further enhanced his image as a tenderhearted man of passion. "You Are the Sunshine," featuring his nine-year-old daughter Charlesia on guest vocals, closed things out on an unexpectedly cute but heartwarming familial note.

As if to herald the prodigal's return, in 2008 Mardi Gras released a DVD, *Sir Charles Jones: His Life & Times,* which Charles himself directed. It included an autobiographical vignette (complete with rare photos from his past, live concert footage, and fascinating ephemera such as a section devoted to his love for fishing and "a special 'For Ladies Only' photo slide show," which featured shots of a bare-chested Sir Charles ["A Young King"] posing, sexy and soapy, in a frothy Jacuzzi).

In a somewhat uncharacteristic public display of humility, the young king then put out *A Tribute to the Legends,* a set that probably came close to reproducing what he sounded like during those long-ago performances at Birmingham's French Quarters. The eclectic CD included standards by likes of Sam Cooke ("Bring It on Home to Me"), Billy Paul ("Me and Mrs. Jones"), Teddy Pendergrass ("You're My Latest, My Greatest Inspiration"), Tyrone Davis ("Mom's Apple Pie," "Do You Feel It"), and Bill Withers ("Ain't No Sunshine"), along with the Jackson 5 ("Never Can Say Good-bye") and J. Blackfoot ("Taxi"). "I always wanted to give back to some of the great legends of song," he says. "All those songs I used to actually sing on my local gigs. That was me giving back, to let them know I thank them for the great songs that they gave me, how much they inspired me. And Warren loved the idea of it and put it out for me [in 2009]."

It was certainly a magnanimous gesture, although it's difficult not to see it in some ways as an attempt to mollify some of the criticism Charles has endured through the years. That cocksure onstage nonchalance of his, along with his occasional tendency to shoot from the lip when he feels cornered (or simply doesn't care enough about the consequences to censor himself), has earned him a reputation for arrogance among some observers, including more then a few within the business itself. "I'm criticized out here," he admits. "They call me the young motherfucker out here, because I'll tell the truth, and I'll tell them to their face."

Most of it, he believes, is due to jealousy. "At first," he says, "when my music started being played and heard, there was a lot of older genre blues singers—ain't gonna call no names—criticized what I done and made things hard. Maybe it was a threat to them, that it would be something that would take over, and there would be less work [for them], but they didn't approve of it too kindly."

It's a common enough scenario: The young lion with new ideas gets hazed by oldheads protecting their turf. But then Charles concludes with the kind of self-serving rationale that seems all too typical and that is almost guaranteed to draw even more criticism: "Only thing that made 'em approve of it is that when we started out creating this Blues Is Alright tour [Memphis-based promoter Julius Lewis's annual all-star multicity revue], I was the majority of the draw that pulled the audiences in. That created work for them, and so they learned to accept [me]."

His tone is matter-of-fact, just as his demeanor seems so disarmingly casual when he saunters out of the wings after his band has warmed up the stage for him. Gentlemanly ease or kingly disdain? Good manners or noblesse oblige? It's hard to tell, and maybe Sir Charles likes it that way. After all, it's no secret that the music world is fraught with jealousy; more than one soul-blues artist has complained about the "crabs in a bucket" mentality—people climbing over one another and trying to pull down anyone who manages to get ahead—that sometimes seems to permeate it. It's also understandable how an ambitious young artist like Charles, whose role in modernizing southern soul and making it more marketable to younger listeners has been beyond question, might chafe at still being treated like the new kid on the block after over a decade as one of the genre's leading hit-makers.

But it also seems pretty bold for him to insist that a revue that's featured, at various points, such legendary figures as Bobby "Blue" Bland, Denise LaSalle, Millie Jackson, Shirley Brown, Latimore, and Bobby Rush has depended on him to "pull the audiences in" and ensure employment for the others. That same tendency toward egocentrism, according to a fellow singer, got Charles in hot water when the Blues Is Alright tour made a stop in Jackson, Mississippi, a few years ago.

"To say what he said!" the singer fumed. "In essence, that he's the youngest blues artist out here that has as many fans as he has [a not indefensible claim: Charles is, in fact, one of the youngest frontline stars on the circuit]. And then he takes it a step farther, says he put Jackson on the map. How's he gonna say something like that, man, when you got folks like Medgar Evers, a lot of civil rights leaders, Walter Payton, a lot of great people come out of Jackson, Mississippi? You put this city on the map? They responded to it in a very, very rough way in Jackson."[17]

But did they really? And, perhaps more to the point, who precisely were "they"? After awhile, it's hard to tell the honest critics from the haters—and maybe, in some cases, the two are one and the same. It's yet another reason why Charles often seems unable to rest comfortably with the accolades and rewards he's earned, to say nothing of his putative kingship. Another incident that supposedly happened in Jackson, involving thuggish behavior on the part of his crew, was either blown out of proportion or made up entirely, according to him: "That's a rumor, and it was a lie. I was shocked when I heard that one. That never happened, and that was a terrible rumor going around. It kind of took a minute for that to die away, and we had to do a lot of interviews, a lot of radio stations and everything, to let people know I was all right and it never happened. People gonna say things like that about you." But who? And why? "I don't know. To this very day we're still trying to find out."

In a sense, it's not all that different from the way it was so many years ago, running the streets of Birmingham with the Gangster Disciples. If you're trying to move up, there's always someone who wants to take you down. And even if you make it, you never stop looking over your shoulder. That's not to say, though, that Charles has succumbed to bitterness or paranoia or that he's somehow been unable to shake the old thug ways. His pride in having finally lived up to his mother's expectations rings absolutely genuine; he often talks about how "blessed" he's been in music, and when you watch his DVD and see him cruising over the water in his fishing boat (a Mercury-powered Pro Team 175 TXW), it's clear that he's embraced the good life with relish—a relish that becomes even more palpable in the tenderness that warms his voice as he murmurs encouragement to Charlesia in "You Are the Sunshine."

And in fact, Charles emphasizes at every opportunity that he's motivated by love more than anything else. "Man, the fans!" he effuses. "Communication with them is the best thing."

> You know, last night I was exhausted, leaving out of the arena, and there was this lady. She was crying; she wanted an autograph. And as much as it hurted for me to get [up] and peel myself out of that van—you want to rest after you did the show, let your respiration go down, [then] you go out there posing and smelling funky breath and signing autographs all night, you be so wore out, man—I jumped back out and did what I had to do and let the lady know how much I appreciated her loving me as well as supporting me. That goes a long way with people. They'll always support you, man, if you just do the right thing.

Still restless, still determined not to be reined in, Charles decided to return to his own label not long after the release of *A Tribute to the Legends*. With a characteristic blend of workmanlike dedication and self-confident flair, he describes his follow-up project as foreshadowing a new stage in both his life and his career. "I'm only about five tracks into the album," he explains, "'cause we're recording a lot of it live. We're contemplating, I would say, another two months [this was in March 2011]. I got youth and, God willing, I got time to try to pull something off good. We're gonna put this one back on Jumpin.

"We're gonna entitle it *Glow.* After the success of my career—all the ups and the downs—I feel like I can glow."

8

Ms. Jody

"Just a Little Bit Won't Get It"

It's mid-August 2009, and a crowd of soul-blues lovers has packed the DeSoto Civic Center in Southaven, Mississippi, a few miles outside of Memphis, Tennessee, for the Seventh Annual Tri-State Blues Festival. Ms. Jody, one of the fastest-rising stars on the circuit despite her newcomer status (her debut CD, *You're My Angel,* came out on Ecko in 2006, and when it was released she hadn't even done her first show yet), is on the bill along with veterans like J. Blackfoot, Shirley Brown, Marvin Sease, Bobby Rush, and Sir Charles Jones. It's a pretty packed lineup—at least eight acts are scheduled to appear—so Ms. Jody knows she won't have much time to get the house.

Her drummer kicks into a sassy "striptease" beat, and Jody launches into "Sugar Daddy," a popular track from *You're My Angel.* As she sings, she prances back and forth across the stage and caresses her body, pausing coquettishly when her hand gets close to her crotch. After a few verses, she signals the band to quiet down and launches into her sermon: if you're a woman and you want to capture a sugar daddy, you'll need to "keep your hair lookin' good, keep your nails lookin' good, keep your deodorant good . . . and keep that 'cat' smellin' good"—a backhanded reference to "You're Dog's About to Kill My Cat," a song from another of her Ecko CDs.

She continues: "When Ms. Jody's man goes out and works hard all day, he don't do it for nothin.' He comes home . . . get in that shower, washes that body all-l-l-l over . . ." [she rubs herself down with her hand, gasping and panting with pleasure, as the crowd screams for more] "Oooh! That feels good, right there!" After her man emerges from the shower, she says, he calls her name—"And you best believe, I come Jody-on-the-spot. And when I get there, that man is standin' just like the proud man he is, y'all [she pantomimes an exaggerated, three-foot-long jerking-off motion]—just the way I like him!"

By now the women in the audience are shrieking so loudly that it's hard to keep up with Jody's spiel:

> Now that man say, "Jody, I want you right here on your knees. And it ain't prayin' that I want you to be doin', either." . . . I take that joystick into my hand, y'all—and I like to call it a joystick because it brings me so much joy, keeps that smile on my face. Y'all, that thing is so pretty to me! I just look at it, and I kiss it [she plants her lips on the head of her microphone and smooches it with a loud slurping sound] . . . I say, "Baby, you been missin' me, baby?" And it jumps [she jerks her hands upward, snapping the mic erect in her first] . . . I say, "Baby—are you ready for what I got to give you?" [another mic jump] . . . Now I'm gonna show y'all just what Ms. Jody do . . . [and suddenly she's licking the microphone cord, her tongue extended to an almost cartoonish length, inch by inch, all the way up to the mic itself. She laps and slathers it as the room explodes into ecstasy].

But that's just the preliminary. A bit later, in the middle of another song, "Big Daddy Don't You Come," she quiets the band again and calls out to an assistant: "I need a big daddy, and I need a chair, right about here." After the prop has been put in place, a man emerges from the wings, hobbling on crutches. She feigns dismay: "Ohhh, shit! Are you sure?" But he looks game, so she lets him sit down. Leaning against him, she coos: "Is it all right if I maybe straddle you? And I ride you?" Yes, he answers. "Would it be all right if when I straddle you, and I'm riding you, and my cat accidentally strokes your leg [she's standing in front of him now, fondling her crotch and thrusting it toward him]—would that be a problem?" No, no problem at all.

"Well," she continues, "if while I'm straddlin' you, and I'm ridin' you, and my cat accidentally strokes you leg, are you gonna give it back to me?"

As the screams and applause cascade around her, she cues the band, breaks into the song again ("I'm gettin' in the saddle, takin' you for a ride"), and struts back toward her "Big Daddy" volunteer. Leaning all over him as he reclines in the chair, she takes his head into her arms and caresses it, vibrating her breasts and body against him; finally, she stands back in a pose of triumph and asks him if he's all right. He points to his bad leg; she goes back to work, wrapping her own legs around it and undulating atop it. Suddenly he rises to his feet, grabs the crutches from the assistant who's been holding them, tosses them to the floor, and breaks into a gyrating bump-and-grind with Jody. The crowd erupts into sanctified fervor. The emcee shouts, "The power of coochie, y'all! The healing power of coochie!" before leading the stooge back to the wings.[1]

"That was my backup singer's boyfriend," she'll later explain. "This was all set up." Usually she invites her "Big Daddy" from the audience without preparation and with no "miracle healing" finale.

. . .

Vertie Joann Delapaz is still, she maintains, a country girl at heart. By her own account, she is also a strong-willed, independent woman who has learned the hard way to stand up, fight for herself, and demand her due, and who is now determined to spread that message in song.[2] "I'm gonna tell it like it is," she likes to say, "and I'm gonna keep it real." And if that means celebrating the raw as well as the tender side of life and love; if it means putting on "skits," as she calls them, which she admits would probably have offended her father (a man of faith who became an ordained minister in his later years) had he lived to see them; if it means incurring the wrath of some of her more old-school colleagues; even if it means running the risk of being stereotyped as a one-trick pony whose "trick" just happens to be whoever she's straddling and rubbing against on stage at any given time (she insists she's never felt typecast, but several of the artists profiled in this book immediately mentioned her name when I brought up the music's ongoing "raunch" controversy)—well, that's why they call it the blues.

"Ms. Jody is just a character that Vertie plays,"[3] she has said, and as she reminisces about her childhood on the family farm in Bay Springs, Mississippi, and her struggles and triumphs since then, it's not hard to believe her. She was born Vertie Joann Pickens ("Jody" is a childhood nickname based on her middle name), not in Mississippi but in Chicago, on November 10, 1957. "My parents were working there," she explains. "My grandfather, my mom's dad, had a construction company."

Figure 21. "Telling it like it is": Ms. Jody, Sunflower River Blues and Gospel Festival, Clarksdale, Mississippi, 2008. Photo by Gene Tomko.

[But] within two years' time, we came back South. We have a big farm; my grandfather purchased it. When I was really, really young, my dad used to raise cotton. We raised corn, peas, butter beans, okra, all type of vegetables, watermelons. That's when I learned to drive the tractor. We would do some of the plowing with the tractor, and we also had mules to plow. And my dad would hire people to come in and help work the farm, work the crops and stuff. We raised our own chickens, so we had our own poultry, our own eggs, and we raised the corn to carry us across the winter and feed the livestock.

Farming families have traditionally been anchored by strong women, and the Pickenses were no exception. "My mom, Vivian," Jody says, "she was the heavyweight around the farm. My dad usually just worked to bring the money in, and my mom ran the farm."

> Wasn't much of nothing she couldn't do. She could tear down a tractor motor and rebuild it. And you know where you have the gasket to go between the parts and stuff? Well, she would get the sheet of gasket paper and make her own gaskets. She did our own plumbing, and I learned that from her, and she was good with a gun, and I learned that. I used to go coon hunting with my dad when he was living. And we fished a lot and just did, basically, country stuff. Most of all, she taught us how to survive. I hear so many people complain about, "What are we going to do if the electricity go off?" That doesn't bother me. Like I said, my mom taught us how to survive.

"Give me a good sharp knife, and in fifteen minutes I can skin [a side of] beef all by myself,"[4] she brags, adding that "just by watching my mom" she also learned how to make short work of the raccoons, squirrels, and rabbits she can still bag and bring in if she needs to.

When she wasn't hunting, fishing, or doing farmwork, young Vertie Joann absorbed a diverse array of popular and vernacular music, both black and white. Country music was all over the radio, of course, and any Mississippi child who was raised right in those days absorbed a healthy diet of gospel and religious songs, but there was plenty of R & B in the air, as well. Vertie came of age doing dances like the Twist, Rufus Thomas's Funky Chicken, and the Bus Stop, and she remembers Marvin Gaye as one of her favorite singers. She also shared at least one infatuation with her Caucasian counterparts: "I was in love with Elvis Presley as a kid," she admits, in a tone that indicates the flame hasn't entirely died out. "I mean, I was in love with Elvis Presley. Oh, God, I can't recall any particular songs that I liked at that time, [but] oh, he was just so beautiful, and he danced and moved, and—oh, God, I just fell in love with it."

But it was her mother, once again, who lit the spark that would eventually ignite into a lifelong passion for singing. "When we were kids, I remember, Mom used to sing to us all the time. And in the evening time, when we got all our work done and we're outside playing, she would sing songs for us, we would get out there and play, and we would sing along. She would sing little nursery rhymes and stuff like that, and little things kids play by, and then sometimes we'd sing gospel songs. I used to tell people it was my dad, because he and my aunties had a gospel group, but my mother is who instilled me with music, singing."

In those days, though, she had no dreams of becoming anything more adventurous than "a mom and a housewife," albeit a housewife as handy with a rifle, a hunting knife, and a pair of alligator pliers as she'd be with a spatula and a vacuum cleaner. Strong-willed from the first, she quit school in the eleventh grade to get married at seventeen. But she didn't allow any teenage romantic fantasies to hold her back when harsher realities came calling. "It didn't last," she says. "I confronted with him about something that he was doing, and he hit me. And when he got in from work the next day, I was halfway to Chicago." The daughter of Vivian Pickens was not about to let herself be used as a punching bag.

Living on the west side of Chicago with her sister and her sister's husband, though, Vertie soon became restless. Unfamiliar with the city, she stayed home most of the time. As much as she loved music, she says, and as lively as the local blues scene still was, she ventured out into the clubs only occasionally. After someone tried to break into her sister's apartment, she took stock and realized that "this [was] too much for me. Shortly after that, I came back home."

She came home, though, to one of the poorest regions in the country. Opportunities weren't plentiful for an eleventh-grade dropout. But, as she says, her mother had taught her how to survive. She trained as an inspector at a chicken processing plant ("I got that down pat really good and thought about going and applying for my license. I submitted an application, but I didn't follow through with it"), and she also worked in home health care for a while. She remembers that she used to soothe her elderly patients with a cappella versions of the gospel songs and spirituals ("Amazing Grace," "Jesus Gave Me Water") she'd sung as a child. And despite her harrowing early experience with matrimony, she tried it again—and again, and again—until she'd been married and separated five times ("twice to one guy—I guess maybe you could sum it up as four").

"Each one of these husbands," she maintains, "were hardworking men. They were hardworking men who would provide for the family."

But they had ways she couldn't countenance. Her song "Loving You Is Like Doing Hard Time," which appears on her 2009 Ecko CD, *It's a Ms. Jody Thang!*, arose out of one of her marriages, to a man who was so jealous and possessive that "I was to stay in the shadows. . . . It was like doing hard time. I wasn't locked behind bars, but the life I had just wasn't mine."[5]

She eventually decided that marriage simply wasn't for her. "I don't want to go that way again. It gets lonely sometimes, it does. It gets lonely, but I don't want to go back that way anymore."

In retrospect, though, it almost seems as if life was simply clearing a path for her. In 2005, about two years after her fifth marriage came to an end, she had the experience that propelled her into a world, and eventually a career, whose existence she'd barely suspected before then. "My brother and I—his name is Dale Pickens—were very close," she says. "I was driving truck with him. He took me to this blues show. It was a festival in Bassfield, Mississippi. O. B. [Buchana], Willie Clayton, [the late] Jackie Neal, L. J. Echols, and Denise LaSalle. I have always loved Denise. Oh, God almighty! I have! And then getting a chance to see her live, and see her perform—oh, man. That just rocked my world."

Riding home with her brother that night, "I said, 'You know, I can do that.' He said, 'What?' I said, 'What those people was doing on stage.' I said, 'You know what? I'm gonna do that.' And that just tickled him so. He said, 'All right. I heard you, girl.' I went home, and I started writing songs. I talked to one of my sisters about it, and she started writing also. And here I am."

First, though, she had to get those songs heard. "Every year, [Dale] would put on a blues show there on the farm," she explains. "So he knew some artists. And so this particular CD release party [was] going on in Meridian, Mississippi, for [vocalist] Carrie Carter. We went up there, and that's where we met William Day, who is my manager today."

Despite her professed determination to emulate Denise LaSalle and the others she'd seen at Bassfield, though, she didn't exactly push herself into the spotlight. "She was sitting there in a corner by herself, humming a song," Day told *Living Blues* magazine in 2010. "I could tell she had some rhythm to her voice. I told her, 'You sound pretty good humming that song. Can you sing?' She said, 'Maybe.'"[6]

"I had never met them before," she explains, when asked why this uncharacteristic surge of shyness seems to have possessed her at such a crucial moment. "They were all strangers. And we were sitting there. They asked who I was and everything, and I told 'em, and they were pickin' at me, saying, 'Oh, she probably can't sing anyway.' So I didn't say anything, and [they] said, 'I'm tired now; I'm getting ready to go.' And I started singing 'Sugar Daddy'—'I'm lookin' for a sugar daddy'—and they stopped, and they just looked." ("All of a sudden," marvels Day, "you hear this big voice coming out of this quiet person."[7]) "I said, 'I've sung my song,' and that was it. And I went back into my little quiet zone. And they walked back outside. [Day] knew some people who were working at Ecko Records. My brother and he were talking, and William suggested to him to bring me to Memphis. The following weekend, we went to Memphis, Tennessee."

In Memphis, Day introduced Jody to Ecko arranger and session musician Morris J. Williams. Williams took her "out somewhere to a studio" where she recorded a demo of the song that would eventually be known as "Ms. Jody" ("I'm Ms. Jody, I'm the new freak in town") and serve as the opening track for *You're My Angel,* her debut CD on Ecko. Other demo tracks were recorded at the Ecko studio itself. When label owner John Ward heard them, he acknowledged that the singer had chops, but he wasn't sure she was ready to join his roster.

"Singing ability is not the main thing we look for," he has explained, perhaps inadvertently revealing the lack of emphasis on artistic quality that critics of southern soul—and pop music in general—have long suspected too often affects front-office decision making. "The main thing we look for is somebody who is really working in the field. If you're out there and you're known, it really doesn't matter how great a singer you are. . . . She had never done a gig or been in the field."[8]

This time, though, the aspiring vocalist who'd already adopted Ms. Jody as a stage name (even though she'd never been on a stage) decided she'd waited long enough. As Ward tells it, he ended up releasing her first CD almost in self-defense. "She was really persistent," he admits. "She called me again, and she called me again. Even when I told her, 'We're gonna pass,' she called me again and said, 'Well, I really would like to be on Ecko Records.' So I said, 'Okay.' I said, 'Hey, we'll do it, then.' She was a pretty good singer, but I just didn't have confidence that she was going to be an artist or back it up, y'know, to get out there."[9]

You're My Angel provided at least a few foreshadowings of the wanton-woman-with-a-wink persona that Jody would eventually claim as her own. "Ms. Jody," which was written by her sister Lillie Pickens, craftily name-checked Marvin Sease, one of southern soul's biggest-selling stars at the time. That, along with its burbling synthesized backing track, virtually assured it both jukebox and radio action, despite its somewhat unwieldy length—over five minutes—and the lyrics' PG-13 descriptions of how "the new freak in town" could satisfy her man. In the jazz-tinged "Love Shop Mechanic," Jody extolled the virtues of her boudoir handyman ("Talkin' about a man who know just how to lay his pipe . . . and he knows how to use all the tools that he's got") in a sexy purr that was nonetheless full-bodied and sure.

"I Never Take a Day Off," lushly produced by Morris J. Williams, was country-flavored: the melodic line was honky-tonk simple, and Jody's

Mississippi drawl made the tale of conjugal dedication ("I never take a day off from lovin' my baby") sound like a bedrock declaration of country values. "Get Drunk Party," penned by brother Dale, was based on a melodic theme extending at least as far back as Solomon Burke's 1965 hit "Got to Get You Off My Mind"; the lyrics told of a wronged woman determined to drink her blues away, reflecting the kind of good-natured fatalism that has always belied the blues' reputation as "sad" music.

Perhaps most tantalizing, though, were the ballads. "Quiet Storm," with its wafting strings and fuzz-tone guitar lead (courtesy of John Ward), created a sensual bed for Jody's voice as she praised the joys of long-term commitment with understated yet fiery intensity. "I Had a Good Time," again caressed by strings, was a celebration of love, life, and perseverance that reflected both hard-won wisdom and unbending faith. Regardless of any doubts the Ecko brain trust might have had, the breadth and depth of ideas, emotions, stylistic influences, and musical personas that Ms. Jody attained on her debut were both impressive and rich with promise.

Meanwhile, it was time to begin to make a name for herself as an entertainer. In vintage dues-paying fashion, she ended up traveling almost halfway across the country to do it.

> My very first show on the road was in Oklahoma City, Oklahoma. O. B. Buchana and [Memphis-based vocalist] Booker Brown were on the show. William [Day] and his partner Leo Johnson called me up and asked me would I like to go to Oklahoma and perform on the stage. And I said, "Sure I would!" And that's how it came about. Oh, God, I was totally excited!
>
> I worked with O. B. a lot. And I enjoyed that, and I thank him so much for allowing me to come along, tag along, and a lot of times he would call me up, he said, "I've got a special guest here with me tonight, Ms. Jody," and, "Ms. Jody, you come out here and do something for us." I thank him for that. I really thank him for that.

As Jody was establishing herself as an entertainer, several tracks from *You're My Angel*—"I Never Take a Day Off," "Ms. Jody," "Get Drunk Party," the generically titled "Shake Your Booty"—began to make some encouraging noise on southern soul radio. John Ward became a believer in a hurry: "I said, which is what I always do, 'Let's go get another CD; let's record one on her.' We got that CD [*What You Gonna Do When the Rent Is Due?*] out, like, within about six months after the first one. We came up with 'Your Dog's About to Kill My Cat' and got her in here, recorded it, and that's [what] really did it for her. Once that came out, she really got more popular."[10]

This time around, most of the songs were written by Ward and his compatriots at Ecko (bassist Leo Johnson co-wrote the title song with

Jody). In fact, although she'd continue to bring at least a few original creations to all of her subsequent sessions, it would be a long time before Jody would record another disc consisting mostly of material emanating from the Delapaz/Pickens family. Whether or not that's the main reason, not all of her subsequent recorded output fully lived up to the artistic promise of *You're My Angel*. Although her career as a frontline entertainer has maintained a steady upward trajectory in the wake of "Your Dog's About to Kill My Cat," for at least several years, in purely artistic terms, her albums sometimes seemed to be marking time.

Despite the commercial success "Dog" garnered after its release, there was little to distinguish its lyrics from boilerplate nudge-nudge/wink-wink soul-blues silliness ("You gotta realize, this kitty ain't all yours / But you wanna stroke and poke 'til she can't play no more"), and the lazy two-chord vamp on which it was based broke little new ground either melodically or rhythmically. Listeners attuned to the subtleties of gender politics might also have found the song's story line problematic: "Your dog," Jody mewed, "shows up at my door every day, wanting to play with my kitty, whether she's tired or not / And when it's all worn out, you still don't want to stop." Some may hear this as striking a good-humored sisterly blow for "a sexually-beleaguered woman saddled with a man with unquenchable appetites," as one critic suggested.[11] Others, though, might find joking about "unquenchable" male libido disturbingly close to laughing off the threat of sexual violence ("I don't know how much longer I can take this abuse," Jody sang at one point, ostensibly with tongue in cheek), whether within or outside a relationship.

There were, nonetheless, quite a few promising moments on Jody's sophomore disc. "Big Daddy Don't You Come," the song that soon provided the soundtrack for her most notorious stage routine, was energized by a jaunty, pseudo–New Orleans strut. Its double entendres did double-duty, proclaiming a woman's determination to be satisfied ("Big Daddy don't you come too soon, because the night is still young") as well as to satisfy ("You can take the high stool, I'm a-gonna take the low," she sang, in obvious homage to Bobby Rush, "While I'm workin' on the head of things / don't you even move a toe").

The title tune showed even more depth; an uncompromising throw-down to a trash-talking player, it inspired her to summon her most blistering vocal fire. "I'm Puttin' Love on the Shelf" reflected her self-proclaimed determination to forego the temptations of romance for the lonelier but safer rewards of self-reliance, and again both her vocal delivery and the production were robust. Her kiss-off to a no-good cad in Raymond Moore and John Ward's "Get Up and Move On" was biting and effective. But what was missing from this disc, overall, was the emotional vulnerability that had characterized such earlier outings as "Quiet Storm" and "I Had a Good Time."

Meanwhile, as she continued to appear on shows with O. B. Buchana and increasingly on her own, she was perceptive enough to realize that not all the excitement she felt on stage was finding its way into the audience. "She came to me," recalls William Day, "and said, 'I gotta add to my show to make it live and exciting.'"[12]

Fortunately, she had a good role model in Buchana himself, a husky-voiced soul man from Clarksdale, Mississippi, whose risqué stage antics and penchant for barnyard-humor lyrics sometimes run the risk of belying the smoldering sensuality of his vocals ("The people are loving it," he explains, "so if that's what's selling the album, that's what you got to do. You've got to do whatever it takes to sell the album."[13]) She began to copy his trademark lascivious tongue-wags, and before long she was applying them to her microphone. "That just happened," she asserts. "I was talking to the women, telling them about some of the things they can do to keep their man at home, and it just happened on stage one night."

Over the next year or so, as she added more songs to her repertoire, her act grew into what it is today. "I thought about the song 'Big Daddy Don't You Come,' and I said, 'I can work with that. Get me a man, put him in the hot seat, and ask him if it would be all right for me to ride him and a few more questions.' I gave it a try, and the people loved it."[14]

But she also says she wanted to expand her range—emotionally and thematically, as well as musically—and to do so, she had to bring new songs and ideas to the table. Even some of the things she'd already recorded gave her pause, at least initially. "'Your Dog's About to Kill My Cat,'" she admits, "I really didn't know how it was going to come across to the people. I didn't know whether they were going to like it or not. After we did 'Your Dog's About to Kill My Cat' and—let me see, there were a few other ones in there—I told John, 'I want to clean it up some.' I want to be proud of what I got and not be embarrassed or bashful to [hand] the CD to anybody and say, 'Listen to this. You'll like it.'"

Her next recording, *I Never Take a Day Off*, which came out in 2008, showed encouraging signs of depth, and true to her vow the material mostly avoided blatant sexual innuendo. This time, though, the production seemed disturbingly uneven, and too many of the songs were saddled with lyric clichés. Raymond Moore and John Ward's "Energizer Bunny" revisited the conceit of "Your Dog's About to Kill My Cat"—praising the prowess of a partner whose sexual desire is so insatiable that it's virtually predatory—and at the end, when an uncredited male vocalist came in playing the role of a threatening husband ("I don't wanna hear that, woman! Lay down!"), the singer ended up succumbing meekly to his desires, belying any hint of irony that might have been implied until then.

But there were still some fine moments. The title tune, which laid Jody's vocals from the earlier version over a remixed backing track, was as effective as it had been the first time around (she says it was reissued by popular demand). "Lonely Housewife" was charged with bluesy intensity, and on it Jody attained what sounded like genuine desperation. "Two Strikes You're Out" overcame run-of-the-mill backing to showcase her feline snarl at its most uncompromising. "I Might Be Your Part Time Love but I Won't Be Your Full Time Fool" again spurred her to hone a passionate vocal edge. "I'm So Thankful," which she co-wrote, was a church-inspired love ballad in the great tradition ("I love you from deep down in my soul . . . That's a sacred place where only you and God can go"). Her sanctified fervor on this, the final cut, made it clear that she'd lost none of the fire or vision that had originally impelled her into music.

The following year's *Ms. Jody's Thang!*, though, seemed to represent a rethinking on either her part or Ecko's. The cover portrayed her as a dominatrix-cougar: a tiny silver key dangled from her fingers as she smiled imperiously down at a bare-chested young man who appeared to be on his knees, his right wrist locked in a handcuff. With titles like "You've Got to Play with It Before You Lay with It" and "He's Coming in the Backdoor," it seemed as if her determination to "clean it up some" might have wavered a bit ("I try to give 'em what they want," she has said, echoing O. B. Buchana's fatalistic attitude toward both aesthetics and ethics when it comes to getting heard). "He's Coming in the Backdoor," as it turned out, was a song about an illicit lover sneaking into the house, rather than an ode to kinky sex. The title song, a variation on the popular line-dance theme exemplified by such better-known songs as Marcia Griffiths's "Electric Boogie" (a.k.a. "The Electric Slide"), DJ Casper's "Cha-Cha Slide," and Cupid's "Cupid Shuffle," found Jody doing a credible dance-master DJ turn, shouting out instructions in a muscular bellow.

On "The Better the Goods the Higher the Price," Jody revisited the vintage blueswoman's theme of demanding both erotic and financial props from her man in return for satisfaction; once again, though, the backing seemed oddly tentative—it laid bare her occasional timbral uncertainty on more challenging melodic runs. The rich-grooved danceability that usually characterizes the best soul music seemed more implied than realized. Her

Figure 22. Ms. Jody flashes her "come-hither" doe eyes at the Sunflower River Blues and Gospel Festival, Clarksdale, Mississippi, 2008. Photo by Gene Tomko.

sole self-written contribution to *Thang!* was "Loving You Is Like Doing Hard Time," the song she'd penned about an overly possessive husband; lyrically, it was uncompromising, even stark ("I got to give an account of everything I say and do. . . . I may as well be in hell"), and as the song built, her voice intensified into a ragged, angst-ridden scream. But the bouncy soft-soul melody, muted synth backing, and generic-sounding rhythm track drained it of most of its urgency.

Meanwhile, though, her reputation as a live entertainer continued to spread. And then, on *Ms. Jody's in the Streets Again,* her next release, the Jody whose potential had shone so brightly on her first recording reemerged. Her vibrato-laced wail sounded surer than ever; the mix was rugged, roomy, and powerful; and the emotional range of the material had rewidened. The title song, with its echoes of the Ann Peebles classic "Breaking Up Somebody's Home," was as bluesy and robust as anything that had emanated from Ecko in years; the ballad "I've Got the Strength to Walk Away" found Jody's voice at its most bittersweet, and the story told was both heartrending and inspiring. "I Won't Be Back" throbbed with pent-up outrage as Jody announced her determination to break free, supported by an ironically lilting girl-group accompaniment.

"The Bop," a bouncy midtempo dance tune, emerged from the pack to take on a life of its own; it's been embraced as a dance-floor favorite, at least in the South, and it's been posted several times on YouTube. The disc's centerpiece, though, was another ballad, "You Had It All." Jody, who co-wrote the song with her cousin, Mario Ferrell, summoned a riveting mix of heartbreak, resignation, and redemptive determination as a synth-string backing billowed around her. Contrary to what some cynics might think about the inability of soul-blues fans to stop lickin' it and stickin' it long enough to appreciate music of substance, Jody says that this song and some of her other more thoughtful material have become among her most requested, both on stage and on radio.

"When the CD first came out," she affirms, "I got a lot of calls from different DJs and different people, telling me how much they loved those songs. I know when we went to Flint, Michigan, this past weekend [in April 2011] and did 'You Had It All,' I got a great response. The people really loved it."

Consistency, though, doesn't come easy. Jody's next Ecko outing, *I'm Keepin' It Real,* only occasionally revisited the emotional depth and storytelling eloquence that had made *In the Streets* so impressive. "Move On," yet another riposte to a no-good man, allowed Jody to bring forth her full armamentarium of cat-scratch fierceness. "I've Got the Strength to Stay Gone" was a more somber-minded version of the same story— a wounded but resolute woman proclaims her independence—and it echoed the bruised soulfulness that had made songs like "You Had It All" and "I Won't Be Back" so memorable. The title tune, although saddled with an annoying faux-"live" audience soundtrack, effectively cast Jody as a relationship counselor imparting advice to both the trapped and the lovelorn.

Elsewhere, though, *Keepin' It Real* seemed tentative; rhymes were strained and often clichéd, the production was tepid, and Jody's phrasing sometimes sounded stiff. "I Wanna Rock It in Your Rocking Chair" and the twelve-bar "I Thank You for a Job Well Done" ("You've got a sugar tit right at the tip of your tongue") revisited well-trod Jody territory; "The Spank," for all its "old-school-meets-new-school" bluster, sounded almost painfully out of touch with contemporary R & B values: Jody's callouts to various soloists seemed mannered, and the overall production invoked neither James Brown and other vintage-era "Spank" purveyors nor modern street dance culture. Several of the songs' backing tracks sounded as if they could have been lifted from any of hundreds of anonymous southern soul predecessors; in places, even Jody's vocals sounded hollow and too low in the mix.

A lot of these problems might have been rectified by taking a little more time to fine-tune the songwriting, fill out the production, and allow for a few more in-studio run-throughs. The promise that had seemed close to being realized on *In the Streets Again* and the best of Jody's previous work felt suddenly muted, if not a little betrayed, by a lot of *Keepin' It Real*. Even some critics who had been among Jody's most avid boosters were less than enthusiastic about the turn her recordings now seemed to be taking.[15]

But does it really matter as long as the product keeps selling, enough songs get airplay and club action, and people keep coming to the shows? Jody remains one of the hottest-drawing live acts on the southern soul-blues circuit. In performance, her voice is clarion-toned and sure, and her prestige as a rising soul-blues celebrity allows her to hire some of the most accomplished backup musicians on the circuit. Her stagecraft, of course, is deft and imaginative; for all her lascivious carryings-on, she conveys a sense of steadfastness, even dignity, in her refusal to back down or compromise as she demands both satisfaction and respect.

For her part, Jody professes nothing but delight with what she's accomplished so far. "I'm really excited about it," she asserts. "I am still excited about it."

> And I'm looking forward to the future. I would like to see Ms. Jody become a household name everywhere. I want to get out of this little southern circle. I would like to hit Detroit, Michigan; Pennsylvania; and Chicago. Those are three main places I would like to get. I'm willing to try just about anything, because I just love music. Whatever brings about a change, or whatever the change is, I'm willing to give it a try. [At a recent show], I called some of the women, about eight or twelve women, up on the stage to dance with me. And before they left off the stage, they all gave

me a hug and kiss and said, "Ms. Jody, thank you so much for calling us up. We've never done anything like this before." And oh, Lord, that just touched my heart.

I'm happy. I'm happy with what I'm doing. Just about everywhere I go, people give me good receptions. I guess that's what makes me continue to do what I do and enjoy it so much, because they give me so much love.

A similar serenity—or maybe it's simply a refusal to allow her hard-earned sense of equilibrium to be violated—informs her personal life. These days, performing as Ms. Jody, she spends a lot of her time in cities and on the road. But she clings to her country roots. Heidelberg, Mississippi, the town she calls home, is a hamlet of fewer than nine hundred people about seventy-five miles east of Jackson. The 250-acre Pickens family farm is nearby in Bay Springs, and it remains her emotional and spiritual center.

Some of my siblings still live there. We have horses, and in the springtime, we plant peas; people come in and pick the peas. And [on] some part of the land, we do mud bogs. It's when they get on their four-wheel bikes, and we go into the mud and the creeks and stuff, and, man, we have a ball. We have a ball! Mud bogging [she chortles]—you need to pull it up on the Internet, mud bogging. Sometimes we have, like, three or four hundred bikes there. [Does she climb on a bike herself and join the fun?] Yes, Lord! And if I can't get muddy, I don't wanna do it. I love it!

As for her stage act, she maintains she has no difficulty keeping Ms. Jody, the character that Vertie plays, safely separate from Vertie herself. She admits, though, that some of the things Ms. Jody does violate the sense of propriety with which Vertie was raised. "I do believe that my father would be proud of me singing and doing something with my life," she avers. "He always wanted my sisters and I to have a gospel group. My dad became a minister; it was in the '80s when my dad became a minister. As far as my act on the stage, my little skits, he would have had a problem with that. And if he had been still living, no doubt I wouldn't have been doing those little skits on the stage, because I really respected him."

She insists, in any case, that there's a deeper purpose behind what she does and that her true audience understands it. Like the trickster of myth, she may violate or transgress the bonds of propriety during the ritual of her show, but it's all in the name of asserting, not defiling, the values that her upbringing and her life have taught her to embrace. After all, when she licks her microphone or offers her "cat" to Big Daddy, she makes it clear that she's showing women how to keep their men, not flaunt themselves as wanton hoochies. "When I hit the stage," she maintains, "I like to tell 'em,

'A lot of people think Ms. Jody is nasty.' I say, 'I'm not nasty; I'm nice-ty.' I try to keep it on the real. I let 'em know there is another side."

> I have had fans to come to me and ask me for advice. I have had fans to come up to me and tell me how much they love my music, and that they have gone home and did some of the things that I advised 'em on, and about [how] their relationship is so much better, and I will tell 'em, I say, "Give thanks to God for that." And I [also] let 'em know it's more to life than just jumpin' in bed; you've got to build on your relationship.
>
> This last CD that we recorded, [the song] "I'm Keepin' It Real"—well, the first thing I said was, "This is Ms. Jody, I'm back, and I've got something I need to say. I got something that you all need to know." I said, "Well, first of all, I want to say, if you're in a relationship and you're not happy, get the hell out." Short. It's time out for all this—abusive relationships, and flow just to be going, and making folks happy while you're miserable. Just come off of that!
>
> Those things I said in that song are true. I mean, those things really happen. No matter who you are, you're going to have ups and downs in your relationship. There were two women that came up to me and said, "Ms. Jody, you said that you like to keep it real." I said, "Yes, I do." They said, "Well, what's so real about 'Your Dog Is About to Kill My Cat'?" I said, "Well, I'm talking about, when most women and men get together, if they get wild and carried away with it, when they're finished up, that cat is either bruised, swollen, beat down, or just downright tired, and that dog's just 'bout killed that cat." And they burst out laughing. They said, "You're right! You're right!"
>
> As long as I can relate to it and apply it to my life, I can deal with it. Ms. Jody's going to tell it like it is.

• • •

In late 2011, after this chapter was written, Ecko released *Ms. Jody's in the House,* a straightforward and gimmick-free blast of Jody at her most assertive and soulful. The tentative-sounding mix and clichéd lyrics that marred parts of *Keepin' It Real* had given way to forceful production, thoughtful storytelling (Jody once again took a major songwriting role), and a seriousness of purpose that harked back to the best of *In the Streets Again.* Whether reinhabiting her role as a life-wizened personal adviser ("When Your Give a Damn Just Don't Give a Damn Anymore"), promising a hot young tenderoni a night of no-strings ecstasy ("I Just Wanna Love You"), or plumbing the torment of erotic and emotional infatuation (Raymond Moore and John Ward's "I Never Knew Good Love Could Hurt So Bad"), Ms. Jody again sounded like a soul woman on the move—a life traveler who'd come back with stories to tell.

The "Raunch" Debate

Hoochification or
Sexual Healing?

Spend even a little time in the soul-blues world, and you're likely to find yourself in the middle of conversations, if not arguments, about the current proliferation of graphic lyrics and stage turns in the music. Songs like Sweet Angel's "The Tongue Don't Need No Viagra" and the various "cat"/ "dog" ditties in recent years, as well as more explicit outings like Ms. Jody's "Lick if You Can't Stick" and L. J. Echols' 2009 "From the Back" ("Do you want me to get it from the back . . . do you want me to lay up in it from the back") and the onstage antics of Jody, Angel, O. B. Buchana, and some others, have been blamed for everything from defiling the music's legacy to driving away respectable—and, by implication, profitable—listeners.

But such conceits are nothing new in blues. Blind Lemon Jefferson's nightmarishly phallic "That Black Snake Moan" in 1926 was one of the earliest blues hits. "Classic blues" women such as Bessie Smith, Ma Rainey, and Lil Johnson, to name just a few, recorded sexually unexpurgated songs that violated their eras' taboos. Hattie Hart and the Memphis Jug Band invoked oral sex in "Memphis Yo-Yo Blues" in 1929 ("Bring your yo-yo, wrap the string around my tongue"); so did Peetie Wheatstraw in his sacrilegiously titled "The First Shall Be Last and the Last Shall Be First" seven years later ("The first woman I had, she made me get on my knees / and had the nerve to ask me . . . did I like Limburger cheese"). Tampa Red (accompanied on his early sides by pianist Georgia Tom Dorsey, who went on to become the founding father of modern gospel) recorded such titles as "It's Tight Like That," "The Duck's Yas-Yas-Yas," and "Let Me Play with Your Poodle" between the late 1920s and the early 1940s. And when Howlin' Wolf bragged about the exploits of his "little red rooster" in 1961, few could have missed the fact that his "rooster" was nothing more (or less) than a "cock."

Are the soul-blues songs that Tommy Couch Jr. derides as "lick-it-and-stick-it" abominations actually revitalizations of this tradition? Are stage routines like Sweet Angel's and Ms. Jody's merely updatings of the celebratory carnality that has always charged blues and soul performance? Or do they represent the same nihilistic assault on respectability and values that some decry as hip-hop's most troubling legacy, to which soul is often seen as being in opposition? This argument, raging in the southern soul-blues world today, is actually the most recent version of a discussion that's been going on among both admirers and critics of the blues for many years.

• • •

"Fever Started Long Time Ago": Sex, Love, and Blues— A Brief Historical Overview

> Romantic love is seldom romanticized in the blues. No authentic blues woman could, in good faith, sing with conviction about a dashing prince whisking her into the happily ever-after. . . . The classic blues women sang of female aspirations for happiness and frequently associated these aspirations with sexual desire, but they rarely ignored the attendant ambiguities and contradictions.
> —Angela K. Davis, *Blues Legacies and Black Feminism*

> There's never a dull moment once you're in my bed,
> I'll rock and sock you and have you screamin' out your head,
> I've got more to offer, and I don't come cheap
> —Ms. Jody, "The Better the Goods the Higher the Price,"
> written by Raymond Moore and John Ward

> I wanna lick you till you come.
> —Marvin Sease, "Candy Licker"

Figure 23. Ms. Jody and her "joystick." Photo by Pat Ryan at Business Visuals, Memphis, Tennessee.

Perhaps no facet of the blues tradition has been so widely noted and so seriously misunderstood as its sexual expressiveness. It's a cultural artifact with a complex history that extends, in many ways, back to pre-Middle Passage practices in which, as noted earlier, the dualistic thinking characterized by European Cartesianism was not the dominant paradigm. Spirit and flesh—or, more specifically, spirituality and carnality—were usually understood, and ritually celebrated, as complementary, rather than oppositional forces.

Those values, of course, were assaulted under slavery. Not only were all freedoms, including the freedom to express Africanist beliefs and aesthetics, now under attack, the white slave-owning class also did its best to harness black sexuality itself as a tool of subjugation. Sometimes it was used to humiliate: "marriage" ceremonies in which a man and woman were forced to copulate in the presence of the master and other spectators were not unknown;[1] often as well, slave owners used their slaves as "breeders" in an effort to create better and more profitable "stock," as well as to control, to the greatest extent possible, slave familial and social relations.[2] And, of course, masters had license to take whatever sexual liberties they chose with their female slaves.

Emancipation did not bring the kind of freedom most slaves had hoped for. (As one former slave put it, "Slavery was a bad thing, and freedom, of the kind we got, with nothing to live on, was bad. Two snakes full of poison. . . . Both hit the nigger, and they was both bad."[3]) Among the overclass, black sexuality—no longer safely under white control—became an object of both near-phobic dread and obsessive fantasy. On the one hand were the innumerable lynchings of black men accused of consorting with, or even looking at, white women; at the same time, white southern men could still rape black women with virtual impunity. Also common were clandestine, allegedly "consensual" sexual relations between powerful white men and African American women—often maids, housekeepers, or other employees—who might then be castigated as sexual predators or insatiable, home-wrecking Jezebels.

Within the African American community itself, though, the liberty to choose one's own partner(s) and freely express one's sexuality emerged as at least one clear-cut difference between pre- and post-emancipation life. It was a difference that made itself known in song and storytelling (e.g., the prevalence of sexual boasting in rhymed "toasts," the Dozens, and other vernacular art forms); by the time the blues emerged as a distinct form in the early years of the twentieth century, this new tradition of open sexual expression—often harshened by an emotional bluntness at least partly arising from the stress and trauma of living under the ongoing burden of oppression—had become well established. As Angela Davis has noted:

> The former slaves' economic status had not undergone a radical trans-formation—they were no less impoverished than they had been during slavery. It was the status of their personal relationships that was revo-lutionized. For the first time in the history of the African presence in North America, masses of black women and men were in a position to make autonomous decisions regarding the sexual partnerships into which they entered. Sexuality was thus one of the most tangible domains in which emancipation was acted upon and through which its meanings were expressed. . . . [F]or African Americans during the decades follow-ing emancipation, sexual love was experienced as *physical and spiritual* evidence—and the blues as aesthetic evidence—of freedom.[4]

Thus, a blues singer who boasted of sexual prowess was often sending a coded message of social, as well as personal, liberation. Women, especially, were conveying multiple, layered signals: they were proclaiming their agency as African Americans *and* as women, determined to live (and love) on their own terms in the face of both white racism and the patriarchal values that suffused their own culture as well as the dominant one.[5] But for men as well, struggling under the lash of a white ruling class intent on emasculating them—either literally, through castration during lynch-ing, or figuratively, by such strategies as addressing them as "Boy" until they were finally old enough to merit the encomium "Uncle" (but never "Mister")[6]—the blues could offer a declaration of erotic independence. "Sex," as Robert Gordon pointed out in his biography of Muddy Waters, "became the analogy for a kind of freedom, a freedom to serve himself, to damn the torpedoes, the shift supervisor, and the overseer's big gun."[7]

This historical context—the "political" side of the "personal"—has gen-erally been understood intuitively by most African American blues artists and audiences: as Muddy used to say, "I got a long memory."[8] Nonethe-less, the deromanticization of eros had its dark side. Most blues tended to downplay (or ignore) the "higher" emotions of love and romance in favor of images of sexuality that not infrequently packed an erotic tension which threatened to explode into unpleasantness or even violence. As effective as this may have been in challenging bourgeois propriety, it was probably also one reason why the younger generation of the twentieth-century postwar years began to move away from the music as their drive for upward mobility and assimilation intensified.[9]

Whites, meanwhile, "discovering" the blues during this same period, often harbored unquestioned (or unacknowledged) racial stereotypes.

They commonly misread the sexual forthrightness of many blues lyrics as evidence of a kind of holy primitivism—the old "buck"/"Jezebel" image in slightly more idealized garb. (The leering reaction of some white fans to Bobby Rush's stage routine, as described earlier in this book—"Hey . . . where the booty girls at?"—illustrates all too clearly how some of these attitudes have carried on into the present day.) And when they weren't fantasizing about black blues eroticism, whites often tried to mimic it: Mick Jagger, according to critic Mike Jahn, was a better "imitation black blues singer" than other white rockers largely because he was endowed with "more aggression, more obvious sexuality . . . he was skinny with big flappy lips."[10]

Lady in the Street (Freaky in the Bedroom)

Soul music was seen by many as a corrective to stereotypes such as these. As suggested earlier, at its best soul retained the carnal honesty of the blues while summoning exultation both spiritual and worldly—a return to a nondichotomous, essentially Africanist view of flesh and spirit as dialectical rather than oppositional forces. Thus, for instance, an artist like Wilson Pickett, who boldly proclaimed himself "Wicked" and cultivated an image of virility, even coarseness, that harkened back to the grittiest back-alley blues (he revived the old protogangsta outlaw tale "Stag-O-Lee" for a 1967 hit), could appear on all-star shows, as well as on the charts, as a member of the soul community in good standing alongside wholesome purveyors of love songs such as Carla Thomas and inspirational, gospel-infused visionaries like the Staple Singers.[11] Aretha Franklin could extol the erotic prowess of "Dr. Feelgood" while at the same time demand conjugal "Respect" from her man ("Give me my propers when you get home"), and then a few years later record a live gospel album at the New Temple Missionary Baptist Church in Los Angeles, with no apparent compromise of either her power or her faith. James Brown's lascivious ode to "Hot Pants," his admonition to "stay on the scene like a sex machine," his anthemic "Say It Loud—I'm Black and I'm Proud," and his harrowing antidrug sermon "King Heroin" could coexist in his oeuvre as harmoniously as his pugnacity and onstage machismo coexisted with the pleading vulnerability he exuded on showstoppers like "Please, Please, Please" and "It's a Man's Man's Man's World."

Some songs, like Pickett's 1978 "Lay Me Like You Hate Me," although they didn't represent the soul mainstream, reaffirmed the link between the modern sounds and the more explicit blues that had come before. The stage patter and some of the lyrics sung by women like Millie Jackson and Denise LaSalle likewise harked back, even if they were usually interpreted at the time as displays of modernist transgressiveness. But these, by and large, were exceptions, and by their very uniqueness they proved the rule: soul was for folks—rural and urban poor and middle-class alike—bent on "movin' on up" in the world. Their musical values and public behavior were going to reflect these aspirations.

It's a different world today, of course, and what's considered tasteful or "appropriate" can't be judged by the standards of earlier eras. But it's safe to say that one of the appeals of what's now called southern soul, at least at first, was that it seemed to represent an affirmation of the idea that popular music could again attain this balance between funky good times and higher aspirations. That many of its most successful artists were veterans of the same deep-soul era that had helped codify the sexual/ spiritual dialectic outlined previously indicated how deeply both the artists and their listeners wanted to recapture this feeling. This desire transcended demographics and market categories. Plenty of younger fans, weary of the chrome-plated sterility of disco on the one hand and skeptical of the nihilism and phallocentric thuggery already arising among the first generation of rappers on the other, were eager for music that had danceable grooves, was sexy and fun, yet didn't insult or condescend to its audience. They bought records and attended shows alongside older soul and blues lovers who celebrated this new music as a reaffirmation of cherished values.

Denise LaSalle pretty much hit the ground running when she restyled herself as a soul-blues artist in the early 1980s; *A Lady in the Street,* her 1983 Malaco debut, included the sexual throw-down "This Bell Was Made for Ringing" (a takeoff on Anita Ward's 1979 disco hit "Ring My Bell"), and her stage shows, if anything, embraced the rap-era zeitgeist by becoming more explicit than ever. For the most part, though, the new hybrid genre continued in the deep soul tradition by avoiding outright raunchiness, at least on record. The main exception was probably Clarence Carter, whose dirty-old-man chuckle and uncanny ability to look as if he were leering, despite his blindness and dark glasses, were as much a part of his persona as his bluesy guitar work and blackstrap molasses baritone. After Carter signed with Ichiban in the mid-1980s and broke through with "Strokin'," he released a series of follow-ups in the same mold ("Love Me with a Feeling," "I'm Not Just Good, I'm the Best," "Dr. C. C."), alongside relatively standard fare like his remake of "Too Weak to Fight," a 1968 hit that many of his newer fans had probably never heard.

The Turning Point

But Carter was a beloved old-schooler who'd managed to recast himself in a contemporary light; he wasn't about to lead a revolution. It took a younger man to do that. Not long after Carter debuted "Strokin'," a journeyman soulster (and erstwhile gospel singer) named Marvin Sease had a dream in which he heard the lyrics to what he immediately recognized might be a new kind of soul anthem. "Candy Licker," the song he created out of that inspiration, changed the face of southern soul-blues forever.

"I'm Jody, baby!" Sease proclaimed, invoking the mythical backdoor trickster/lothario:

> I will lick you up, I'll lick you down
> Turn around baby, and I'll lick you all around
> Oh, I'll lick you good, girl, like your lover should . . .
> I wanna lick you til you come.[12]

Set to an ironically romantic midtempo melody, "Candy Licker" ran for over ten minutes and featured a woman gasping and panting in the background along with extended quasi sermons from Sease, in which he expanded on his theme in joyously profane detail. It hit the soul-blues world with a force almost as powerful and unexpected as "Down Home Blues"; before long, almost everyone in the field seemed to have jumped on the bandwagon (or, perhaps, the bed). Denise LaSalle's "Long Dong Silver" came out in 1992; other delectable offerings such as Sease's own "Condom on Your Tongue" and "I Ate You for My Breakfast," Luther Lackey's "I Smell Funk," and Sheba Potts-Wright's "Lipstick on His Pants" also followed in "Candy Licker's" wake. Not to be outdone, Denise herself weighed in with such fare as "Dial 1–900-Get-Some" in 1994 and "Lick It Before You Stick It" in 2000. Many of these songs were tucked away on CDs instead of released as singles, but they still made their impact on the soul-blues ethos. (When Sease announced that he harbored a desire to return to his church roots, one wag suggested that he and Denise LaSalle should record a gospel CD together and call it *Speaking in Tongues*.)

Maybe it was all an attempt to beat hip-hop at its own game (although it's difficult to imagine street-hardened gangsta rappers being amused by such antics); maybe some singers simply decided that the old sexual bluntness of the blues had been missing from "soul-blues" for too long and it was time to take things back into the alley; or maybe it was simply a matter of following the money (Sease became one of the music's biggest

Figure 24. Marvin Sease, LaMont's Entertainment Complex, Indian Head, Maryland, August 26, 2006. Photo by Ronald Weinstock.

draws, and he remained so until his death in 2011). Whatever the reason, by the time Theodis Ealey unleashed "Stand Up in It," his juke-joint Kama Sutra, in 2003 ("You can lick it, and you can stroke it / Now you can kiss it, and you can eat it / But you ain't did a doggone thing until you stand up in it"), soul-blues had become inundated with double- (and single-) entendre sex songs. On their own terms, some of them were pretty funny (in "Stand Up in It," a man praises his woman's lovemaking by telling her, "That thing is so damn good I wanna put it in my pipe and smoke it!"), but over time, as the analogies grew stale and the humor less subtle, a lot of the southern soul world started to sound more like a junior high school locker room than a juke.

Almost from the beginning there was criticism, and it's intensified since then. Tommy Couch Jr. waxes nearly apoplectic in his denunciation of what he calls the "lick-it-and-stick-it" school of songwriting. "Maybe ['Stand Up in It'] was a big deal," he fulminates, "but maybe it was also the beginning of the end. Because how can you drive a carpool, you're a thirty-five-year-old lady, how can you drive carpool with your children in the car, listenin' to 'you can smoke it, you can eat it, you can roll it up, but you ain't done nothing 'til you stand up in it'? I mean, these women—my mother wouldn't want to hear that. And neither would 99 percent of these black mothers."[13] (That, however, didn't stop Malaco from signing Marvin Sease in 2004 and releasing CDs on him that included such titles as "The Power of Coochie," "Pump My Juice," and "Everything You Eat Ain't Good.")

At least some artists would probably concur with Couch's professed conservatism. Both Latimore and Bobby Rush are adamant in their criticism of singers who spew raunchiness for its own sake. Little Milton, one of the music's most revered figures, was even more outspoken about it in an interview he did a few months before his death in August 2005. "To me, it's a disgrace," he fumed. "It's vulgar. Especially on the so-called chitlin' circuit. There should be some principles, some class, and some common sense. There were so many people, man—black people, white people—that lost their lives trying to elevate the image of the black man. And now, the black people are doing it [to] themselves."[14]

It's not only the oldheads who feel this way. Floyd Taylor, for instance, has made it clear that he doesn't want to compromise his principles for the sake of a hit ("That works for some people, and for some people it don't. . . . I hope I never have to go that route"). Sir Charles Jones, although he's wary of knee-jerk condemnations ("You're going to have your people that's going to criticize music; I've even heard people who say negative words about 'Down Home Blues'"), also emphasizes his own pride in having attracted listeners of "all ages, man, from children all the way up to senior citizens. That's why I try to keep the music clean. You got a lot of frank songs that people put out and give [the music] a black eye."[15]

Bobbye "Doll" Johnson, who released her first CD, *Been There, Done That,* in 1998 and has since built a promising local and regional following in the South, says she's had to put her foot down a few times to drive the point home. "Some people did say," she recalls, "that there could be things that I would have to do to make it."

> One of the things I was gonna have to do was to be a little grittier than what I was, because I was too sweet and too soft. [But] there are some things I will not do—some of those hard things, like be X-rated—I'm not going to even pretend or say I'm gonna do whatever I have to do.
>
> I don't want little girls and boys saying, "Well, Auntie said that word; if it's a bad word, why would Auntie say it?" Or other people's little girls and boys saying, "Well, Bobbye 'Doll' said blah-blah-blah in that song." I don't want them to hear that. My daddy and mother would slap me in the mouth if [I] used vulgarity around them. I was brought up to be respectful, and I think when you do that sometimes, you tend to be a little disrespectful. Every artist have their own way of thinking about it; I think it's disrespectful.[16]

But it's doubtful whether things will clean up in the near future. As the ever-pragmatic Denise LaSalle has noted: "Tommy Jr.—that's all we talk about—he says, 'I'm tired of 'lickin' it and stickin' it' and so and so and so.' I say, 'I tell you one thing: you may be tired of it, but other people are not. So as long as they like it, you got people out here'll buy it forever.'"[17] And at least some industry spokespeople say the whole issue is basically a red herring anyway, propagated mostly by white critics who don't understand the historical context of sexuality in the blues. "White folks don't know anything about this stuff," insists Ecko's John Ward (who happens to be white himself). "The music is just tied to the culture. It's so closely tied to the culture [that] it has a hard time translating over to being accepted widely."[18]

Ecko's own releases, of course, have included more than their share of "lick-it-and-stick-it" lyrics, and Ward will admit that he's not above imposing his will (or at least his commercial instincts) on some artists who may have misgivings about them. "Sometimes they're uncomfortable with some of the themes of some of the songs," he says. "A lot of time you have artists go, 'Well, I don't like that song.' And you're going, 'Well, this is a great song.' 'Well, I-I-I don't think I want to sing that one, because it's not me.' It may not be 'them,' but it may be the right song for 'em."[19]

Nonetheless, plenty of artists, including some who've succeeded with this kind of material, seem ambivalent. Virtually every southern soul-blues entertainer I've spoken with has insisted on his or her preference for songs that invoke genuine emotion and feeling; many cite their ballads as the creations of which they're most proud. Even some who've been accused, themselves, of further "hoochifying" the music, like Ms. Jody and Sweet Angel, have attempted at times to negotiate with label owners and producers for a change in direction, or at least a wider thematic range.[20]

While it's clear, then, that standards have loosened over the years, and while Tommy Couch Jr. is probably on to something when he says that the trend has become a rut and that it's been made worse by a lack of vision, if not talent, in some quarters ("They're puttin' garbage out because they can't do any better"[21]), most singers insist they're as serious about their art as they are about making money; the professed belief in "songs that really tell stories" is almost universal, even if it sometimes seems honored mostly in the breach. It's apparent as well that this isn't merely a generational conflict (compare Denise LaSalle's relative permissiveness to Bobbye Johnson's conservatism); virtually all southern soul CDs, by veterans and newcomers alike, contain at least a few serious-sounding songs. According to the singers, these are often the ones most requested. The raunchy stuff draws the people in, they'll admit, but then, once you've got them, you can hit them with something more real. In other words, the old dialectic between the flesh and the spirit is still being negotiated, but the terms of that negotiation are a lot more complex and difficult to delineate in the post–hip-hop era than they were during the golden era of deep soul.

Meanwhile, though, things have also heated up on stage.

What Makes a Man Go Crazy

Blues performance has never been a genteel art form. Although some entertainers, such as B. B. King and the late Jimmy Witherspoon, have made it a personal mission to convey an image of dignity and class, explicitness—to put it politely—has characterized a lot of blues shows almost from the beginning, especially shows put on by men. Delta pioneer Charlie Patton was known to pound his guitar and shout, "This is the way I beat my woman!" to the amusement of his case-hardened juke-joint audiences.[22] Howlin' Wolf, who patterned his stage show after Patton's, used to crawl across the floor in an imitation of his lupine namesake, stopping occasionally to grind his midriff, ogle the women sitting nearby, and entreat them with improvised lyrics like "Let me hump you, baby!"[23] As recently as the early 1960s, Muddy Waters would shake up a bottle of beer or pop and stuff it into his pants while one of his sidemen was taking a solo; at the song's climax, he'd unzip his fly, uncap the bottle, and spray the room. By most accounts, the women gathered around the bandstand enjoyed the shower.[24]

The tradition has persevered, and it's gotten more outré as cultural standards have loosened. Marvin Sease, when he wasn't wagging and rolling his tongue with cartoonish lasciviousness, spiced up his act with a routine featuring a saddle fitted with a monstrous stiff dildo in place of a saddle horn; he used the rig as a visual aid during his song "Sit Down on It." Today, in some of the more permissive venues on the soul-blues circuit, O. B. Buchana will invite a woman onto the stage and coax her into nuzzling her head in his lap or hoist her into the air and lower her crotch onto his face. And in at least some instances, things cross over into realms usually associated with the more controversial extremes of hip-hop: A video clip shows Buchana and fellow vocalist Mr. Sam ogling a woman on stage, apparently a volunteer from the audience, who's turned her back and bent over so far that she looks like nothing more than a butt with legs. By the end of the routine, Mr. Sam has taken the bait and begun humping her.[25]

Most women, though, have been more restrained in their performance styles, at least until relatively recently. (Shake dancers and even drag revues have long been featured on shows starring blues artists, but in most cases they haven't been part of the headlining musical acts.)[26] Even during the "classic blues" era, when women's proclamations of sexual independence most strongly resonated as manifestos of social liberation, certain standards were maintained. As profane as the lyrics might get, or as hardscrabble as the settings could be (Lucille Bogan's scabrous "Shave 'Em Dry" is a good example of the kind of thing women might sing in some of the less tony venues[27]), most singers remained relatively conservative in their stagecraft. Displays of opulence (e.g., Ma Rainey's famous necklace of gold coins) and theatrical emotionalism were common, but we have little evidence of any outright sexual provocation on the part of the performers themselves.

After the "classic" era came to an end in the late 1930s, most women who sang the blues were accompanied by jazz or jump-blues (later rhythm and blues) bands, and again they usually comported themselves with appropriate reserve, no matter how spicy some of their songs might become (even Memphis Minnie, who "played guitar like a man" and performed largely in the same jukes and gin mills as male bluesmen like Big Bill Broonzy and Muddy Waters, usually conducted herself in this way, at least on stage).

More recently, in the wake of the 1950s/1960s-era move toward middle-class respectability (and before the hip-hop insurgence), women soul and R & B singers became, if anything, even more careful not to confuse the bandstand with the bordello. Probably the most transgressive in this regard was Millie Jackson. As early as the 1970s, she'd begun to pepper both her stage patter and her lyrics with cuss words, interspersing even the most emotionally fraught love ballads with profanity-laced signifying. For any listeners who'd disparage her for being "dirty," she created her "Phuck U Symphony"—a pseudoclassical number complete with strings and choir, whose entire libretto consisted of the title phrase repeated over and over—and dedicated it to them. Her contemporary Denise LaSalle was usually more reserved on record, but by her own admission she'd been taking things about "as far as the law allowed" in her stage act since her early days in Chicago. Most soul women, though, played it clean. Tina Turner might be considered an exception, but by the late 1960s, when she'd become famous for performing fellatio on microphones, she'd embraced a rock-and-roll aesthetic far removed from the soul mainstream, despite her ongoing success on the R & B charts.[28]

"This Ain't Your Ordinary Pussy Cat"

It's difficult to pinpoint the precise moment at which soul-blues women began to get more physically explicit on stage, but the common assumption that Ms. Jody broke the taboo single-handedly isn't quite accurate. Shirley Brown has long been known for her toned-down version of Tina Turner's microphone routine, in which she cradles the mic between her breasts and caresses it (although, to be fair, she doesn't do it for long, and the focus of her show is still her spectacular voice). Sheba Potts-Wright, a Memphis-based artist who also records for Ecko, used to act out her song "Lipstick on His Pants" in a routine similar to Jody's "Big Daddy" turn. "What Ms. Jody do," she says, "I used to do that; I had that spotlight, when I was doing that kind of stuff. What I would do—they sit on stage, [I would] move around like I'm getting ready to kiss him down there, and I go wipe my lipstick off my lip and wipe it on their pants."[29]

But Sheba insists that those days are gone. "I have turned myself around," she attests. "I'm not gonna do it no more." That applies to her recordings as well: "There's certain things I'm gonna say and not gonna say now." In fact, she maintains that she turned down the opportunity to be J. Blackfoot's foil on his now-notorious *Woof Woof Meow* sessions, a gig that eventually went to Ms. Jody herself.[30] That leaves Jody and, to a lesser extent, Sweet Angel pretty much on their own, and as a result they're the ones who seem to be bearing the brunt of censorious scrutiny.

As both Angel and Mike Dobbins point out, and as the history related here illustrates, much of this scrutiny is the result of a double standard; antics like Muddy Waters's pop bottle routine, Marvin Sease's saddle dildo, or even Michael Jackson's trademark crotch-grab have usually been accepted, if sometimes with a shudder, as legitimate expressions of masculine feistiness. It's important to remember as well that "macho" in the southern soul world has usually had more to do with being a satisfying lover than strutting one's prowess as a weapon (Mr. Sam's ogle-and-hump routine notwithstanding). Sease, like most male soul-blues sex symbols, cultivated his image as a man bent on pleasing his woman, first and foremost ("I wanna make you feel good, like your lover should"). In the context of his act, the purpose of that rigged saddle and the lyrics that accompanied it was to motivate men to be attentive to their women's needs, even if it meant letting the women take the active role in lovemaking; Theodis Ealey's stud-lover might "stand up in it," but Sease's protagonist did him one better by lying back and letting his woman "sit down on it, ride it like a pony."

Women have traditionally both promised and demanded satisfaction as well; in this sense, at least, the double standard has not been universally applied. But, as we've seen, they usually haven't acted out their promises (or their demands) through physical onstage business. A performer like Ms. Jody presents a more brazen, and more threatening, image. Her relationship to her own body is erotic: she caresses, touches, and teases herself as she prances across the stage; the message, whether intentional or not, is that she'd be perfectly capable of satisfying herself with no help from anyone, if that's what it took. And when a man enters the picture, she's no less in control. She may get down on her knees when he steps out of the shower in her story, and she may run her tongue and lips up and down her microphone to show us what happens next, but her pose is one of triumph. Not even Tina Turner proclaimed victory over the phallus as aggressively as Jody does when she snaps the mic erect in her fist, grabs it even tighter, and goes at it again, all the while declaring her ongoing infatuation with her "joystick." Tina, as Philip Norman noted, "teased" it; Jody seizes it and literally bends it to her will.

Ultimately, though, it might be the active soliciting of male participation that sets Jody's act apart, especially now that Sheba Potts-Wright has toned things down. It's one thing to exploit the phallic implications of a microphone (or, in Sweet Angel's case, an actual phallus), and sacrilegious signifying like Jody's "healing power of coochie" routine also has plenty of precedents in blues, R & B, and even jazz. But displays of sexual license on the part of women, to the extent they've occurred, have traditionally been presented as—and carefully packaged to represent—fantasy. Any onstage flirtation has been just that: smiles, winks, or maybe a sway or a "sock-it-to-me-one-time" pelvic thrust in the direction of male admirers seated safely beyond the footlights.

Even when women have been used as eye candy by male entertainers, the boundaries have usually remained intact: When Bobby Rush parades his dancers out from the wings, he often invites the men to "Look!" But he also warns them that they "can't do nothin' else *but* look," and to drive the point home he invokes an old "Dozens" routine: "Your eyes may shine, your teeth may grit / But ain't shit up here you gon' git!" Not even Ike Turner physically offered up Tina or the Ikettes to individual men in the audience. At least as far as male contact has been concerned, the physical bodies of women have usually been pretty much off-limits.

Apparently uninhibited by any of the doubts that compelled Sheba Potts-Wright to clean up her own act (Sheba says she made the decision after performing a G-rated show for an all-ages festival in Memphis and being moved to tears by the love she felt coming from the children[31]), Ms. Jody has broken through this final wall and brought in-your-face (or, perhaps, in-*my*-face) seduction out of the bedroom and onto the stage. But she's as in control with her "Big Daddy" as she is during her solo routines. Her come-ons to him ("If while I straddle you, and I'm riding you, and my cat accidentally strokes your leg, are you gonna give it back to me?") sound more like ultimatums than offers, and once again, when he finally responds, she's the victor—he rises from his chair like Lazarus resurrected and pays homage by dancing obediently in front of her before returning to his seat, satisfied (if not sanctified) by her erotic power.

Jody, as we've seen, has become one of the most popular acts on the southern soul circuit, even as some accuse her, along with Angel and a few others, of cheapening the music to the point where it no longer presents a safe, adult, and relatively respectable alternative to gangsta culture and the other perceived excesses of hip-hop. For her part, she insists she's unaware of any serious criticism of either her act or the overall trend toward raunchiness ("No, I haven't heard too much of that. . . . I try to give 'em, you know, what they ask for"), but she's equally adamant that neither her shows nor her songs "hoochify" herself or women in general.

In fact, she insists, they do the opposite: they're living parables that she enacts, using the license afforded her by the trickster tradition of ritually transgressing norms and standards in the name of a higher purpose. And that purpose, she maintains, is to counsel women on what they need to do to keep their relationships strong, a mission she takes seriously, both on stage and off.

"I wear my skirts up to my knees," proclaimed Clara Smith in 1926, "and whip that jelly with who I please."[32] That stance of claiming one's own sexuality as a force of womanly agency continues to resonate through R & B and other popular music; today, though, it's usually assumed by singers who either are, or portray themselves as, hot-to-trot adolescents like most of their ostensible target audience (Destiny's Child, with Beyoncé at the helm, virtually reprised Smith's boast word for word in their 2001 hit "Bootylicious"). But soul-blues, like the blues that preceded it, is—as so many have proclaimed—a "grown folks' party." In this spirit, Ms. Jody, along with others like Sweet Angel (with her "Lady Libertine" dildo act juxtaposed against romantic ballads and anthems of empowerment), has reclaimed this venerable role of the sexually defiant blueswoman and adapted it to an age when aspiring to security and respectability, both financial and personal, is no longer an impossible dream or an ideological compromise for most African Americans.

In this way, southern soul-blues continues the soul tradition that dates back at least as far as the early gospel-blues fusions of Ray Charles: offering a holistic and essentially Africanist alternative to the reductionist dualisms that have for so long both defined and limited Euro-American cultural perspectives, the corrupting influences of which are evident in (among other things) the more extreme poses of hip-hop, in which "keeping it real" too often translates into reifying, not rectifying, externally imposed contradictions between spirit and flesh, thus serving to conflate righteous rebellion against repressive moral codes with nihilism and a full-scale assault against morality itself.

Part IV

The Crossroad and Further On

Where Do We Go from Here?

Too Late to Stop Now

It's been over three decades since "Down Home Blues" kicked off the modern soul-blues renaissance. Since then, the music has succeeded to the extent that it has on a unique fusion of hipness and anomaly. While drawing on decades of soul and blues tradition, its producers and artists have also attempted to mainstream their sound by incorporating stylistic and technological features borrowed from contemporary R & B. These days, even when it's extolling "down-home" virtues like slow-paced living and small-town friendliness, southern soul-blues usually employs cadences and vernacular that bespeak a modernist sensibility.

At the same time, though, seemingly in the face of all logic and even survival potential, the music has staked its claim as a regional phenomenon. The very appellation *southern soul* exemplifies this regionalism. So do CD covers, such as several that Ecko has designed for O. B. Buchana, which portray the artist posed in front of cotton fields or bucolic rural vistas. Lyrics of songs like Floyd Hamberlin Jr.'s "Mississippi

Boy" (which Denise LaSalle transformed into "Mississippi Woman") or Mel Waiters's "Down Home People" praise putative country values; a lot of the ubiquitous paeans to all-night clubbing are set in back-roads juke joints where the aroma of "whiskey and chicken wings" fills the air along with vintage jukebox fare ("Johnnie Taylor is still the favorite / Bobby Bland is still the blues . . . the smaller the club, the bigger the party"[1]). So powerfully is this context evoked that even many of the songs' more scabrous story lines, for all the disparagement they get from more conservative quarters, often sound closer to *Tobacco Road*–like backwoods ribaldry than exercises in hard-core transgression.

Most working soul-blues performers tour along what remains of the old "chitlin' circuit"; virtually the only festivals that book them in significant numbers are also located below the Mason-Dixon Line (Benton Harbor, Michigan's, on-again, off-again Old-School Blues Festival is a rare northern exception). This kind of regional focus can segue into provincialism, of course, and in fact it's reflected in some artists' outlooks. For every Willie Clayton or Sir Charles Jones with well-defined ideas about what national or international fame might entail, there's a Ms. Jody, who speaks longingly of becoming "a household name everywhere" by expanding her territory as far as "Detroit . . . Pennsylvania, and Chicago," or a Sweet Angel, who effused to me during our conversation in Memphis about the audience responses she'd been getting "up North"—meaning, as it turned out, Virginia.

Nothing Good Comes Easy

Even during the best of times, then, a genre like southern soul-blues would find itself struggling to attain long-term commercial viability, no matter how popular it might be among its core listeners. These, obviously, are not the best of times. Although major pop acts continue to tour and record successfully, the implosion of the recording and broadcast industries under the dual onslaughts of corporate retrenchment and Internet technology has left much of the rest of the music world a scorched earth of failed enterprises, obsolete business models, and orphaned entertainers wandering dazed through the wreckage. Despite the ongoing vitality of the music itself and the depth of talent that continues to be available ("You can walk in any black church in Mississippi," marvels Tommy Couch Jr., "and find three people that are the greatest singers you've ever heard—until you walk into the next black church. You'll find three more"[2]), few sectors of this world have felt these effects more severely than the southern soul industry.

Virtually every southern soul-blues artist I've spoken to still expresses confidence in the music's potential to reach a wider audience, but they're also adamant that to do so will take a lot of initiative and creative thinking on the part of artists and labels alike. "It could be huge," says Sir Charles, "if the radio was involved [and] more TV time, because younger generations listen to the radio, and a hundred percent, often, television. We need to . . . get more control of teaching our artists [about] paperwork, publishing, and how to take care of themselves out here and learn better business. Things will pull out better with your iTunes and your Amazon; they'll see that this thing is generating capital, and they'll put more initiative into helping promote it."[3]

At the same time, there's a palpable frustration—and not a little resentment—about the music's apparent inability to grow beyond its status as a moderately lucrative (at best) local and regional phenomenon. Some in the field are simply giving up. Tommy Couch Jr. has become convinced that between changes in the industry and what he sees as a decline in the quality of the music itself, what looked for a while like a new golden age was really just a boomlet. As far as Malaco is concerned, he laments, "southern soul has basically died."

> There's no outlets for it. There's no radio for it. There's no place to go to the stores to buy. You can't make it available, just about. And [then] the problem is, a lot of these little acts are still throwing stuff out, some of these little labels [are] just slammin' shit out there that ain't any good.
>
> I feel like [Malaco] had a major, major, major role in it, and it's just like somebody's ripped your heart out and laid it on the table and stepped on it right in front of you. . . . Any man can hit his head against a wall once, thinking he can move it. If he stands there and repeatedly does it for years, he's an idiot. We can't just make something happen just because we want it to happen, no matter how much money you throw at it. In these economic times, you just can't keep betting on a horse with three legs. I don't know how it can get better.[4]

Others in the industry, though, aren't so pessimistic. Larry Chambers, a forty-year-plus veteran of the R & B and soul music industry who now handles Ecko's media relations and promotion, agrees that the music is going through some rough times. What he sees when he's out in the field, though, gives him reason for hope. "It's falling," he admits, "and probably will fall even more, but long as the music goes on, the people will always be around that want to hear this." Among other things, he believes, the stereotype that this is music for "older" listeners may actually work in its favor.

> The people that are at least twenty-four, thirty, thirty-five right now—ten years from now, they're not going to be listening to R & B. I've already seen it happen down through the years. They migrate into southern soul music.
> When you go to the shows now, there was a time where you didn't see many in their late twenties. Now when you go to shows, you gonna see a lot of late twenties. I go around to some of the clubs, and I see some of the young people, and I'll say, "Wow—you're into this music?" "Yeah, I like this music; it has more substance than just a beat." It will always be around. It will never die.[5]

And yet again, most artists as well are convinced that southern soul, if given a chance, can succeed among mainstream listeners and make enough money in the process to remain viable. To many, the salient issue isn't just how little exposure the music gets; it's how popular it manages to be despite that scanty publicity. When Stan Mosley's "Anybody Seen My Boo" began making noise on Malaco in 2000, Mosley discovered that even in places where soul-blues was virtually ignored on the radio, people were familiar with the song—most likely from hearing it played on jukeboxes or spun by club DJs—and liked it. "I did a show at the Regal [in Chicago]," he said, "and when I was singing 'Anybody Seen My Boo,' every time I got to the hook, I would see people sitting out there singing. So I said to myself, 'They had to have heard this song!' They come out, they hear this music—you'd be surprised at the young kids that be at my concerts. I'm talking about kids, now, teenagers—'So how come I can't hear this on the radio?'"[6] Similar stories are told by virtually every active artist on the circuit, and since they're usually based on firsthand experience, it's difficult to write them off as mere wishful thinking, ego, or whistling in the dark.

They do, though, embody a spirit close to the heart of what the blues has always represented. Historically, blues has never been a music that admitted defeat. Survival through hard times has been the essence of its message since the beginning. In this spirit, this section looks at some of the issues facing southern soul-blues as it attempts to maintain both its appeal and its commercial viability in the face of the problems outlined here. We'll look at some of the issues concerning songwriting and selling songs in contemporary soul-blues; then we'll expand our scope into a broader discussion of the challenges confronting the genre as it attempts to evolve in today's volatile, high-risk marketplace, technology-driven, and youth-obsessed, largely defined by neohipster aesthetics and ideologies that don't necessarily coincide with the core cultural values represented by southern soul and held by its primary audience. Finally, we'll see how one artist, Louisiana native T. K. Soul, is negotiating these commercial, artistic, and technological challenges to create an image, a sound, and a self-reliant business model that he hopes will both sustain his career and enable him to craft a legacy of lasting value. These, in fact, are the same challenges the music itself must surmount if is to maintain (or perhaps reassert) its place in the blues and soul tradition, appealing to listeners of diverse ages and backgrounds yet remaining true to its cherished regional, cultural, and historical roots.

9

Blues with a Feeling

Writing Songs for the Market and the Heart

"Go back to that little change, George . . . let me put the solo in here. . . . Play it where you did two bars, right there where you [played] 'di-di-di-di. . . .' Okay, hold it, I got you now, I see where you're going there. Okay . . . is it right? It's a two-flat, major seventh. . . . Yeah, that'll probably be the guitar—let that part be the guitar. . . . Let's see if I got it, George. . . . Take it from the solo."[1]

It's a quiet afternoon at Malaco in Jackson, Mississippi. There's no session scheduled today, so house writer George Jackson and arranger Harrison Calloway are in the studio, working out ideas for a song. Jackson is one of pop music's most accomplished songwriters; his credits include Bob Seger's "Old Time Rock and Roll" and the Osmonds' "One Bad Apple" (which he originally wrote for the Jackson 5), as well as southern soul classics such as Johnnie Taylor's "Last Two Dollars," "Down Home Blues" itself, and hundreds of others. Trumpeter/keyboardist Calloway is an alumnus of the famed Muscle Shoals horn section; aside from his session work and his tours with such names as Elton John (in 1972), he has probably orchestrated and arranged at least as many songs as Jackson has written.

Jackson sits at an acoustic piano and locks eyes with Calloway, who's playing an electric keyboard with a pad of sheet music paper sitting atop it. Jackson hums above the chords he and Calloway are playing; Calloway listens, writes, asks questions, makes suggestions, listens again, and writes some more. Here, inside Malaco's barnlike studio complex, safely isolated from the stultifying Mississippi summer heat, esoteric (or even commercial) arguments over nomenclature and "authenticity" seem far removed. Jackson and Calloway, as they've been doing for decades, both individually and as a team, are simply trying to write a hit.

The Songwriter's Craft

"I'm a songwriter," Jackson declares, giving little shrift to ideological or terminological niceties.

> I'm not a blues writer, not a pop writer. Songwriter. I write all of it. [Success] been in all fields. When I first started writing songs in Muscle Shoals, I was writing for Clarence Carter. Me and Clarence collaborated on [Carter's 1969 hit] "Snatching It Back." I did [Carter's] "I Can't Leave Your Love Alone" [from 1970]. These were just, I call it soul music. "Old Time Rock and Roll," I was inspired by people like Little Richard, Fats Domino, Jerry Lee Lewis; I always wanted to write a rock-and-roll song, write something a little bit different. I wrote the song, and [Muscle Shoals guitarist] Jimmy Johnson knew Bob Seger, and Jimmy gave the song to him.
>
> I just write what comes to my mind. I don't start out trying to write this kind of song, that [kind of song]. Sometimes the melody comes, sometimes the lyrics; I might hear a good line or something that might be a good title of a song. You could sit here [at] the piano all day and can't think of nothing. Then sometime, when you can just [be] in a different mood or different situation, a song will come to you. I've done this; that's how it be.

As for what's variously labeled soul-blues or southern soul, Jackson is equally noncommittal—or perhaps nonplussed—about such categorizations. "It's confusing me, also," he admits.

> I know that it all comes from gospel. It used to be called R & B. It is now called blues. Me, I always consider a blues song as being twelve bars. The difference is, you know, like [he plays a few bars of Ben E. King's "Stand by Me"]—you couldn't call that no blues song. But nowadays they will call that a blues song. Now what the young people doin' now, they call it

Figure 25. George Jackson. Malaco Publicity Photo, courtesy of Malaco Records.

something else, too. Some kinda soul—neon soul [*sic;* "neosoul"]. The era I came up through, with the Sam Cookes and the Jackie Wilsons, people like that, it was always called soul music, 'cause they sang from the heart. That was [also] called rhythm and blues.

To hear Jackson and Calloway discuss their work is akin to listening to a glassblower talk about creating elegant flutes and decanters from molten bubbles. It's anomalous, perhaps, yet captivating—master craftsmen testifying their love and dedication to a dying art.

"There's not but a few," muses Calloway. "Me, the George Jacksons, some of the older guys that kept the tradition. He and I are [among] a few who are still keeping it around."

> See, I worked with George back in the [Muscle Shoals] Fame [studio] days, and we've been working together for over thirty years. I played on some of his biggest hits, and I helped to arrange some of his biggest hits. So he and I are family; when he come in with a song, I can just feel where he's at. George has the basic ideas. It's his little baby. And he's such a good writer that he comes in—I help him, sometimes, with his structure and beefing up some of the chord changes—but basically, he has his own thing. And we put it into a structure from what he's written. That's my job, put it in a structure and make it come out in the session.

Like many pop songwriters, Jackson sees himself as both savvy and sincere. "I want it to be a hit," he professes. "That's the main thing. If it's a hit, it's good for me. But I have to like the way they cut it [because] I'm a fan of the music. It might be a hit, but if it don't sound good, even if I wrote it, I ain't gonna listen to it."[2]

Sam Cooke, he says, remains his lodestar. "The way he would write songs—'Wonderful World' [he sings]: 'Don't know much about history . . .' That's timeless. The lyrics are as relevant today as they were then. That's what I still try to write, songs that have that impact."[3]

That "impact" is what some commentators and critics believe is missing in a lot of soul-blues songwriting these days ("The quality of the music isn't there," grouses Tommy Couch Jr. "The quality of the singing isn't there, the production isn't there, the songwriting isn't there, it's just a different deal."[4]) This, of course, is a generalization; plenty of southern soul artists, as we've seen, continue to show themselves capable of writing songs that can both move product and stir the emotions. And once they do, they've made a lasting mark; one of the unique things about this genre is how long a song can remain popular. Even today, it's possible to tune into a radio station in Mississippi or Tennessee and hear a decades-old classic like "Let's Straighten It Out," "Someone Else Is Steppin' In," or Cicero Blake's mid-1970s hit "Dip My Dipper" inserted into the rotation between the latest offerings from artists like Sir Charles Jones, Ms. Jody, Omar Cunningham, or T. K. Soul.

Nonetheless, the perception persists, and it's not limited to nostalgic survivors of the deep-soul era. Floyd Taylor, son of the legendary Johnnie Taylor, came of musical age during the time when southern soul-blues was forging its modern hybrid identity. Although the deep-soul emotionalism his father helped codify remains the driving force behind his sound, his recordings make it clear that he has an ear for contemporary R & B and hip-hop as well as the earlier styles. Nonetheless, he shares some of the older generation's concerns. "Some of the stuff I hear," he says, "I wonder why they even took the time to even put it out here. Everybody is trying to use whatever tool they can [just] to get them a hit record."[5]

Bob Jones, a veteran Chicago-based songwriter whose credits include Artie "Blues Boy" White's 1977 breakout song "(You Are My) Leanin Tree," Willie Clayton and Pat Brown's "Equal Opportunity," and Cicero Blake's "Caught in the Wrong Again," among others, believes that the problem isn't lack of talent as much as limited vision. "There's a little bit more to songwriting," he maintains, "than clashing a bunch of words. It's good to have a hell of a vocabulary, but you need a good story. You got some young cats that's coming up that can write, but they don't have a reason to stretch their imagination—write a one-line verse and put a three-line hook to it and rap that hook for seven minutes. A lot of them don't really have an imagination because they ain't lived no life."[6]

Woman's Gotta Have It

The songwriting process itself, like much else in music, is easier to criticize than to define. Sir Charles Jones, perhaps not surprisingly, sees it as an activity requiring dedication and prowess similar to lovemaking. "If you're making love to your woman," he explains, "everything from the beginning—[from] when you first look at each other, through when you're finished—that's the song. You know, you got your beginning, you got your middle, and you got your climax. That's how I write the story lines; that's the thing you want to do—you want your audience to get captured off into what you're doing and try to touch people's hearts."[7]

George Jackson is somewhat more cryptic about his own techniques, but he will say that he often tries to write "from a woman's point of view, because women buy the records more than the fellas do." Even "Down Home Blues," although originally written for a man to sing, consisted mostly of a woman's narrative. "I had a lady friend in Memphis," he remembers. "She was typical of that type of person. She'd come to my home and say, 'George, fix me a drink. I've been working all day, let me hear some of your good songs. . . . Play me some of your bluesy stuff.' She would give me that type of idea."[8]

Jackson's Malaco colleague Frederick Knight echoes his view. Knight, like quite a few others in the field, has written hits in mainstream R & B and pop as well as southern soul. His recording of his own "I've Been Lonely for So Long," on Stax, peaked at No. 8 in 1972; later, after Stax folded, his "Ring My Bell" was a career-defining hit for disco diva Anita Ward in 1979. Knight's ballad "Be for Real," originally released by Marlena Shaw in the mid-1970s, was covered by Leonard Cohen, of all people, on Cohen's 1992 album *The Future*. He has also penned such modern soul-blues classics as Stan Mosley's "Anybody Seen My Boo," Shirley Brown's "(I've Got to) Sleep with One Eye Open," and Johnnie Taylor's "Big Head Hundreds."

"You have to think like a woman," Knight maintains.

> First you got to understand, you're going to have a lot more women buying the product, so the last thing you want to do is be offensive to women. We're not talking about hip-hop and certain things that they get away with. I wouldn't want to do it anyway; [even] if I was going to get away with it, I wouldn't do it. You don't be offensive to women. And a woman's basic nature [is] she wants to be loved, she wants to be needed. And if you can tap into that and you stay in it, that's the safety zone. And if you can stay in there, your odds of having consistency are going to increase.

(Whether it's the old double standard at work or simply the dictates of the marketplace, most soul-blues composers who write for others tend to be male. Songs actually written by women usually end up getting sung by the writers themselves; artists ranging from Denise LaSalle through Ms. Jody and Sweet Angel exemplify women who've honed the art of crafting songs that will "deliver to each one of those individuals out there," as Sweet Angel has put it, "something that is going to touch them." In most cases, though, others haven't recorded their songs; Z. Z. Hill's hit version of Denise LaSalle's "Someone Else Is Steppin' In" is, arguably, the most notable exception. This represents at least one difference between modern soul-blues and earlier deep soul. Although men dominated the field then as well, women such as Bettye Crutcher, Valerie Simpson [usually in tandem with Nickolas Ashford], and Joshie Jo Armstead were also in demand as songwriters. Some, like Armstead, also recorded their own material.)

Knight, perhaps because he came of age in that earlier era (the perennial complaint that "these kids today" don't know what's going on is as pervasive among pop elders as it is anywhere else), believes that contemporary southern soul songwriters too often lack the patience to hone their craft. "People are in too big of a hurry with the creation of the song," he maintains. "It's almost become a lost art."

> Have you sat down and listened to the lyric that you write? Does the lyric move you in a way, without music? Does it say something to you? Does it make you smile, just hearing the lyric? This is what I had to learn how

to do. It wasn't just [that] the hook was good and I just put some stuff in to get to the hook. You've got to approach a lyric line by line. Most people think just because they rhyme that it's okay. But then, when you start going through the lyric, you won't find a lot of substance. You might have a hit record, but a lot of people won't reach back and say, 'That was a great song.' If it's not saying anything that really triggers a response from people, you won't get a lot of covers out of that song.

See, the whole thing about a song, you're pretty much gonna be writing about the same thing that's been written about for years and years. But what makes it different, and what makes it unique, is the approach that you take to get to where you're trying to go. For example, "I love you." We've heard that a million times. But what makes this "I love you" that I'm getting ready to do is the road that I take that makes it unique. Gamble and Huff, Smokey [Robinson]—"Like a snowball rolling down the side of a snow-covered hill [from the Temptations' 1965 hit 'It's Growing']"—they'd go out and create all these vehicles knowing that the approach is going to bring you right back to talkin' 'bout how much you love somebody. But it's the journey and the approach to the journey that make those records so great.

The Right Stuff

Of course, successful songwriting means more than just thinking like a woman or finding new ways to say "I love you"; a song also has to fit the person singing it. This means that a songwriter needs to come up with material—words, melody, that elusive quality of "feel"—that another person can adapt and make sound as if it's coming out of his or her own life. Some writers, in fact, consider this the essence of the craft. "A good songwriter, to me," says Bob Jones, "is: you can write a song and make it for yourself, but what can you do for somebody else? Can't just say that a person is a good writer because he wrote the song for himself." According to Jones, though, exactly who that "somebody else" might be isn't always clear when the song is being written.

> I don't really write for any particular person; all my songs don't really fit the same person. I've written for [Little] Milton, I've written for James Carr, Lee "Shot" [Williams], [but] when I was writing a tune, I wouldn't say I had those guys in mind.
>
> When I write, my first thing I do—some people say they get a title, [but] I don't really have a title. I might have a line, but I got a story; my line brings a story to me. And I try, in my writing, to make every line mean something about the story that I'm trying to tell. Once I've finished a tune, then it might come to me who to send it to or who I think might do it. So it really depends on what I'm doing at the time and what

Figure 26. Bob Jones, 2007 Chicago Blues Festival. Photo by Paul Natkin/Photo Reserve, Inc.

I'm feeling. You cannot get away from that woman thing—money and love—you can't get away from that. So you write something that's going to appeal to the public.[9]

It shouldn't be surprising that some singers, who already know what it takes to live inside a song, might also be adept at creating material others can inhabit. Sir Charles Jones, for instance, penned "Slow Roll It," an easy-riding, medium-bounce ode to sensitive lovemaking, for a former radio disc jockey named Lewis Clark, who recorded it on Mardi Gras in 2001 as the Love Doctor. The song has since become a southern soul standard.

"Senator Jones brought me in the studio," Charles remembers.

> We recorded his first album [*Doctor of Love*],[10] and I wrote ["Slow Roll It"] for him. The song blew up so big, everybody loved it so much, 'til Universal came to Warren [Hildebrand] and offered him a gigantic deal to distribute the album, and that was my first, actually, gigantic check that I ever got.
>
> Then Sheba [Potts-Wright], she had some success with it [on her debut for Ecko that same year]; after that, I just ventured off into writing and bringing out a lot of other southern soul entertainers. Andre' Lee, La'Keisha [Burks], Reggie P.—I wrote one called "Ps & Qs" for Reggie P. [which appeared on Reggie's 2010 CD *The Rude Boy of Southern Soul*] that stayed on the charts for about nine weeks.[11]

Charles isn't the only one. Mr. Sam—Sam Fallie—was already a noted southern soul composer before he released his own first album in 2007, having penned songs for J. Blackfoot, the reconstituted Bar-Kays, and Theodis Ealey, among others. It wasn't until vocalist Terry Wright passed on his song "Lookin' 4 Love" that he realized he had enough material on hand to embark on his own recording career.

"I wrote these songs for other people," he explains. "Since I hadn't [had] anybody use them, I just put them on my album."[12] "Lookin' 4 Love" became that album's title song; the disk was issued on the MiLaJa label, owned by Jazzii Anderson (a.k.a. Jazzii A.), one of Bobby Rush's dancers. Fallie has since proven himself a first-rate interpreter of his own material—"Picking Up Pieces," from his 2008 CD *Voicemail*, was a neosoul-styled ballad that should, by rights, have been a mainstream R & B hit—and he has also continued to write for others: his "Just a Little Bit Won't Get It," co-credited to Ecko president John Ward, was a highlight of Ms. Jody's 2011 release, *Ms. Jody's in the House*.

Fallie, despite his youthful sound and modernist production techniques, is as adamant as Frederick Knight and other veterans that much southern soul songwriting today seems uninspired, or at least unmotivated. He points to the proliferation of songs extolling the joys of partying to old-school blues and R & B (as if southern soul were nothing more than a reunion for aging nostalgists), as well as the post–"Candy Licker" onslaught of double-entendre novelties, as the kind of thing he tries to avoid. "It's an easy way out," he maintains, "and I don't respect that. . . . I want to do a new story, with a twist. I do sex songs, [but] if I am going to put one on my album, it's going to be interesting. It's not just going to be plain. I love to tell stories. I love to tell life experiences. True life experiences. I got a lot of my learning skills from [former Bar-Kays producer] Alan Jones. He [taught] me to write, how to put a story together, to make it like a book. You got a beginning, you got your meat in the middle, and you got your good ending."[13]

Despite the grumbling, though, and despite the assembly-line lyrics and sounds that some labels and artists seem content to churn out (a problem hardly limited, of course, to any single pop genre), the professed belief in honest emotional expression—and the faith that blues and soul are among the music best equipped to convey it—is virtually universal among southern soul-blues songwriters. "That's why it was called soul music," as Sweet Angel has noted, echoing George Jackson almost word for word, "because it was coming from the soul." Bob Jones, who still considers himself a "blues" writer even though most of his songs these days are in the southern soul mold (whether or not they fit into the twelve-bar structure), is even more convinced that genuine storytelling in music will eventually win out. As far as he's concerned, it represents something close to a basic human need, and whether it's called "blues" hardly matters in the end. "The blues is still there," he maintains.

> The blues is a sound, a feeling; it's still there. The stories are still there. You get some [different] arrangements, all that digital stuff, it's the same. It's just a change in the music and the people who are listening to it. Before Muddy Waters, back in the '20s—just look at the changes in what they were calling blues. Listen at some of that stuff that Ma Rainey was doing and how it has changed. The vocals, the sound, the melodies were different. It's the same thing now. The blues has taken a change.
>
> But the blues itself as we know it is gonna always win out, because everything has to come back to the blues, period. All of it. You get your good blues, telling a story, a good story that has touched most everybody will get through. Get something new, the basis of it is going to be blues.[14]

10 Music and the Marketplace
Getting Heard, Getting Known, and Staying on Top of the Game

The paradox is undeniable: despite their almost universal belief in southern soul's potential, even its strongest advocates will recite a list of problems so daunting—diminishing media exposure, plunging CD sales, uncertain quality control at some labels and from certain producers, and an aging fan base, to name just a few—that after a while, simply thinking about the future can feel like an exercise in blues forbearance. Even as mega-events like the Blues Is Alright tour, as well as smaller regional showcases featuring many of the same artists, continue to sell out auditoriums and civic centers in the South and elsewhere; even as local venues ranging from Memphis, Tennessee's, Vineyard Entertainment Center (formerly the Whitehaven Celebration Complex) and Greenville, Mississippi's, V Spot to Mr. G's in Chicago pack the house for shows by the likes of Denise LaSalle, Willie Clayton, Sweet Angel, T. K. Soul, and Bobby Rush; even as Sir Charles Jones, with his R & B–fueled sound and hip-hop–flavored onstage insouciance, can speak confidently of being one of the hardest-working roadmen in the blues ("We're actually around about a hundred and eighteen dates a year; Bobby Rush is the only one ahead of me"[1]) and Ms. Jody continues to pursue her dream of expanding her territory by traveling as far as Milwaukee and Boston ("Oh, man! We had a ball! We were at a country club, and it just blew me away. Those people paid $200 a ticket there!"[2]), the overall mood remains uneasy, if not grim.

The contrarian voices, in this case, are the hopeful ones. And some of them come from a sector of the industry that even many of its staunchest advocates have all but given up on: radio. It's all the more surprising when one realizes that radio play, or the lack thereof, is often cited by southern soul artists and record industry people as the number one issue confronting the music.

The Radio Conundrum: Airplay, Ad Money, and Ratings Games

Virtually everyone agrees that southern soul radio has taken some serious hits in recent years. The reason usually given is that the music won't attract either the listenership or the advertising necessary to make it worthwhile; sometimes that complaint is modified to suggest that when it does earn good ratings, southern soul appeals mostly to "older" listeners (i.e., thirty-five and over), and advertisers won't support programming that attracts that demographic.

It's not just southern soul that's been affected, of course; the entire medium of radio has been transformed and, in the eyes of many, seriously compromised ("Who listens to the radio anymore?" scoffed one singer's manager, as she explained why attempting to garner airplay was no longer the major thrust of her artist's career strategy).[3] Especially problematic has been the decline of radio's identity as a voice for local tastes and community concerns. Historically, one of its primary strengths as a cultural force has been its role as a kind of modern-day tribal drum around which listeners could gather to participate—culturally, socially, politically—in what might be described as an alternative public sphere, no less vital than more physically defined, traditional public gathering places such as churches, fraternal lodges, and political and civic clubs.[4] This has been especially true in African American communities, at least since WDIA virtually invented "black radio" by switching to an all-black format in the late 1940s. Although local stations continue to do their best to keep their fingers on the pulse of the community, their incentive to do so has diminished since Reagan-era deregulations removed mandatory minimums on the amount of "nonentertainment" programming (i.e., community service and public affairs) a station would be required to schedule.

A lot of those local stations, moreover, are "local" in name only. In 1996, President Bill Clinton signed the Telecommunications Act, which virtually eliminated previous restrictions on how many stations a single corporate entity could own. Today, companies such as Clear Channel Communications own hundreds of stations across the country, often holding near monopolies in entire local and regional markets; in most cases, they exact strict control over programming, and their emphasis is on nationally known, big-money acts with multimillion sellers on the charts. Gone are the days when an artist could break a song into a small or midsize market by getting airplay on a handful of stations, and then eventually see its popularity expand to the national level.

Southern soul has felt the impact particularly harshly. It's almost a mantra in the business: "Everything now is programmed by someone that's twenty, twenty-one, twenty-two years old, or maybe in their early thirties, and it's all automated now" (Floyd Taylor).[5] "It all goes back to radio. They don't understand the blues. The major stations have young guys as music directors and program directors, so they haven't got the feeling for the blues. So the records can't get out" (Bob Jones).[6] "It's in jeopardy, man. Advertisers don't [support] the blues. . . . They're only heard on certain stations that's not going to bring in the attention of people to go buy 'em" (Harrison Calloway).[7] "If the radio was like it was, I could probably really move some product" (Latimore).[8] "The radio stations now, if you listen, you hear this song; wait two minutes, and you can turn to the next FM station and hear [the same song] over there" (Millie Jackson).[9] "For someone to say, 'I'm a southern soul artist,' you've just limited yourself off of 200,000 radio stations" (Sweet Angel).[10]

There's reason enough for the anxiety. Even in the South, stations that have programmed southern soul for years have begun to move away from it, and others don't seem to be rushing in to fill the void. Tommy Couch Jr., as might be expected, has strong opinions on the subject. He blames some artists and labels, at least as much as corporate consolidation and demographics-obsessed program directors, for the trend. "What has been accepted as southern soul," he avers, "most of the listeners have abandoned a lot of the stations that were playing that."

Because of technology, anybody can make a record now for not very much money. And, unfortunately, most of 'em sound like somebody made 'em for not very much money; the song isn't any good, the singer can't sing,

Figure 27. Floyd Taylor gets intimate with the audience at the 2002 King Biscuit Blues Festival, Helena, Arkansas. Photo by Gene Tomko.

the musicianship or the computer programming is horrible, it hasn't been mastered, and the song is saying nothing. There's a lot of lickin' and stickin' and standin' up in it and "she likes it from the back" and just a lot of stuff that should not be played on radio.

And the deejays and some of the program directors, they can't tell the difference. As that started to happen, you started to lose listeners, then you got more guys that couldn't afford to pay the good jocks, and so these [other] guys would play it and say, "Well, you don't understand—we get requests for that." I say, "*You* don't understand. The majority of the public ain't listening to it, and the people that are calling you, you got three hoochie-mamas that don't even have a job, and all they have time to do is sit around and call the radio station all day. The people who are listening to it aren't the people who are going out and buying the records. They're not the people with means to go buy records. They are not representing the public." [11]

Not so fast, says Bobby O'Jay. O'Jay, WDIA's longtime program director, is a forty-year veteran of the industry, and he's one of the most venerated figures in southern black radio. Unlike some of the naysayers, O'Jay has data, and they contradict a lot of the common wisdom about southern soul's radio potential. His station, although owned by Clear Channel, has retained a healthy measure of autonomy in its programming, and it still programs blues and soul-blues all day on Saturdays, a weekly eighteen-hour marathon. "Saturdays, we're in the top five [ratings]," O'Jay reports. "Demographics are anywhere from [ages] twenty-five to fifty-four, and thirty-five to sixty-four. Before we got the PPM meters—that's the new Arbitron rating system; they use meters now, like the old Nielson ratings for TV—we were No. 1. Before the PPM, they were just using diaries; folks would write down their favorite station, what they listened to. And in that system, on Saturdays, our station was always No. 1."

(It may still actually be No. 1. PPMs, or Portable People Meters, are pagerlike devices worn by listeners who agree to participate in Arbitron's surveys. As explained by Chris Beck, founder of the online media consultant group 26DotTwo, "The device picks up embedded codes to ascertain a real time analysis of signals you are actually exposed to, versus stations you wrote down in a diary." Beck believes that this system is not as reliable as the old one; among other problems, the new methodology records the listening habits of approximately 50 percent fewer people than the direct-reporting technique did. It also tends to measure broad geographic regions such as "metro areas" rather than discrete localities. In Memphis, where the majority of WDIA's listeners are clustered in geographically delineated, primarily African American communities, it's likely that this results in some undercounting.) [12]

Radio's significance also goes beyond merely getting songs played on the air. Despite the proliferation of online communication technologies, broadcast media are still the most powerful advertising tool for promoters. "When you bring a show into an area," said Kim Cole, former manager of vocalist T. K. Soul, "you [put] your commercials on TV or you [place] radio ads." T. K. himself has no doubt that on-air exposure is still vital: "Thank you for buying my CDs," he tells his audience at almost every show, "and for calling those radio stations and telling them to play some T. K. Soul." He even gives out his cell-phone number ("I'm doin' it like Mike Jones!") to encourage them to stay in touch and let him know they're following through.

"You Don't Even Know My Name"

Radio, then, still plays an important role in getting the word out about music, perhaps especially in the South, where median incomes tend to be somewhat lower than average, populations are aging in many regions, and not everyone has the resources to stay fully wired into computers or handheld media. (And, lest we forget, even a lot of "wired-in" folks are still listening to the radio, both terrestrial and satellite, over their various devices.) So why is it so difficult for southern soul to get significant airplay? Even the staunchest radio advocates admit that most of the stations that deign to give southern soul a slot are, as Bobby O'Jay puts it, "AM stations with a limited signal and a limited audience." About the only station of significant thrust that carries the music on a regular basis is Jackson, Mississippi's, 100,000-watt WMPR, a public radio outlet that doesn't have to worry much about advertising. (The 50,000-watt WDIA, for all its legendary status and high ratings, is only medium-strength by modern standards; at night, moreover, it's restricted to only 5,000 watts.) And with a few exceptions—WMPR and WDIA being probably the most notable—most stations that do play soul-blues limit their programming to a few hours a week, usually Saturday mornings or around lunchtime. Some stream on the Internet, but it's questionable whether most of their core listeners—who may have the radio turned on while driving or at work or maybe while cleaning the house on Saturday—will be listening via computer.

"The majority of the stations that play the southern soul," Larry Chambers confirms, "are the independent stations. I've been doing promotion since 1984; a lot of the places where we had good radio, we no longer have radio. Basically, our primary market is Mississippi, Alabama, Louisiana [O'Jay would add Arkansas and Texas to the list]. If the song doesn't hit in those markets, then you don't have a southern soul song. That's the largest percentage of our black listeners, the largest-selling market for southern soul."

It doesn't seem to make sense. Virtually everyone who works on a day-to-day basis with southern soul radio, whether in record company promotion (like Larry Chambers) or in broadcasting, insists that the music can—and, when given the opportunity, already does—draw healthy numbers of listeners from a comfortably wide demographic range. O'Jay, reflecting former Stax co-owner Al Bell's theory about "Mississippi River Culture," adds that "anywhere you have a huge number of black people [with] deep southern roots—Chicago, Detroit, Milwaukee—southern soul should definitely have a spot on the radio."

The problem, many insist, is not that the music (or even radio itself) has such limited potential; it's that the men and women who hold the purse strings and control the programming have limited vision. Corporate hegemony doesn't reside only in the central office; it defines virtually the entire marketplace. Mainstream radio's true "customers" are advertisers, at least as much as listeners. Despite the evidence provided by Arbitron ratings in cities like Memphis that a significant majority of music lovers will gladly tune into southern soul, blues, or some other "niche" music, most sponsors seem reluctant to consider those listeners as lucrative a target as the (primarily young, fashion-driven) audience who tune into more "mainstream" programs and structure their shopping habits around the commercials they hear. Better, in fact, to hone one's demographic—keep those kids listening by whatever means necessary so they don't get gobbled up by YouTube and Pandora—by reinforcing prejudices based less upon the music than upon aggressively marketed stereotypes about what a particular genre is supposed to represent. In too many cases, these stereotypes have already been accepted by the decision makers at the stations.

"A lot of the people are younger people that are running these radio stations now," says O'Jay, echoing what Bob Jones, Floyd Taylor, and many others have said, "and they don't know anything about the music. That's the problem, right there. I think that the people you're talking [about] don't know the music."

"They're definitely cutting back," agrees Chambers. "No doubt about that. They're cutting back on the programming."

I've been doing this for so long, I know how this works. They'll say, "Well, we can't sell that show." That's what they'll say, but basically it comes down to somebody within the organization don't care very much about this music. Or the consultant advised them that this music is not going to do anything for their ratings. But they didn't get this opinion from the listeners.

I think it comes down to the program director, [who] feels that the show is hard to sell, as far as advertising. [But] I don't see why they would lose dollars, because advertising, when you go from [age] thirty-five up, these are older, mature people, and they're working people. They're the ones that's going to go out there and go to Walmart; these are the people that's going to go do Home Depot . . . the thirty-five and up, you've passed that juvenile age where you're dealing with these minor advertising products. You're dealing with serious product now, when you've got to buy a stove, refrigerator, air conditioners, and houses and cars.

"A lot of the [ad] agencies," O'Jay adds, "don't understand the [musical] product; they probably just shy away from it because they don't understand it. This music, all it needs is an avenue."

Searching for a Demographic That's Already There: The Conundrum Continues

On the face of it, at least, these would seem to be irrefutable arguments. According to the online consultant group Strategicmedia, the advertising categories most successful in direct marketing via radio include retail and discount stores (Home Depot is "one of the biggest radio advertisers"), financial services (including debt consolidation and brokerage products), intellectual property and informational products (ranging from "wealth building" and parenting through weight-loss products and anxiety/stress reduction), beauty (skin, hair, teeth, etc.), fitness (primarily home fitness products and regimens), and "hard goods" (computers, radar detectors, and other personal technologies).[13] Virtually all of these advertisers should find Larry Chambers's "older, mature, working people" an attractive target demographic.

At the same time, though, most ad strategists seem to have a limited notion of exactly what appeals to the populations they want to reach. Strategic Media, in its listing of which formats are attractive to different demographics, focuses primarily on age, not ethnicity, although within its formatting categories it is possible to extrapolate ethnic breakdowns. Here's a sampling, spanning roughly the age groups that O'Jay, Chambers, and others have identified as most likely to listen to southern soul:

Adults, 25–34: Alternative; Rock; CHR [Contemporary Hit Radio, including—depending on the ethnic/cultural target market—rock, dance music, R & B, and/or hip-hop]; some Urban [primarily black-oriented and comprising mainly R & B and hip-hop as well as dance tracks and the neosoul/smooth jazz/slow-jam "quiet storm" format]; Adult Contemporary [including, for an "urban" demographic, R & B and neosoul but little hip-hop or rap]

Adults, 35–44: Rock; Adult Contemporary

Adults, 45–54: Oldies; Adult Contemporary

Adults, 55–64: Classical; New Adult Contemporary[14]

It's a pretty inflexible-looking set list; there's not even any country and western in the mix, let alone blues or southern soul.[15] The occasional B. B. King standard or deep-soul chestnut will pop up in an "oldies" or adult urban contemporary rotation; the few southern soul-blues artists who've crossed over into "mainstream" R & B, such as Willie Clayton or Sir Charles Jones, will have their moment of glory on an urban or possibly adult contemporary playlist. But that's about as far as it goes, at least according to the taxonomy outlined here.

If we address ethnicity more directly, things still don't look much better. According to research cited by another online consultant, MichaelD. Communications, urban adult contemporary is the "most popular . . . more than 11% ahead of the next-most-listened-to format" among African Americans, accounting for over 30 percent of all radio listening among this demographic.[16] One could make a case for blues or soul-blues fitting into this slot (and, at least in the South, it occasionally does), but it would take some imagination and creativity to do so. If a station's program directors are the "young guys" and culturally myopic business school grads of Bob Jones and Floyd Taylor's description (or if they're located in a corporate office in Los Angeles, with little incentive to modify business plans that are already reaping profits), it's unlikely they'll consider trying to work a genre like southern soul into any of these standardized formats, even if such a case could be made.

The problem, though, isn't just radio myopia. Historically, new or unknown artists and genres have broken through largely due to the enterprise and vision of record industry mavericks. Many were at the helm of small independents such as Chess, King, or Stax. But even at some larger companies, big-eared executives (e.g., Jerry Wexler and Ahmet Ertegun at Atlantic; John Hammond Sr. and Clive Davis at Columbia) often made it their mission to discover and develop artists and styles not yet considered "mainstream" for their time, and in the process helped fuel revolutionary changes in both the industry and popular culture.

Today, though, outside of the rap world, where freethinkers and visionaries continue to chart the future, such figures are in short supply, at least among the major labels. (Indie imprints still exist, of course, but the majority are shoestring operations, if not vanity projects on the part of their owners; few have the resources to create hits.) And without big-label prodding, it's unlikely that most stations, whether independent or owned by a conglomerate like Clear Channel, will be motivated to give a listen to a relatively unproven, unprestigious genre like southern soul; the fabled days of independent record pluggers traveling the highways and back roads in search of radio station antennae and then conning disc jockeys into taking a chance on a new record are long gone. It takes major-label clout to even get an appointment with program directors at most stations, and the majors today don't seem to be much more imaginative than those same program directors when it comes to opening their ears to untested sounds. Bobby O'Jay, with decades of hard-won industry savvy to back him up, believes they're making a serious mistake. "Southern soul," he maintains, "I think that's the genre of music that people are overlooking. I think that genre of music is something that could really make a lot of money for record companies."

> If a major record label would search out these artists and market them the way they market a Beyoncé or Rihanna, that music would do a lot for radio, [and] it would do a lot for the record label. That's the genre of music that could save a lot of these labels. If they walked into the radio station with a Willie Clayton or a Sir Charles Jones—T. K. Soul, he's another one—if these guys could get on major record labels, and the major record labels walked 'em into a radio station, hey man, it'd be all over. Absolutely! Some smart guy from a label, all he would need is one guy that he'd sign to make it on the charts, and I guarantee you every record label in this country'll be lookin' for some southern soul artists.

Meanwhile, many of those artists themselves believe that the music's fans need to make their preferences known in order for both radio stations and labels to realize what they're missing out on. That's why T. K. Soul makes it a point to urge his audiences to bombard their local disc jockeys with requests for his music. Floyd Taylor agrees, emphasizing that "what people have to do is, they have to call those radio station . . . flood their lines so much that they gonna say, 'You know what? We got to give these people what they want.'"[17]

Whose "Mainstream" Is It, Anyway?

Southern soul, though, faces other contradictions and paradoxes as it attempts to widen its popularity, some of which may be more difficult to surmount. Much contemporary pop music—even (or maybe especially) putatively transgressive genres like hip-hop and indie rock—is marketed and promoted in a cultural context shaped by a disingenuous, if not outright hypocritical, stance toward matters of "art" and "commerce." This is not a new phenomenon; it follows a pattern set at least as early as the 1960s, when "underground" became a lucrative brand in the music industry. Since that time, few recommendations have carried as much pop cachet as being so "alternative" that you've spent most of your career playing for a handful of aficionados for little or no money, preferably in either a ghetto housing project or in dingy lofts and garages hidden away in a hipster enclave such as pre-Nirvana Seattle or pre–Frankie Knuckles/Ministry/Smashing Pumpkins Chicago.

In this context, becoming "mainstream" may be equated with selling out; artists strive to maintain their "alt" cred, even as many still welcome major-label deals if they can get them. For those who want to ramp up the outlaw image even further, Internet technology has made a way: they can make their music available solely to a self-contained, self-sustaining online fan base, bypassing the corporate music industry entirely to retain that all-important aura of in-group exclusivity—a cyber updating of the hipster fan club model pioneered by the Grateful Dead and their legion of Deadheads, who styled themselves as avatars of alternative values even as their symbiotic adulation generated millions of dollars annually.

(Today, of course, those dollars probably won't flow as abundantly as they did then. "The practice of selling music," notes Miles Raymer, music critic for the Chicago *Reader,* is "looking more and more outdated" as file sharing, free downloading, and viral YouTube celebrity increasingly command the attention of the young, the hip, and the trendy.[18] Some see this as a victory. "Music wants to be free," according to the post–Napster-era slogan, a kind of faux-anarchistic manifesto that virtually guarantees prolonged "heroic poverty" status for musicians if they can't sustain perennial tours or beat the freebies by glomming on to the success of one the few record industry monoliths left standing.)

But such techno-hipster idealization of "underground" as a mark of authenticity is laden with ideological and cultural assumptions, many of which don't necessarily apply to southern soul-blues or much of its core audience. Moreover, these assumptions are not new; a lot of whites during the 1960s-era blues "rediscovery" also romanticized that music as an outsider art, as hostile to "establishment" values as protest folk music or acid rock. But few if any blues artists, then or now, have taken pride in their obscurity, equated attaining commercial success with selling out, or faulted record producers for attempting to create "mainstream" hits, the kind of hits that most would dearly love to have. From the beginning, blues artists have strived to make a living by garnering as wide and lucrative a listening audience as possible (however much this might have been downplayed by folkie romanticists over the years). For a rural bluesman like Robert Johnson, this meant including pop standards, novelties, and even polkas in his repertoire; according to data collected by Alan Lomax and John Work, Muddy Waters performed songs like "Chattanooga Choo-Choo" and "Red Sails in the Sunset" for plantation audiences in Mississippi in the 1940s.[19] Later, during the glory days of postwar Chicago blues, as Buddy Guy has remembered, "You had to do that jukebox in all the small blues clubs; if you couldn't play the top ten records on that jukebox, you wasn't gonna get another play for that three or four dollars a night."[20]

In most cases, of course, a musician playing in those small blues clubs was also looking for a way to get a top-ten record of his own on that same jukebox and start making more than "three or four dollars a night." The same holds true today. Cutting a hit record—becoming a "star"—has been the goal of most blues recording artists since Mamie Smith made "Crazy Blues," usually considered the first blues record, back in 1920. It's certainly been the aim of virtually every R & B and soul singer since these more modern forms evolved during the mid-twentieth century. Usually, the way to do this has been to appeal to mainstream, decidedly "above-ground," African American musical tastes.

Even in today's alt-pop world, in fact, "obscurity" doesn't quite live up to its billing. Most of the "alternative" artists lionized for their underground integrity actually purvey variations on once-radical styles that have, in fact, become mainstream—primarily rap/hip-hop or indie rock in its various postpunk/postgrunge permutations. At the very least, they're almost certainly making music and projecting an image reflecting values and life experiences far removed from most of southern soul's primary fan base; someone like Sir Charles Jones's protagonist in "Friday," for instance, a grown man who "just got paid" after "working nine-to-five" all week, is headed for his local nightspot to "get [his] groove on" and will probably also be in church on Sunday morning.

Soul-blues, then, in its attempts to reach a wider listenership, finds itself contending with a musical marketplace driven by standards of hipness that, paradoxically, romanticize the "right" kind of obscurity—being popular among a small coterie of counterculturally correct bohemians or outlaws—while simultaneously castigating the "wrong" kind—in this case, appealing to an audience that's geographically, culturally, and at least to an extent chronologically removed from milieus or attitudes that might otherwise garner them hip cred. A band of white punkers thrashing out noise metal for a few dozen stoners in a Wicker Park loft in Chicago or a posse of gangsta rappers rhyming on a Compton street corner or at an all-night rave party in Bed-Stuy may be an "underground" phenomenon waiting to happen; a soul-blues singer performing in a Jackson, Mississippi, juke packed to capacity with seventy-five or a hundred people is merely catering to "marginal" tastes that don't represent a cutting-edge trend or niche market and thus don't merit serious consideration.

"I'm Going for Myself Now"

It should be no surprise, in the face of these problems, that a lot of southern soul-blues artists, unable to land deals with major labels and frustrated with what they see as an inability (or, perhaps, a reluctance) on the part of independents to adequately promote and support them, are going off on their own. We've already seen artists such as Willie Clayton, Sweet Angel, and Sir Charles Jones declare their determination to take the plunge (although some did return, at least temporarily, to established labels after their first forays outside the fold). Mel Waiters, probably Malaco's biggest seller after Johnnie Taylor died, left the erstwhile soul-blues powerhouse about three or four years ago; he now appears on his own Brittney label. T. K. Soul has been recording on Soulful Records since 2002; Bobby Rush has been appearing on his Deep Rush imprint since the early 2000s; Latimore has been releasing product on LatStone since 2008. But going it alone isn't easy. "It is extremely difficult and extremely expensive," affirms Travis Haddix, a Cleveland-based singer/guitarist who straddles the "blues"/"soul-blues" genre line and recorded for Ichiban between 1988 and 1994. In 1995, Haddix began releasing material on his own Wann-Sonn label. "You're the man," he explains. "There's no middleman. You are the man whether it goes good or whether it goes bad. There's nobody that you can depend on when things are not going well."[21] (Haddix's CDs now appear under the imprint of Benevolent Blues, a subsidiary of Dylann DeAnna's CDS label in California.)

Distribution is a significant expense, of course, although sometimes an artist can arrange a distribution deal with a label without relinquishing either creative or financial control. But it's not the only challenge. In the age of instant CD-burning, bootlegging has become a serious problem for artists and labels alike. Quite a few of the mom-and-pop stores that have traditionally been outlets for blues and soul-blues records have been caught selling bootlegged CDs; vendors set up shop in shopping malls, at street fairs, and at festivals, often peddling product so slickly disguised and packaged that it's virtually impossible to distinguish from the legitimate article. Some bootleggers even advertise on the Internet and distribute directly to retail outlets.

"It's major," confirms Tommy Couch Jr. "At one point, Malaco sent someone undercover through Texas, Louisiana, Mississippi, and one or two stores in Arkansas. He went into thirty-one stores and was able to purchase bootlegged product in twenty-nine of 'em. We turned around and fought it on our own and sued the stores and this and that, but that's kind of a double-edged sword thing, because those guys are supposed to be your partners, but if your partners are stealing from you, then they're not your partners anymore. That's another thing that has really hurt that part of the business."[22]

It's even harder on artists who are trying to make it without the financial cushion of a record company. Millie Jackson, who formed her Weird Wreckuds label over a decade ago, has said she's not going to bother recording anymore, even on her own imprint, because of the bootlegging situation. "I put out 'Butt-A-Cize' as the single [from *Not for Church Folk!* her 2001 CD on her label]," she recalls. "I was going to put out the CD a month later."

> Before the CD got put out, "Butt-A-Cize" was in a compilation album [released] by somebody [else]. I called 'em up. I said, "I'm opening a record store, and I see here you have a lot of records, so I want to order some records from you." The woman informed me, she said, "Well, we don't sell less than a hundred per order." And I'm saying to myself, here I am up here, sending out five records to somebody in Milwaukee, another six or seven to a music store somewhere in Rochester, New York, and this bitch gon' tell me I gotta order a hundred copies of my own record!
>
> So I did some investigating, and I put the law on their ass. But I don't have time to play cop. After I spend the money that I spend to make an album, and then [I] gotta promote the album, you just gon' go and get all the goodies from me? I've been to the shopping mall several times, and guys are selling the records out there, and they go, "Millie! I got ya, girl! I'm keepin' you alive!" I said, "Thank you," and keep on walking. They don't [even] know they're doing something wrong. They paid the money to buy the records; they legitimately bought it from somebody, from a store somewhere, and they don't know that they're doing anything wrong.[23]

Nonetheless, between the implosion of the mainstream recording industry and the temptation to control the means of production as much as possible, more and more artists are seeking independence. Ironically, going independent can also mean going old school. A lot of people are rediscovering what earlier blues artists accepted as a fact of life: hard work, hustling, and constant taking care of business are the only ways to survive. T. K. Soul, for instance, sponsors, organizes, and performs on an annual "Soul Ship" sea cruise that departs from southern Louisiana every January. Quite a few artists will affirm that they spend at least as much time glad-handing and making contacts as they do performing, recording, or songwriting. "A lot of cats," agrees Bob Jones, "are going back to the old-fashioned way, from the grassroots—that walkin' the street, knockin' on doors, and puttin' the stuff in people's hands."[24]

These days, when an artist isn't making contacts by walking the streets, he's probably doing it online. "You're personal now," emphasized Kim Cole. "You cannot rely on even your distributor to let people know what's going on. You got interactive [media], interactive with the fans, and you have to continually let them know what's going on. You got to let those people know what's going on with you."

But that works only when those people already know who you are. The amount of music on the Internet is staggering, and the odds of a random surfer stumbling across a particular artist's Web site, Facebook page, or YouTube video are virtually nil. The odds of that surfer actually purchasing some of the artist's music are even lower. According to a study done by PRS for Music (a British association of songwriters, composers, and music publishers roughly analogous to BMI and ASCAP), there were at least thirteen million songs available for sale online in 2008. Ten million were never downloaded at all. Overall, approximately 52,000 songs—less than 1 percent—accounted for 80 percent of all revenue generated by online music that year.[25] It's likely that a significant percentage of those were by well-known artists, or at least artists with substantial fan bases already in place.

There is a way, though, to reach new listeners, and it's not radio. "Clubs," says Larry Chambers. "We get more exposure now from club DJs than we do from radio. And for those that didn't go to the club, word of mouth takes over: Woman sayin' to another, 'Girl, you should have been to the club last night, I heard this song . . . .' The club DJs are total assets to us now."

"I'm going to distribute to club DJs every time," affirmed Kim Cole. "If we go into a place and I don't know that DJ, I'm going to make sure

Figure 28. Millie Jackson, Greensboro Coliseum, Greensboro, North Carolina, February 2009. Photo by Gene Tomko.

I have that contact information. These guys share music back and forth. They share, and their networks are large. There's a guy named DJ Sugalove [Johnnie Armstrong, who also books and promotes shows] in Louisiana. He's got 260 DJs in his organization. They are [like] radio deejays, they really are, at the end of the day. You MP3 them that music, and it's all right there."

Cole also believes that freelance CD burning, as reviled as it is throughout most of the industry, may not be an entirely bad thing. Although she's as adamant as everyone else about the damage done by big-time bootleggers like the one Millie Jackson confronted on the telephone, she's come to accept what she calls low-level "bootlegging"—individual burning and sharing of CDs—as a means of free publicity. T. K. Soul, in fact, has whipped together a few anthologies of his older material to distribute, knowing full well that at least some of it will get copied and shared. If nothing else, it gets people to his shows. "He recently went into an area where he doesn't get much radio play," Cole said. "He sang a lot of his early material, and the audience cheered and sang along with almost all of it. They just somehow knew his stuff, and I have to say it was bootlegs."

CDs as loss leaders? It hasn't quite come to that, but Cole admitted that even direct-mail distribution to the few stores that still sell recorded music has become risky, at least for an artist who's not signed to a major label. "We did our own distribution," she explained, "where [a store] could call directly to this office and place an order, and it would be shipped out. As the record stores got worse and worse off, they stopped sending the checks back. So when I found myself writing collection letters every day, follow-up phone calls, we pulled them. We started relying totally on venue sales. T. K. works a lot. If you're an active artist—you play Arkansas, you play Louisiana, Texas, Tennessee—I've heard people say, 'Well, T. K.'s regional. He only plays in the South.' [But] you play these places, you've pretty much got distribution."

The Only Way Is Up

Resurrecting the old "regional market" concept and making it work in new ways; building an online network of fans and then reaching new ones by hustling product to club DJs; creating an annual seagoing showcase to expand your reputation; getting fans to take over the job of the old-style record pluggers by "calling those radio stations and telling them to play" your records; reintroducing the single, not the entire album, as the most important unit to push ("One thing about a single," noted Cole, "if it doesn't work, you pull it back and put another one out there. T. K. said, 'You mean I got eight tries, ten tries to make a hit? I believe I can win this one'"), it's a high-risk business model requiring constant vigilance, improvisation, and not a little fearlessness. Even then, there's no guarantee it will succeed. In many ways, it's a throwback to the days when the industry was dominated by high rollers and hustlers, often flinty-eyed and unscrupulous but motivated by a consuming, even obsessive love of the game, who freely made (and broke) the rules as they went along.

Cole, a former nurse who discovered T. K. Soul almost by accident at a J. Blackfoot show in about 2002 and became his manager a few years later, doesn't really fit that profile. Her soft-spoken demeanor, though, may be deceiving; it took awhile, she says, for people in the industry to get used to "that bitch" running interference for T. K. and taking care of his business. But eventually, the gigs and money started getting better, and they've continued along that trajectory ever since. To heighten her optimism, in late 2011 Universal Records signed T. K. Soul to a distribution deal for his single "Zydeco Bounce," to be distributed on Universal's Street Scholar label. (Shortly after the Universal deal, Kim Cole and T. K. Soul dissolved their business partnership. She is now working with other southern soul artists.)

"The vice president picked it up off of YouTube," explained Cole, "and he was just really impressed at the numbers. They signed him for 'Zydeco Bounce' and any other options we want. We still maintain control over Soulful Records. If T. K. decides to drop another single, he can do it with them or he can do it alone.[26] That's up to them, to prove to us that they can offer [something] different from what we're doing. Now there'll be ringtones, and you'll see a video that will be on VH1 Soul. They've hired a publicist and a radio airplay person. It's just going to be a whole lot [put] into just this one song."

She's convinced that southern soul is a bonanza waiting to explode for anyone savvy enough to invest in it and give it the support it deserves. "I've seen these venues filled up by southern soul lovers," she emphasized. "I think we had sixty-five hundred people at the show in Tuscaloosa [Alabama]. We have a show coming up on January first [2012]—'T. K. Soul vs. Sir Charles Jones'—I think it's a forty-five-hundred seat venue [the Washington County Convention Center in Greenville, Mississippi], and it's near sold out [as of December 2011]. No way in the world you're gonna keep missing that money if you're a businessman. You're not gonna do it.

"So what I see in southern soul, I see big money coming to collect this money."

11 Evolution
A Look toward the Future

Media exposure, CD sales, and revolutions in communications and marketing aren't the only challenges facing southern soul-blues. Despite the encouraging signs noted by Larry Chambers, Stan Mosley, and others, the music is also contending with aesthetic and cultural constraints that involve not just geography ("that 'Bama music") and style, but audience as well. The blues, unlike rock and roll (and, at least since the mid-1970s, unlike a lot of mainstream R & B and certainly unlike most rap), has historically been characterized by an adult sensibility.

Back when the blues was first developing, there was no such thing as "adolescence," especially for working-class people and especially in the rural South. By their late teens, most African American southerners were working full time, and they were probably either having children or getting ready to do so. Their music, almost by default, already reflected the attitudes and perspectives of people negotiating their way through a world of adult responsibilities and challenges. Later, in the 1960s and '70s, even as Motown marketed itself as "the music of young America," southern-based deep soul remained primarily ageless in its appeal; most of the singers, to be sure, were relatively young, but the songs themselves could (and still do) speak to listeners of virtually any age.

One of the most distinguishing characteristics of southern soul-blues ("grown folks' music") has been its ostensible return to that kind of adult-oriented perspective. The artists' ages and musical personas, as well as many of their songs' story lines, reflect this, representing yet another commonality with earlier blues (Muddy Waters was thirty-three when he had his first hit; Howlin' Wolf was over forty). Veterans in their fifties, sixties, and even seventies record new material, get radio and club play, and share stages with newcomers, many of whom themselves are somewhat older than most mainstream pop stars (Sir Charles Jones, the self-described "youngest blues artist out here," was almost thirty when he released his first CD in 2000). And despite the recent trend toward youthful-sounding vocal deliveries, plenty still boast voices that sound toughened by experience, if not age itself.

To succeed on its own terms, southern soul needs to find a way to retain its identity as a distinct subgenre rooted in this blues and soul tradition yet still be marketable to younger listeners. The most common strategy has been to season the deep soul, funk, and blues that remain at the music's core with elements drawn from more contemporary styles. But this still leaves unsolved the problems of lyric content and the stereotypes many still have of the performers and the genre itself. Even without the word *blues* getting in the way, southern soul has struggled to shed the generational biases that have hurt it on radio and discouraged at least some mainstream R & B fans from listening at all ("'How old is he?' First thing they ask," as Emmett Garner recounted). Most major labels share these biases. How, in short, is it possible to sell "grown folks' music" in a marketplace that seems to consider grown folks an anathema?

Some artists have attempted to solve this problem by pushing the "grown folks" envelope until it's almost a death letter. Especially since the late 1990s, when Mel Waiters began to hit the charts with his songs praising the heady, smoke-filled atmosphere of "hole-in-the-wall" after-hours joints, we've seen a proliferation of dispatches from fictional jukes and nightclubs where people gather to dance, drink, and party to old-school soul music and blues. The nostalgia is almost as thick as the cigar smoke, and many of the songs name-check entertainers and dance styles from years, if not decades, earlier. Despite attempts to modernize the message with synthesized backings and beats, such fare raises the danger that the artists, if not the music itself, will be pigeonholed as retrograde. At its worst, it threatens to turn southern soul into an old-timers' reunion presided over by juke-joint Lawrence Welks performing for middle-aged audiences who step and slide around the dance floor dreaming of the days when they were young and "real music" was still the thing.

At the other extreme are those who've decided to go "raunchy." Ostensibly, at least part of the idea is to throw down a riposte to the moldy-figgery previously described by reclaiming the transgressive voice that once characterized the blues but has more recently been assumed by hip-hop and rap. "The blues lineage," as jazz critic Giovanni Russonello points out, "with its personal revolutions and community consciousness . . . found new life in soul and funk and, by the late 1970s, in hip-hop."[1] In light of this, adopting a pose of militance and transgression (sexual and otherwise) along with synths and sampling in the studio could help soul-blues move toward forging an alliance with hip-hop in "keeping the blues alive," albeit in ways that many proponents of that notion might resist.

Admittedly, some truly hilarious novelty songs have arisen from this trend. Too many times, though, the result has instead been double-entendre ditties that, despite their putative "adults-only" status, would be dismissed as childish at the average high school jock party. The days of "crawling kingsnakes" and "pig meat papas" are gone; militant sexuality has become the province of rap, and the blues is unlikely to be able to take it back. "Dogs," "cats," "hitting it from the back," and unlocking "coochie keys" simply can't compete with the unexpurgated sexual signifying that remains one of hardcore rap's most cherished badges of transgression.

These are extremes, of course, and most southern soul-blues artists manage to find a balance that allows them to sustain viable, if not quite lucrative, "beneath-the-radar" recording and performing careers for relatively diverse audiences. Nonetheless, it's often the extremes that set the tone. Just as rap continues to draw the wrath of moralists who cite gangsta nihilism as representative of the entire genre and just as both blues and country music have been stereotyped through the years as "depressing" or "unsophisticated," southern soul finds itself damned by detractors (including a lot of radio programmers) who point to these very extremes when they accuse it of being either irrelevant or without substance, unable to decide whether it wants to come off like a nostalgia act or a circle-jerk.

T. K. Soul, born Terence Kimble in Winnfield, Louisiana in 1964, "grew up watching everything from *Hee Haw* on TV to Elvis to Michael Jackson to James Brown to Frank Sinatra, you name it," as he told Dylann DeAnna's *Soul Blues* Web site in 2007.[2] He gravitated to R & B pretty early on. After a stint with a Shreveport, Louisiana–based group called Under

21 (who later changed their name to Profyle and scored in 2000 with the No. 1 hit "Liar" on Motown), he hooked up with the R & B/hip-hop aggregation H-Town before landing his first major southern soul gig as Willie Clayton's keyboardist in the 1990s. After writing and producing several important hits for Clayton, he launched his own Soulful Records label in the early 2000s, and he's been on his own ever since. His style is still developing; unlike some, he seems determined to grow and change with every recording, rather than rely on trademarks that might devolve into clichés. But a look at his recording career—where he's come from and where he seems to be headed—can provide tantalizing glimpses of how southern soul might confront some of the dilemmas that have hindered it

Figure 29. T. K. Soul, 2010 Chicago Blues Festival. Photo by Jim O'Neal, BluEso-terica archives.

so far, simply by playing to its strengths: emotional honesty, groove-rich danceability, and vivid lyric storytelling.

"Bad Boy" Grown with Stories to Tell: The Trajectory of T. K. Soul

One Woman Man, T. K. Soul's 2002 debut, was in many ways a typical freshman effort. It consisted mostly of wafting ballads, hothouse celebrations of eros (with the obligatory shout-outs to oral sex), funk-flavored odes to all-night juking, and rakish tales of hoochified high jinks. "She's Bad," the opening track, was a stylistic pastiche; a savvy listener could ferret out elements of everything from "Billie Jean"/"Bad"–era Michael Jackson to Stan Mosley's "Anybody Seen My Boo" swirling around in it, and the mix was so dense it was almost claustrophobic. Despite the punchy production and the quivering sensuality of T. K.'s voice, it sounded like an effort to be all things to all people rather than carve out a distinct identity. But this was a case of too much ambition, not too little, the kind of thing that usually bodes well even if it doesn't entirely succeed the first time. "Meet Me at the Spot," an exuberant, bass-heavy dance outing, sounded more focused and made some encouraging noise on southern soul radio, but it did little to distinguish T. K. from any of southern soul's other hard-partying dance floor lotharios.

Tucked in among the boilerplate, though, was a gem: "Straight No Chaser," which T. K. delivered in his most emotionally wracked croon, admonished "wanna-be players" to straighten out and stop mistreating women, both for the sake of the women themselves and to give some respite to good men who end up paying for their nefarious brothers' sins. The song was set to a ballad tempo, but hard-jabbing beats undergirded the tenderness with anger. The mature perspective implied in "Straight No Chaser" (as well as "My Life," a school-of-hard-knocks autobiographical ballad) was an encouraging sign that T. K. Soul had more substantial things on his mind than seducing hoochies and establishing his "playa" credentials.

By his next CD, 2003's *The Bad Boy of Southern Soul,* T. K. was already showing signs of fulfilling that promise. Despite his smooth tenor voice and that anomalous "Bad Boy" tag, he sounded increasingly determined to focus on adult-sounding themes, even as he upped his production values to approximate mainstream R & B standards. After setting the party mood with the dance anthem "Shake It Down," he fired down the jets while firing up the passion on ballads like "My Kind of Girl," which revisited the vintage soul theme of a man overwhelmed by his pride in the woman he loves ("beautiful lady, a shining star"), and "Rain," complete with requisite sound effects, which admonished lovers to "try to stay together" in the face of temptation and conflict.

From the beginning, T. K. had mostly eschewed both dirty-joke silliness and macho posing; he was more likely to sing about being concerned about his woman's feelings than strut his prowess. Even when promising to please her orally on "All the Man You Need," from his first CD, he'd sounded more like a generous lover than a self-consciously "freaky" playa. "A Little Love," from *Bad Boy,* found him welcoming his lady home and asking how things had gone at work—a disarmingly tender slice-of-life moment—before inviting her into his arms for an evening of lovemaking. To keep things from getting too precious, he set the song to a bouncy, good-time party beat.

Although on purely musical terms there was little on *Bad Boy* that even the most eclectic-minded listener might call "blues," he often invoked blueslike sentiments. "Sprung" portrayed a man in thrall to a woman's erotic power, playfully insinuating that she must have enlisted supernatural assistance in her efforts. "Where Jody Stay" found T. K. on the trail of the archetypal blues trickster and wife stealer; in "Bedroom Conversations," he admonished his woman to stop bragging about their love life because her girlfriends were getting curious, and he was going to have to satisfy them if things didn't cool down. "She's a Player" warned against succumbing to the blandishments of a street-tough seductress, but it also revealed an undercurrent of compassion, or at least an understanding of her plight—"love won't pay no bills, and sex won't feed the children." Through everything, the grooves were infectious, the ambience techno-modernist but roomy and inviting, and the trigger-drum beats propulsive.

In 2004, T. K. released *Now Playing Love Games,* which most critics consider his actual breakout CD. The opening track, "Cheating and Lying," set the tone: T. K. sang his story of cuckoldry and betrayal with supple melodicism and a hip-hop–flavored rhythmic impetus, supported by a club-friendly dance-track backing. There was a swaggering insouciance to his delivery that bespoke both the bluesman's fatalism and the hip-hopper's defiance, leavened by the soul man's redemptive hope wrought from the vicissitudes of everyday life. On closer listening, though, a darker theme revealed itself: a women swore on the lives of her mother and her children that she wasn't cheating, only to be caught in her lies.

That coupling of crisp production and fearless lyric storytelling characterized the entire set. "Real Love Is Calling," a ballad toughened by leather-fisted beats, featured guest vocalist Myra K. trading anguished meditations with T. K. on the dissolution of a longtime love affair—again, a resolutely adult treatment of a theme too often couched in teen-angst platitudes. "If You Don't Want Me" was shot through with an almost desperate sense of longing as the singer begged his woman to either declare herself or set him free.

"You Ring My Bell," despite its novelty-sounding title (and its obvious reference to the famous Anita Ward disco hit) again found T. K. pledging his devotion in a voice rent with both passion and vulnerability; the leavening touches (a languorous funk bass line, T. K.'s double-tracked vocals crooning "ding, dong, ding, dong" behind his lead singing) served to enrich the mood rather than compromise it. In "Let's Stay Home Tonight"—taken at ballad tempo but ramped to a nearly ominous intensity by its lurking, minor-key synth groove—he sounded on the verge of imploding under the pressure of his own erotic hunger, but he assured his lover that he was "in no hurry," that he wanted to "cuddle up" and "watch a DVD on my little TV" as well as spend the night "makin' sweet love," and that "I don't need no special occasion just to show you my love / for all that you do for me, it's the least I can do." Few others this side of Latimore could have crafted so sly and irresistible a seduction.

Perhaps the most appealing thing about *Love Games,* though, was T. K.'s ability to embrace the ironic playfulness of modern pop without falling prey to the sneering cynicism that often accompanies it. His pose was closer to blues irony, which takes life seriously but then dares to laugh (or at least dance) in its face: ironic engagement rather than ironic detachment. The twelve-bar blues "Single Man" found him manfully refusing to "jump back" into love after surviving a scarring relationship, but, like the bluesman he is, he still gets lonely sometimes, so he'll compromise, at least for a night, "'cause I still like to get it on." "Jodette," with its nods to James Brown's trailblazing on-the-one funk arrangements, threw down the gauntlet to cheating women who fall for "Jody's" charms by unleashing Jody's seductive female counterpart.

T. K.'s sweet double-tracked vocal harmonies helped elevate "I Want You (For Christmas)" above run-of-the-mill holiday fare, and that love-wracked quaver of his, as well as the haunted vulnerability that ran through the lyrics ("Somebody gonna be crying this Christmas / I hope that it's not gonna be me "), heightened the song's appeal. "We Be Sliding," the obligatory dance-floor workout, was arguably the most effective of its kind that

T. K. had yet concocted, full of witty electronic tweaks and pushed by a throbbing drums/bass mix. Overall, *Love Games* erased any doubts about T. K. Soul as a rising star. Two years after its release, both "Cheating and Lying" and "You Ring My Bell" were still in rotation on radio playlists, indicating that T. K. had become a member of the honored brotherhood of southern soul artists whose hits have legs strong enough to stay in the game for years.[3]

By this time, T. K. had embraced the "Bad Boy" persona so fully that he was kicking off his shows by coming onto the stage draped in a hooded boxing robe with "Undisputed Bad Boy of Southern Soul" emblazoned across the back. He posed in that robe for the front cover of *Undisputed,* his next CD; to push the analogy further, the disc's twelve songs were listed as "rounds," not "tracks," on the cover notes. Musically, there was again a noticeable shift in style and emphasis from T. K.'s previous outings, but his core approach remained steadfast.

The production on *Undisputed* made it clear that T. K. was casting a wider net. On several songs, his vocals were distorted by a talk-box, an effect, long common in R & B and hip-hop, that can be either appealingly surreal or annoyingly cartoonish, depending on the context. Most notable in this regard was "Round Six" in the set list, "Love Make U Do Thangs." It was a slow-jam ballad in which T. K. again assumed the role of a streetwise savant abrim with life lessons ("Ain't it funny how love takes control of you / Love will make you do things that you said you'd never do . . . You remember the time she cut your tires / You were at your baby mama's house, she keyed your ride"). Those tweaked vocals, though, came close to diluting his meaning; it's hard to heed a message when the messenger makes himself sound so silly.

At the other extreme was "Party Like Back in the Day," T. K.'s entry in the grown folks' nostalgia sweepstakes (and more or less a reprise of "Party Like We Used to Do," which he'd earlier penned for Willie Clayton). It was among the disc's most successful cuts, at least in terms of radio play. But its title, most of its lyrics, and its bouncy, midtempo lope reflected the Hobson's choice mentioned earlier: a tune that invokes the Electric Slide as a nostalgic artifact and portrays juking as an activity for people living in the past is not likely to catapult either its singer or his genre into the R & B mainstream. It seemed, at this juncture, as if T. K. was still struggling with one of the main contradictions affecting southern soul-blues as a whole.

Paired with "Party" on the single T. K. released, though, was "It Ain't Cheatin Til U Get Caught," which also enjoyed radio success. This song, despite its anachronistic twelve-bar blues structure, indicated that T. K. was beginning to rectify some of those contradictions. In his most sandpapery timbre, he sang of a couple, each of whom had been cheating on the other, neither of whom knew what the other was doing, and both of whom were ridden by guilt and thinking of coming clean. His advice was to keep mum because "you didn't get caught," so it might as well never have happened—returning to that venerable trope of "truth" being manifest only when experienced firsthand—thus salving their marriage and (presumably) their consciences. It was a story as old as the blues: we live in a fallen world, sin is inevitable, so the best we can do is live and groove with it. But at its heart, this was a morality play rather than a street tale of pimps and hoochies; these were plain-living people with families and homes, struggling to do the right thing in the face of temptation, torn between their fallibility and their need to preserve what they cherished most in their lives.

Addressing the same theme with a bit more subtlety was "You're So Special." Its spiky cadence and harsh ambience made the love sound hard-won and the singer toughened by adversity yet brave enough to open his heart; the devotion conveyed was so intense that when we finally learned that the singer's lady was actually tied down to another "sorry man," it seemed almost beside the point. This wasn't a casual backdoor fling but a genuine love affair, the kind of thing that probably led to those heart-tearing breakups portrayed in "Real Love Is Calling" on *Love Games*.

Undisputed also included a pair of seduction songs in which the protagonist was almost chivalrous in his determination not to force the issue. "What does it take to be with you?" T. K. pled in "What Does It Take," a retro-sounding slow jam ballad. "Let's have a conversation . . . let's go out on a date." "Try Me," with synthesized horns and strings washing through the mix, found the singer trying to reassure a reluctant paramour who insisted that she had "her morals" and didn't want to "end up in sorrow." He promised to be "a gentleman" and just "hold her tight" if that's what she wanted, even though he sounded almost choked with desire. "You're afraid to trust me," he sang, "but I gotta draw the line . . . try me tonight . . . this ain't no one-night stand." It was a message that a lot of women in the southern soul world apparently wanted to hear; although it was a little slower out of the gate than "Party Like Back in the Day" and "It Ain't Cheatin Til U Get Caught," "Try Me" also became a radio hit.

The Evolution of Soul, which was issued about two years after *Undisputed*, moved T. K. in yet another direction—or, more accurately, expanded the stylistic scope he'd already established. Several songs from *Evolution* made some encouraging noise, but the big news was "Zydeco Bounce," which eventually made such an impact that it attracted the attention of Universal, who signed their distribution agreement with T. K. and Soulful Records in late 2011.

"It [became] the hottest line dance besides [V.I.C.'s] 'Wobble' dance," Kim Cole asserted. "I've been pulling stuff off of YouTube; people from Connecticut and Las Vegas, Sacramento, that's a national song. Most [radio] people, the southern soul people, felt like 'Zydeco Bounce' didn't fit their format; they wouldn't play it. So it went to the streets, and then the demand came for radio." The reaction to the CD overall, she adds, "has been amazing. It has just been amazing."[4]

"Zydeco Bounce" lived up to its hype; despite the obligatory wheezing accordion, it was a fully contemporary R & B dance number, mixed to sound like a series of mashed-up samples yet coherent and propulsive throughout. T. K.'s shout-outs to southern culture and identity ("Everywhere I go, the people from coast to coast / When they hear I'm from the dirty south, they want to know what it's all about . . . southern soul meets zydeco") sounded like both crafty name-branding and expressions of pride.

Another dance number, the more conventionally styled "Soul Clap," was originally pegged as the potential hit, but for some reason disc jockeys didn't pick up on it. The most provocative club song, though, was "They Wanna Party," which T. K. sang from the point of view of the artist whose music was fueling the festivities (it was a little unclear whether he was performing or visiting a nightclub where the DJ was playing his records). The song brought a resigned knowingness to a theme that's almost always presented with insistent (and often preening) ebullience. "I be up in the club, they be showin' me love," he sang in a voice that sounded both weary and toughened by cynicism. "In the VIP where they can't see me / but they wanna dance with me, and they wanna party with me." The song's relentless, mechanical repetition seemed to reflect the grind the singer had to endure, night after night, to rev up endless parties to make a living: the loneliness of the long-distance musical road man laid bare. "The Days of My Life" was an even harsher assessment of the southern soul man's life; rapping out the lyrics in his streetsiest bark as the rhythm track popped and sputtered behind him, T.K revisited the "crabs-in-a-bucket" theme voiced by so many of his contemporaries, portraying himself as a beleaguered aspirant fighting off haters and jealousy at every turn ("I take ten steps up, they try to bring me ten steps back") but determined to prevail.

A similar resignation, but without the bitterness, colored "You Got to Cheat," a melancholy ballad in which a young man asked an older married woman for advice on keeping his own marriage intact, only to have her answer, "I hate to tell ya, but you asked me . . . you got to cheat, that's just how it is." By the end of the song, the man's wife was getting the same advice from "an old married man," and they'd both apparently accepted the inevitable and gone on with their marriage, hoping for the best. Here, seeking illicit pleasure was portrayed as more of a burden than a thrill, the price to pay for keeping the real thing alive, once again melding the hard-eyed fatalism of the blues with deep-soul determination to find grace in a human condition that's imperfect and flawed.

Elsewhere, though, T. K. cultivated his image as a vulnerable warrior of the heart. "Baby I Love You," which combined sweet doo-wop harmonies with the lushness of Philly pop-soul, included a welcome throwback to the days when love between a black man and a black woman could signify something greater and more powerful ("the color of your skin / and the beauty's all within"). "That's How I Feel," like the best of its deep-soul predecessors, was virtually ageless; if the relaxed ambience and sonic textures seemed geared toward "grown folks," the lyrics portrayed an emotional callowness ("I got this thing for you, for you and only you / It's going straight from my heart") that could just as easily fit an adolescent sensibility.

When the story lines got more complicated, the music and the message nonetheless maintained their directness. "She Told on Herself" found the protagonist eavesdropping on his wife's self-incriminating phone conversation ("I heard her say, 'Girl, I gotta get away with another man'"). Once again, though, a vignette of treachery and betrayal was grafted onto a bouncy, pop-brightened framework—ironic, perhaps, but also tailor-made for dancing sorrows away. "Rehab" cut deeper; the analogy of love as an addiction may be a cliché, but here T. K. showed the pop craftsman's genius for imbuing a well-worn conceit with new potency. The melody, with its ascending and descending passages and minor-key colorations, followed the emotional contour of the song's story line, both reflecting and intensifying its meaning; the instrumentation was sparse—at times, in fact, almost acoustic-sounding by modern R & B standards—inviting, rather than bludgeoning, the listener into the song's emotional landscape.

Probably the most unabashedly romantic outing T. K. has ever undertaken, though, is "The Greatest Emotion," a stand-alone single available as a download on his Web site. It would be easy to write off the song's lyrics as bromides ("Gentle as a baby, treat her like a lady"), but he delivers them with such a yearning ache that they become impossible to dismiss; he sounds as if he's learned these lessons the hard way and is now almost overcome by the very emotions he's come to cherish. The production envelops us in a thickness both comforting and claustrophobic, a sanctuary that threatens to become smothering, not unlike romantic infatuation itself.

Figure 30. Bad Boy: T. K. Soul, 2010 Chicago Blues Festival. Photo by Jim O'Neal, BluEsoterica archives.

"Long as I Got a Toehold"

The persona T. K. Soul has created thus far in his career is that of a survivor, world-tested but still young at heart, capable of belligerence and
egoism when called upon but redeemed by a determination to embrace
higher values—a determination that's constantly challenged and which he
doesn't always honor but which remains his lodestone and guiding light.
The vulnerability he conveys with his vocal quivers and occasional choked
gasps bespeaks courage rather than weakness, and when he does confess
to weakness (most notably in his cheating songs), it's as a tragedian, not
as a cynic. He seldom exults in a feeling or a belief without recognizing its
cost; his love songs, even borderline-bathetic effusions like "The Greatest Emotion," are celebrations of riches gained through struggle, all the
more valuable for being hard-won. His boyish tenor creates tension with
the complex emotional textures his lyrics call forth; this tension both
reflects and deepens the paradoxes inherent in his best story lines, and it
exemplifies the direction that southern soul-blues can take to expand its
thematic scope, its impact, and its audience.

The problems southern soul faces in attempting to summon a voice that
can encompass both youthful swagger and "grown folks" knowingness
reflect pressures and contradictions that weigh on American society as a
whole, especially in the working-class communities that remain the source
of the music's core fan base. These pressures and contradictions are not
new. In *Manchild in the Promised Land*, Claude Brown's autobiographical
novel about growing up in Harlem, he quoted a boyhood friend:

> Man, Sonny, they ain't got no kids in Harlem. I ain't never seen any.
> I've seen some real small people actin' like kids. They were too small
> to be grown, and they might've looked like kids, but they don't have
> any kids in Harlem, because nobody has time for a childhood. Man,
> do you ever remember bein' a kid? Not me. Shit, kids are happy, kids
> laugh, kids are secure. They ain't scared-a nothin'. You ever been a kid,
> Sonny? Damn, you lucky. I ain't never been a kid, man. I don't ever
> remember bein' happy and not scared. I don't know what happened,
> man, but I think I missed out on that childhood thing, because I don't
> ever recall bein' a kid.[5]

As in Harlem in the 1950s and '60s, so in cities, towns, and rural ham-
lets across America now. Young men and women—especially, but by no
means only, young men and women of color—face being cheated out of
their childhoods and their youths, thrust into perils and life situations that

should, by any reasonable standards, be the province and responsibility of adults. And then, without having had a true childhood to grow out of, they may find it impossible to attain or even imagine an adulthood to grow into (Brown's narrator, like many of today's lost souls in the 'hood, was a street hustler approaching middle age bereft of any skills or perspectives that might help him attain a better life).

This is the young man's and young woman's blues of today: facing the tests and dangers of adulthood while still wrestling with the uncertainties, desires, and tensions of youth. It's also the grown folks' blues, negotiating through a life in which those uncertainties continue to loom and "only the strong survive" long enough—and learn enough—to overcome them. With his knack for grafting mature-sounding lyrics onto danceable backing tracks and delivering them in a voice that sounds simultaneously callow and seasoned, an artist like T. K. Soul has it in him to mine this lode of emotion and truth in his music.

He doesn't have to forsake the sexual heat of his boudoir anthems, the longing that suffuses ballads like "Rehab" and "If You Don't Want Me," or the party-all-night exuberance of his paeans to juking and good times. All he needs to do is delve more deeply and fearlessly into terrain he has already mined in fare such as "Straight No Chaser" (a warning to boys and men not to fall prey to misguided macho), "A Little Love" and "The Greatest Emotion" (a grown man's celebrations of love earned and done right), "My Life" (a meditation on survival, strength, and family), and even street-savvy caveats like "She's a Player" and "Love Make U Do Thangs," songs that are emotionally rich, cast in a contemporary setting, and resonant with the wisdom and compassion of the kind that marks their protagonist as capable of facing the challenge of growing from a man-child into a man in a world all too ready to cut him down before his time. Even the cheating songs fit this theme; most portray men and women caught in the grip of their own frailties, struggling to maintain their equilibrium as they reel through the temptations and pitfalls of a fallen world.

It's this kind of perspective—at once burdened and optimistic, resilient enough to admit weakness, and courageous enough to pass through darkness in order to apprehend the light—that has informed and enriched the best blues, soul, and gospel throughout these musics' intertwined history. It's what can help southern soul-blues and its most gifted purveyors earn their rightful place in today's pop music pantheon.

Coda: "Listen to the Voices"

By singling out T. K. Soul for this discussion, I have not meant to imply that he alone represents "The Future" of southern soul. Quite a few artists—Sir Charles Jones, Mr. Sam, Floyd Taylor, Omar Cunningham, and both Ms. Jody and Sweet Angel at their best, just for starters—share many if not all the gifts I've identified as among T. K.'s strongest. Mr. Sam's "12 Steps for Cheaters" song cycle, Sir Charles's "I'll Never Make a Promise," and neofeminist throw-downs like Jody's "I'm Keepin' It Real" and Angel's "I'm Movin' Up" are only a few other examples of songs that reflect the sensibility suggested here. Meanwhile, the tales of stolen love, heartbreak, and erotic gamesmanship fuse vintage blues grit and irreverence with an up-to-date R & B thrust. And when the production is right (as on the 2010 Floyd Taylor/Simeo concoction "I'm 'Bout It 'Bout It" on CDS), the groove remains as infectious as ever.

The time, to paraphrase the Chambers Brothers, has come again today. With imagination, the right decisions, and a little luck, southern soul-blues has the potential to fill a niche in the popular music marketplace not unlike it did in the early 1980s, but on a larger scale. A lot of today's younger listeners, contrary to stereotype, have "big ears," as the saying goes; it's not uncommon to see many of the same faces at rap, roots R & B, indie rock, and jazz shows. Thanks to sampling, even hard-core hip-hoppers are familiar with horn lines, beats, and snippets of vocals from blues, deep soul, and vintage R & B; now more than ever, people know where the music comes from. "I'll go to the Essence Festival or something," Sir Charles Jones relates, "and Mary J. Blige is there, or a lot of rappers, and these guys are actually telling me how much they love to be romantic with their females off my music. They copy a lot off our forefathers—that's what we call them—[and] they really admire and look up to us, and some of them don't understand why we're not considered, promoted bigger, as big as we perceive ourselves to be."[6]

Also perhaps more than ever, a lot of people are looking for something to complement, if not necessarily replace, the hard-edged, cynical sounds and spirit of so much mainstream R & B and pop music.[7] It's not only right-wing cranks or the spiritual descendants of Tipper Gore who are weary of nihilism on the one hand and dumbed-down glitz on the other (it's no accident that rappers are using southern soul, rather than their own misogynistic paeans to street sex, to set the mood when it's time to "be romantic with their females"). Musically literate, savvy listeners, tired of being condescended to by marketers and quick-money one-shots, are again open to, if not actively searching for, something akin to what their older brothers and sisters discovered when soul-blues first made its mark: music that can be sexy and up-to-date, address contemporary concerns in contemporary language, yet also be articulate, mature, and respectful of its audience's intelligence.

The good news is that what they're looking for is already here—"just a musical note away."

Figure 31. Stan Mosley, 2005 Chicago Blues Festival. Photo by Gene Tomko.

Part V

Soul Stew Revisited

In this section, we'll have a brief look at some of the figures who have contributed and continue to contribute to the development of southern soul-blues. In most cases, I haven't recommended specific recordings; representative and often definitive samples of these artists' music can be found on current CDs and/or anthologies. For further information on these and other important figures in the rapidly changing southern soul-blues pantheon, I recommend consulting the Web sites of the major labels: Malaco (http://www.malaco.com) Ecko (http://www.eckorecords .com), and CDS (http://www.cdsrecords.com). I also suggest delving into the informative (and sometimes provocative) writings of "Blues Critic" (a.k.a. Dylann DeAnna, now head of CDS but still objective and focused in his online writings) at the Web site http://www.soulbluesmusic.com and critic/commentator Daddy B. Nice at http://www.southernsoulrnb .com. *Soul Express Online* (http://www.soulexpress.net/index.htm), *CD Baby* (http://www.cdbaby.com//), and *AllMusic* (http://www.allmusic.com/) are also excellent sources for learning about and acquiring both current and historical recordings by southern soul-blues artists. *Living Blues* and *Juke Blues* magazines regularly review southern soul-blues CDs and often profile the genre's major artists in their articles. And, of course, many artists and smaller labels have Web sites and home pages of their own.

12 Leading Lights

When discussing singers and musicians, it's always risky to apply terms such as *major*; the relative importance of a given artist may have as much to do with the evaluator's tastes as with any objective standards. Nonetheless, for this section I have selected artists (several from earlier eras) whom I consider especially significant in terms of their influence on the development and ongoing viability of southern soul-blues. Obviously, commercial success is part, but not all, of the consideration. Most of the individuals profiled here have been among the genre's most successful recording artists (whether in the southern soul market or the "mainstream" R & B market); those who are still performing are usually either headliners or near the top of the bill. Those who have retired or passed on are acknowledged as important, and in many cases pivotal, figures in the music's development.

Bobby "Blue" Bland

Though usually categorized as a bluesman, Bobby Bland was actually singing "soul-blues" decades before the term was ever imagined. Bland's first hit, the loping twelve-bar "Farther up the Road," predated Sam Cooke's "You Send Me" by about two months in 1957. The following year, Bland virtually defined the blues (or soul-blues) ballad with "Little Boy Blue," which built from intimacy to full-gospel fervor over the course of less than three minutes and codified the soul man's persona as a wounded and fallible man of love, exuding both passion and vulnerability as he pleaded, screamed, and importuned his lady for mercy.

Aside from the occasional house-rocker like 1961's "Turn on Your Love Light," Bland has pretty much stayed with that approach ever since, charting over sixty times in the process. Although through the years his voice has thickened and become less supple (and his gospel "squall" become more intrusive), his sound has also become more intimate, and he's further honed his gifts as a stylist (e.g., 1985's "Members Only"). Today he appears on shows with soul-blues artists decades younger, to the adulation of fans young and old and the respect, if not reverence, of virtually everyone on the bill.

Shirley Brown

Shirley Brown's multioctave range and her genius at shading her vocal timbre to express both subtleties and extremes of emotion mark her as one of soul's most gifted vocalists. Born in West Memphis, Arkansas, in 1947, she grew up in St. Louis, where she crossed over from gospel to R & B in her teens. She cut a few sides under the auspices of noted St. Louis saxophonist Oliver Sain; the story of how Albert King then introduced her to Stax, and how her first recording there, "Woman to Woman," was both an instant classic and virtually the label's swan song, is related earlier in this book. After Stax folded, she soldiered on, occasionally charting but never realizing the commercial success she'd hoped for and deserved.

Shirley signed with Malaco in 1989, and she's been a southern soul mainstay ever since; her 2004 recording of Frederick Knight's "(I've Got to) Sleep with One Eye Open" became a modern standard virtually overnight. Feisty and untamable both on stage and off, she remains one of the music's most galvanizing presences; her vocal gifts, although she may use them a bit more sparingly these days, are virtually undiminished. As she showed at J. Blackfoot's funeral in December 2011, when the spirit hits she can still ascend into realms of glory that few, if any, of her contemporaries can aspire to.

Clarence Carter

In his prime, Clarence Carter boasted one of the most sexually charged voices in soul or blues, all the more so because he never had to gasp, pant, or otherwise use histrionics to get his point across. (He did, however, perfect a lascivious chuckle that sounded as if it had been brewed in a cauldron of pot likker, rotgut whiskey, and Spanish fly.) On guitar, he combined fatback soul fretwork with stinging, bluesy leads.

Blind from birth, Carter attended Alabama State College and began to record in the mid-1960s. His first Top Ten hit was "Slip Away" in 1968. In 1970, he released "Patches," a lachrymose tale of a hardscrabble rural childhood that nonetheless invoked some of soul music's most deeply held values. His calling card, though, will always be "Strokin," which was in his repertoire by the mid-1980s but didn't get officially released until Ichiban included it on a 1989 sampler called *Nasty Blues* (Carter later put it on a couple of his own albums). He followed it up with a series of even more graphic boudoir vignettes that helped solidify his status as southern soul-blues' most beloved dirty old man. Although he's become somewhat frail in recent years, he continues to tour, reprising his hits (and his chuckle) to the delight of longtime admirers and newcomers alike.

Otis Clay

Otis Clay never quite attained superstar status, but among aficionados he's as revered as anyone in soul. In his early years, Clay sang with several notable gospel groups, including the legendary Sensational Nightingales; after crossing over in the 1960s, he charted moderately for both One-derful and Cotillion before moving to Hi, where he succeeded with "Trying to Live My Life without You" and the gospel-tinged "If I Could Reach Out." His last chart hit was 1977's "All Because of Your Love" (on Kayvette); since then he's expanded his international reputation as a house-wrecking live performer while appearing on various independent labels, including his own Echo imprint (not to be confused with Ecko in Memphis, Tennessee); his covers of standards like O. V. Wright's "A Nickel and a Nail" are modern classics.

Clay has also recorded several spiritual albums; in 2007, he garnered a Grammy nomination for the Joe South–penned title track from his inspirational CD *Walk a Mile in My Shoes*. But he's not about to give up the

Figure 32. Otis Clay, 2007 Pocono Blues Festival, Lake Harmony, Pennsylvania. Photo by Gene Tomko.

show lounge for the pulpit. In 2011, he joined St. Louis songstress Uvee Hayes on the cheating song "Steal Away to the Hideaway," demonstrating that even the godliest soul man can strut his rakish side as long as he does it with class and style.

Tyrone Davis

Mentored by Chicago soul singer Harold Burrage, Tyrone Davis released a few singles on the Four Brothers label (as "Tyrone [the] Wonder Boy") in the mid-1960s, but his first national hit was 1968's "Can I Change My Mind" on Dakar, an up-tempo ballad that established his musical persona as a wayward lover pleading for forgiveness. Davis ended up with over forty chart hits between 1968 and 1988, and along the way he played an important role in defining 1970s- and 1980s-era soul music as well as what came to be known as southern soul-blues. His voice was supple and mellow, tinged with vulnerability—perfect for the image many of his songs cast and ideal in a field where women are the primary audience.

Unlike many of his contemporaries, Davis was able to adapt to the changing tastes of the disco and postdisco eras without losing much soulfulness. His stints in the 1990s with Ichiban and Malaco then solidified his stardom on the burgeoning southern soul circuit. He never lost that status; such latter-day outings as "Kiss You" (2000), "Who's Been Rockin'" (2002), and "Bangin' the Headboard" (2003) are still among his most beloved. To many southern soul devotees, Davis, who died in 2005, is second only to Johnnie Taylor in the music's pantheon of immortals.

Theodis Ealey

Theodis Ealey was a forty-year veteran by the time "Stand Up in It" made him a star. Born in Natchez, Mississippi, in 1947, he got his start playing locally in bands with his brothers YZ and Melwin. He cut a few singles on his own IFGAM ("I Feel Good About Myself") label in the 1980s, and he released four LPs on Ichiban between 1991 and 1998. In 2003, he put out "Stand Up in It" on IFGAM, which not only established him as a soul-blues force but hit No. 1 on *Billboard*'s national R & B and Hip-Hop singles sales charts the following year.

"Stand Up in It" was so formidable that Ealey couldn't concoct an equally strong follow-up; as a result, although a few of his subsequent releases have made some decent regional noise, he's been hovering closer to Soul Limbo than Soul Heaven ever since. Still, he continues to tour, strutting his African American good-ol'-boy persona—gambler hats, unreconstructed Mississippi drawl, country-fried blues guitar licks—and spicing up his act with cornball props like the miniature mechanical dogs he sets to humping his mic stands during his finale. But even if his eventual fate is to be relegated to something like "one-hit wonder" status, that one hit has been enough to earn Theodis Ealey a permanent spot in the soul-blues firmament.

Z. Z. Hill

Z. Z. Hill was no overnight sensation, no matter how unexpectedly "Down Home Blues" might have changed the world in the early 1980s. Born in Naples, Texas, in 1935, he released his first sides locally in the mid-1960s. His first chart hit was "You Were Wrong" (on his brother Matt's M. H. label) in 1964; he didn't strike pay dirt again until 1971's "Don't Make Me Pay for His Mistakes" (on the Hill imprint, also owned by Matt) and "I Need Someone (to Love Me)" (Kent).

All told, he charted fourteen times before he signed with Malaco in 1980. In 1981 he released "Down Home Blues" (it became a hit the following year); his follow-ups—"Cheatin' in the Next Room," "Someone Else Is Steppin' In," "Right Arm for Your Love," "Everybody Knows About My Good Thing," "Shade Tree Mechanic," and others—with Hill's gristle-and-fatback vocals and deep-pocket rhythmic sense augmented by the roomy production and skintight arrangements Malaco provided him, further codified the southern soul-blues aesthetic. In Z. Z. Hill's music, you can hear the precise nexus where blues and soul tradition met soul-blues innovation—a point of encounter as thrilling to experience now as it was then. He suffered a heart attack and died in Dallas in 1984.

Millie Jackson

For all her reputation as a provocateur, Millie Jackson has always been more than just a potty mouth; even at her most acerbic and profane, she's a storyteller capable of both tearing and melting the heart, often over the course of a single song. Along with Isaac Hayes, she was instrumental in introducing the "concept album" to the R & B market; her mid-1970s LPs *Caught Up* and *Still Caught Up* were cinematic, multisong vignettes of betrayed relationships and stolen love (sung from the points of view of both the "other woman" and the girlfriend/wife being cuckolded). Among her highlights from that period were her eleven-plus-minute tour de force on "(If Loving You Is Wrong) I Don't Want to Be Right" and her torrid reading of Merle Haggard's "If You're Not Back in Love by Monday."[1]

All told, Millie charted thirty-nine times between 1971 and 1988. For years, she hosted a daily afternoon talk show on radio station KKDA in Dallas, and she still tours fairly consistently. Although she loathes terms like *soul-blues* and *southern soul* (she's an R & B singer, she insists), along with Denise LaSalle and Shirley Brown she is recognized almost universally as a founding mother of the genre.

Etta James

Etta James's secular music career kicked off in high gear in 1955, when she and her co-singers in a trio called the Peaches debuted with "Roll with Me Henry" (on Modern), her sassy riposte to Hank Ballard's 1954 hit "Work with Me Annie." Renamed "The Wallflower," "Henry" hit No. 1 on the R & B charts and stayed there for four weeks.

Etta's career really took off, though, after she joined Chess Records in 1960. Over the next sixteen years, she landed twenty-seven hits for the label and its various subsidiaries, showcasing her ability to segue from bluesy rawness to string-sweetened effulgence while never losing her church-honed spiritual intensity (it's said that her in-studio rendition of "I'd Rather Go Blind" moved Leonard Chess to tears). Although she'd eventually delve into genres as diverse as jazz and country, she never abandoned either her gospel or her blues roots, and her life story of struggle and victory has become a modern-day parable of soul survival. In her later years, she garnered several Grammys, and "At Last," her classic ballad from 1961, became a born-again pop standard after Beyoncé sang it (as Etta) in the 2008 movie *Cadillac Records*. Although she resisted being categorized, it's not stretching things to say that Etta James was (and is) the Queen Mother of Soul-Blues. She passed away in early 2012.

Little Willie John

No less an authority than James Brown praised Little Willie John as "a soul singer before anyone thought to call it that," whose recordings could "beat what any dictionary tell you about soul."[2]

Born in 1937, John was a prodigy; he signed with Syd Nathan's Detroit-based King label in 1955 and hit immediately with "All around the World" ("If I don't love you, baby / Grits ain't groceries, eggs ain't poultry / and Mona Lisa was a man"), which he followed up with "Need Your Love So Bad" in 1956. But it was "Fever," also in '56, that sealed his reputation; combining a hipster's finger-snapping insouciance with searing erotic heat, Little Willie John virtually redefined "cool" for a new generation.

His stage presence was as riveting as his recordings. Suave and elegant yet disarmingly baby-faced, the diminutive singer was in command of a remarkably mature and nuanced voice; he mined depths of passion that even house wreckers like James Brown and Jackie Wilson had trouble approximating. But he was always something of a wild child, and in 1964 he killed a man in a fight in Seattle. Convicted of manslaughter, he died in Washington State Penitentiary in 1968. He's too seldom remembered today, but his spirit can still be felt whenever and wherever soul, soul-blues, or R & B is sung.

Albert King

Albert King became a soul-blues pioneer almost by default after he signed with Stax in 1966. Born in 1923 on a plantation near Indianola, Mississippi, King taught himself drums and guitar early (being left-handed, he created his own versions of standard chords and tunings). In Gary, Indiana, in the early 1950s, he worked as Jimmy Reed's percussionist; he also recorded for the Chicago-based Parrot label. He eventually relocated to St. Louis, where he signed with Bobbin and finally hit the charts in 1961 with "Don't Throw Your Love on Me So Strong."

The St. Louis scene, with its soul-powered R & B bands led by the likes of Oliver Sain and Ike Turner, was a perfect finishing school for King. After he joined Stax, all it took was funkified comping from Booker T. & the MGs and some brawny horn arrangements, and the fully realized Albert King blues-and-soul crossover sound was complete. His voice, gruff and aggressive but underlain with tenderness, conveyed both machismo and vulnerability; his trademark reverse-action string bends and descending note clusters became among the most imitated guitar techniques in blues. When King died in 1992, he was one of the few straight-ahead blues artists equally popular among both black and white audiences.

Ronnie Lovejoy

When Ronnie Lovejoy died in 2001 from the effects of diabetes, southern soul-blues lost one of its most eloquent songwriters and vocal stylists. Born in rural Alabama in 1950, Lovejoy learned the ropes while serving as Latimore's keyboardist; he broke out on his own in the early 1990s and earned a reputation as a gifted lyric storyteller whose smoldering baritone conveyed tenderness, joy, and erotic power with equal facility. In 1999, he released *Nobody's Fault but Mine* (Avanti), which featured his all-time triumph, the rogue's anthem "Sho Wasn't Me." Tyrone Davis eventually covered the song and had a hit with it, but Lovejoy's remains the definitive version. Lovejoy never tasted that kind of triumph again, but his catalog includes several oft-covered classics—"Giving My Love to the Other Man," "Live-in Woman," "In Need of a Good Woman"—as well as others (e.g., "Nothin' Bother Me" and the achingly compassionate "My Time," both from his final CD, 2000's *Still Wasn't Me*) that deserve similar status. A legend within his field yet virtually unknown outside of it, Ronnie Lovejoy exemplifies both the glories and the conundrums of southern soul success.

McKinley Mitchell

McKinley Mitchell was a hard-soul belter of considerable talent, but he might be almost forgotten today were it not for "The End of the Rainbow," his epic parable of despair and redemption, which he released on the Malaco subsidiary Chimneyville in 1977. It only reached No. 71 (Mitchell's other chart hit, "The Town I Live In," had peaked at No. 8 in 1962), but it's become an undisputed southern soul classic; many have covered it, countless more still include it in their stage acts, but few have managed to approximate Mitchell's gristle-and-bone rawness and intensity in their readings. Mitchell, whose career began in Chicago in the early 1960s and continued until his death in 1986, maintained a steady club-based touring schedule despite his relatively meager record sales, thus helping set what's become the style for southern soul-blues careers ever since. "Rainbow," though, is his monument; whether it's his version on a jukebox or another singer's cover on stage, all it takes is beginning of the first verse—"We're running to the end of a rainbow"—for even the rowdiest juke or show lounge to fall silent, except for the angelic harmonies that begin to fill the room as the song builds to its climax.

Little Milton

In his later years, Little Milton Campbell was known as a bluesman with a soulful edge. But his influences were broad, ranging from his early blues mentors in and around Greenville, Mississippi, through country singers like Eddie Arnold to uptown-styled blues artists like Roy Brown and T-Bone Walker.

On his early recordings (for Sun, Meteor, and Bobbin), Milton sometimes seemed to be imitating the styles of other, better-known vocalists. Only after finding his own voice at Chess in the early 1960s did he blossom into full maturity. His sinewy vocals and sharp-toned guitar style—which combined T-Bone–like musical intelligence with the emotional focus Milton had honed accompanying bluesmen like Eddie Cusic in Mississippi jukes—became instantly recognizable. His later tenures at

Stax and Malaco cemented his reputation as one of his era's leading blues (later soul-blues) artists. Many of his records (e.g., "If Walls Could Talk," "Walking the Backstreets and Crying," "The Blues Is Alright," "Annie Mae's Café") have become standards.

Milton always presented his music—and himself—with dignity; he was passionate about honoring the noble heritage he believed the blues represented. His death in 2005 robbed the music of one of its proudest and most gifted ambassadors.

Marvin Sease

Marvin Sease's career is summarized in chapter 7. Once again, though, don't be fooled or put off by "Candy Licker" and its kinky progeny. Sease was a soul man in command of an emotional and thematic range both broad and deep. At least some of his versatility comes through on almost every CD he ever made, but if you want to experience him at his most soulful (i.e., relatively free of hoochie-man gimmickry), outings such as 1989's *The Real Deal* (London) and 1991's *Show Me What You Got* (Mercury) are probably the best places to start. To get a feel of how beloved he was (and still is) by his contemporaries, check out Sheba Potts-Wright's tribute, "Mr. Jody You Did Your Job," from her 2011 Ecko release *Let Your Mind Go Back*.

Scott Brothers/World Band/Platinum

Backup bands and session musicians usually don't make it onto lists like this, but the Scott Brothers and their legacy merit an exception. The Scott Brothers Band, who got their start as the doo-wop group the Masquerades, evolved into one of Chicago's most sought-after show bands in the sixties and seventies, accompanying major soul and R & B acts both locally and on the road. When bass singer Howard Scott broke free to work as a stand-up vocalist, he assembled a new group that eventually incorporated his brother Walter on guitar and became christened the Scott Brothers World Band. They eventually joined forces with the Young Scotts, who included nephews Jerome and Kenneth "Hollywood" Scott (on bass and guitar, respectively) to serve as Tyrone Davis's backup aggregation. In about 1983, when the Scott Brothers half of the contingent departed, Hollywood and the others re-christened themselves Platinum. They remained with Davis until his death in 2005. Walter's versatile guitar work has graced countless Chicago soul recording sessions through the years; now dubbed Sir Walter Scott, he continues to work with the Chi-Lites, among others, as well

Figure 33. Genius at work: Sir Walter Scott (accompanying vocalist/harmonica player Cyrus Hayes), 2009 Chicago Blues Festival. Photo by Gene Tomko.

as fronting a reconstituted World Band behind various vocalists on local shows. Hollywood is a first-call guitarist on the southern soul circuit (he also continues to lead Platinum, often accompanying Otis Clay, when he's in town); Howard still sings occasionally, and he has become an esteemed mentor to young artists. The Scotts, in their various permutations, with a track record extending back over five decades, represent one of R & B's most enduring and robust family legacies.

Johnnie Taylor

It is virtually impossible to overstate Johnnie Taylor's importance in this music. Online critic Dylann DeAnna, known as "Blues Critic," calls him the "Godfather of Southern Soul/Blues. Period."[3] Daddy B. Nice lists Taylor as his "#1 Ranked Southern Soul Artist."[4] Born in Crawfordsville, Arkansas, in 1934,[5] Taylor sang gospel in West Memphis and Kansas City before moving to Chicago, where in 1955 he joined Sam Cooke's old gospel group, the Highway QCs. In 1957, he followed Cooke's footsteps again to join the Soul Stirrers after Cooke, their erstwhile leader, made his famous crossover into secular music. Taylor recorded with the Stirrers in 1959 for SAR, the label Cooke co-founded with J. W. Alexander; five years later, he landed his first secular chart hit on the SAR affiliate label Derby. In 1966, he joined Stax and proceeded to become one of the nation's premier deep-soul artists, charting twenty-four times before leaving the doomed company in 1975. The following year, now on Columbia, he leaped aboard the disco bandwagon and came up with the biggest-selling hit of his career, "Disco Lady."

By 1984, he'd joined Malaco. "Good Love," which peaked at No. 39 in 1996, was his most successful latter-day recording, but some of his most important songs from his Malaco days (e.g., "Crazy over You," "Last Two Dollars," "Big Head Hundreds," the prophetic "Soul Heaven") never saw chart action at all. Today, though, many of them are probably better known, at least in the southern soul world, than a lot of other artists' million-sellers from those same years.

Like Marvin Sease, Taylor recorded what would eventually become his own musical obituary ("Gone On" in Sease's case, "Soul Heaven" in Taylor's), bringing an added poignancy to his story. But it's the full body of his work, spanning nearly four decades and ranging from blues testimonials like "Little Bluebird" to house wreckers like the immortal "Who's Making Love" as well as ballads such as "Crazy over You" and his other genre-defining sides on Malaco, that represents his true legacy and monument.

Little Johnny Taylor

It's unsure exactly when or why Johnny Lamont Merrett (or, possibly, Johnny Young) adopted the name Little Johnny Taylor, but it wasn't to cash in on Johnnie Taylor's fame. Little Johnny, who was probably born in Arkansas (Memphis has also been suggested) in 1943, first recorded for the Los Angeles–based Swingin' imprint in 1960 (when Johnnie Taylor was still singing gospel); in 1963, he hit No. 1 with his now-classic "Part Time Love" on Galaxy. Although he charted only twelve times between 1963 and 1974, several of his songs ("Part Time Love" itself, "Everybody Knows About My Good Thing," "It's My Fault Darling") have become modern-day blues (or soul-blues) staples.

Little Johnny's producers usually provided him with modern-sounding backing, and the ease with which he laid his keening, angst-and-irony-drenched blues vocals over their arrangements presaged the downhome/ uptown stylistic blend that Z. Z. Hill and those who followed would eventually claim as their own; he was, in fact, a major transitional figure between older blues styles and the soul-blues synthesis. Perhaps for that reason, until his death in 2002, Little Johnny was among the few no-frills bluesmen who retained a substantial African American fan base.

Mel Waiters

San Antonio native Mel Waiters was a regional journeyman when he signed with Malaco's Waldoxy subsidiary in 1997 and released "Got My Whiskey," the first in his series of party-at-the-club dance tunes that have since come to represent an entire southern soul subgenre. His "Hole in the Wall" in 1999 reached No. 24 on *Billboard*'s Hot Dance Music/Maxi-Singles Sales chart, elevating him to soul-blues stardom; subsequent entries in the series have included 2003's "Smaller the Club," 2006's "Throw Back Days," and 2010's "They Come Back." More recently, on his own Brittney imprint, titles such as "Hole in the Wall Christmas," "All I Want Is a Beat," and "Got No Curfew" show that Waiters is still pursuing his trademark themes.

But he's also capable of eloquent storytelling, as exemplified by "No Ring," a full-blown soap opera set to music (from 1993's *A Nite Out*), and "If He Don't Care" (on *Throw Back Days*, from 2006), which found him promising to save a lady from a loveless, possibly abusive relationship. It would be a shame if Waiters went down in history as merely a "one-theme wonder"; he has much more to offer than parties at the hole in the wall.

O. V. Wright

Overton Vertis Wright's raspy, emotionally fraught wail invoked the church, the uptown show lounge, and the back-alley juke with equal intensity.

Wright was already well-known in gospel when he cut "That's How Strong My Love Is" for Goldwax in 1964 (Otis Redding scored a hit with

Figure 34. O. V. Wright, Pepper's Lounge, Chicago, March 2, 1980. Photo by Jim O'Neal, BluEsoterica archives.

it the following year). Since Wright was technically still signed to Don Robey's Peacock label in Houston, Robey snatched him back and put him on his Back Beat subsidiary, where Wright proceeded to land twelve R & B chart hits over the next decade, including such classics as "You're Gonna Make Me Cry," the blues-infused courtroom drama "Eight Men, Four Women," and his down-and-outer's anthem "A Nickel and a Nail." Wright's biggest hits were produced by Willie Mitchell in Memphis, and by 1976 he'd moved to Mitchell's Hi label. His 1978 take on Jackie Moore's 1970–71 hit "Precious, Precious," although it only reached No. 50 on the charts, is now considered by many the definitive version.

O. V. Wright died in 1980, just before the soul-blues movement took off. Perhaps as a result, he's too seldom remembered as what he truly was: one of the seminal artists of the genre.

13 Soul Serenade

It's impossible to avoid a certain arbitrariness when compiling a lineup like this. For this reason, the reader should take these listings in the same spirit as he or she might take a label's sampler CD: as a taste, hopefully a tantalizing one, of the pleasures awaiting anyone exploring the southern soul-blues world for the first time as well as an affirmation of how rich the lode of talent is in this still underrecognized musical genre.

Vick Allen

Mississippi-based Vick Allen first made his name in gospel with the Canton Spirituals. Since the early 2000s, he has slowly cultivated his reputation in southern soul; his 2004–2007 stint with the Malaco subsidiary Waldoxy helped further that reputation (he also earned cred as a producer and songwriter during this period). More recently, "Forbidden Love Affair (The Preacher Song)," from his 2009 CD *Truth Be Told* (on Soul 1st), gained considerable radio play as Allen's crushed-velvet vocals, reminiscent of Sam Cooke, conveyed a bracing meld of compassion, righteous outrage, and irony (philandering preachers have long been a staple of down-home humor). Other tracks culled from *Truth Be Told*, such as "I Need Some Attention" and "If They Can Beat Me Rockin'" have helped sustain him since then, and he continues to develop his talents and his reputation via a consistent touring schedule and occasional new single releases.

Cicero Blake

For a full-length profile of Cicero Blake, see my previous book, *Chicago Blues: Portraits and Stories*. In the 1950s, Blake was a founding member of the Goldentones, a doo-wop ensemble who evolved into the now-legendary Kool Gents. His own first recordings were mostly in the buoyant Chicago "soft-soul" style; it wasn't until the mid-1970s that he struck immortality with "Dip My Dipper," a string-sweetened twelve-bar gem that in retrospect sounds almost like the voice of prophecy, foretelling the coming soul-blues insurgency. "Dipper" has remained Blake's signature song, even as he's continued to record for such imprints as Valley Vue, Ace, Mardi Gras, Hep' Me, and CDS. Despite recent health setbacks, he appears regularly at Chicago clubs—showcasing a voice that's occasionally frail but still capable of eloquent musical storytelling—where he's honored with the deferential enthusiasm due a beloved elder statesman and living legend.

O. B. Buchana

Ecko mainstay O. B. Buchana's gruff baritone sounds designed for soul baring and seduction, yet he's spent much of his career purveying fare with such self-explanatory titles as "Booty Scoot," "I'm Gonna Sleep with It in It," "Slow Lick It," and "Put Your Mouth in the South," while his more substantial offerings (ballads such as "Just Because He's Good to You," the show-biz dreamer's anthem "It's My Time") have gone all but unnoticed. It's hard to argue with success—Buchana is one of southern soul's top draws—but it's still frustrating to see a singer of his gifts selling himself (or, perhaps, being sold) short. At his best, Buchana combines country-boy ingenuousness with life-scarred emotionalism, the kind of naïf-in-Babylon pathos that's charged the best country and soul music since the beginning and the hook he could use to elevate himself and his art to a new, more satisfying level.

Barbara Carr

Barbara Carr sang with the legendary Oliver Sain Revue in St. Louis, she waxed a few sides at Chess in the 1960s, and she garnered some modest local and regional success on her own Bar-Car label in the 1980s. But she didn't attain national recognition until she hooked up with Ecko in the mid-'90s and began releasing bad-bitch-with-an-appetite throwdowns like "Footprints on the Ceiling" and "Bone Me Like You Own Me." Lyrics such as "If you can't cut the mustard / I don't want you lickin' 'round the jar" helped codify her persona as a bawdy sister capable of wielding words like a rapier to the groin. She was never happy with that image, though, and in fact her true gifts run much deeper: on her 1999 cover of Gene Chandler's "Rainbow," for example, she summoned a wracked intensity that was almost overwhelming; it's one of the all-time gems of southern soul-blues voice craft. Recently she signed with the Catfood label out of El Paso, Texas; her output for them so far combines the best of the old-school R & B/soul aesthetic (brawny horns, boogie-charged rhythms) with a modernist lyric sensibility that avoids pandering but still tackles mature themes with both bluntness and elegance.

Omar Cunningham

Omar Cunningham's churchy vocals incorporate elements borrowed from such masters as Johnnie Taylor and Willie Clayton, but he adds a youthful-sounding sensual charge. He's also an impressive lyricist; even his most predictable story lines are enriched by humor, self-deprecating irony, and emotional fervor. He can inhabit the loveable-rogue soul-bluesman's persona with unrepentant delight, but he avoids salaciousness; when pleading his case to a recalcitrant lover, he manages to be both heartrending and ironic at the same time; his slice-of-life vignettes (e.g., 2008's "The Beauty Shop") are rife with vivid imagery and witty characterizations. This ability to summon nuance and depth out of even the most well-worn scenarios and conceits sets him apart; along with his no-nonsense yet expressive singing style, it marks him as a valuable and ascendant presence in southern soul-blues.

Lee Fields

The coarse-voiced, emotionally intense Lee Fields had a minor hit in 1986 with "Stop Watch," and some of his other sides have also made noise in various soul and soul-blues markets. "Meet Me Tonight," which he released in 1991 on his own BDA imprint, has become a standard (most notably due to Willie Clayton's 1995 version on Ichiban). His ballad "I'll Put My Life on the Line" was covered by Tina Diamond and the late Reggie P. (as "I'll Put My Life on the Line") on Diamond's *In the Heart of the City* in 1999; Fields's original version, although long unavailable (and possibly unissued), has been hailed as a masterpiece by those who've heard it. Perhaps Fields's resemblance to James Brown—physically, vocally, stylistically—has obscured his own gifts; maybe the vicissitudes of the recording industry have simply been overwhelming. (The jury is still out on Fields's recent attempt to jump-start his career by signing with the Brooklyn-based retro-soul label Truth & Soul; he's now touring the predominantly white revivalist/aficionado circuit with a 1960s/'70s–styled backup band called the Expressions, "adapted for the ears of youngsters whose experiences with soul began with Amy [Winehouse], not Al, Otis, and Marvin," according to the label's Web site.) Nonetheless, if there's ever an elimination tournament for the title of Great Lost Southern Soul-Bluesman, Fields should be a main contender.

Toni Green

Toni Green's dusky mezzo-soprano is both supple and power-packed, and her dignified, almost regal demeanor provides a bracing alternative to the wanton-woman shenanigans of some of her contemporaries. Although she's capable of the occasional naughty novelty like 2002's "G-String and a Toothbrush," she seems more comfortable with more purposeful fare like the punning but serious-minded "No Rang, No Thang" from her 2003 CD *Southern Soul Music*. That disc's title song was one of the first to invoke the term *southern soul* as a badge of musical identity; its real highlight, though, was "Single Mothers," on which Toni summoned her toughest, most uncompromising vocals to update the vintage soul message of perseverance and hope for a new, troubled generation and era.

Bobbye "Doll" Johnson

Bobbye "Doll" Johnson's voice is appealingly tender, and she makes no effort to disguise her honey-chile drawl; in fact, she exploits its flirtatious potential. But she's no retro-belle blushing violet. She may promise a man (in the title song of her 2011 CD *All the Woman You'll Ever Need* on CDS) that she's "all the woman [he'll] ever need" despite the humiliation of being caught in a "three-way love affair," but she won't settle for second best: "Baby Daddy," on the same disc, begins as a wronged woman's lament, but then Bobbye vows that "he won't be comin' 'round here no more," and in the meantime, she'll be going after him for child support. Her eros-charged dance track "Rocking This Boat" ("Give it to me like I want it 'til my well runs dry") is jubilantly seductive but devoid of cheapness—this juke-joint woman is as classy as she is sassy.

Stan Mosley

Stan Mosley rejects the *southern soul* label, insisting that he's a soul singer with no adjectival dilution required. Nonetheless, his earliest successes ("Anybody Seen My Boo," the explosive "Don't Make Me Creep") were on Malaco, and he's known primarily along the same circuit that supports most "southern soul" mainstays. Mosley's Bobby Womack–influenced vocals are among the music's grittiest, and when he's got the right production behind him—as on his recent output on CDS—he can melt and then rip a listener's heart without missing a beat. In early 2012, Mosley announced his intention to forsake his beloved soul music for gospel. His secular catalog, though, is solid; if he does join the ministry, his soul legacy will remain intact.

Sheba Potts-Wright

Sheba Potts-Wright may still be best known for her sassy workout on Sir Charles Jones's "Slow Roll It" in 2001, but a lot of her other output on Ecko, as well as the baby-girl-in-a-bordello cover shots that graced her first few CDs, seemed to indicate that she was angling for a place in the soul-blues hoochie-mama brigade. Her vocals, though, sugarcoated though they may have been, were toughened by an underlying astringency and timbral sureness, and her songs often had a lyric substance that belied their provocative titles ("Lipstick on His Pants," "Big Hand Man," and "Private Fishing Hole," among others). As recounted in chapter 8, in the mid-2000s she decided to forsake the hoochie high jinks for good, and her subsequent output—2008's *I'm a Bluesman's Daughter* and 2011's *Let Your Mind Go Back*—has illustrated her newfound resolve. Both lyrically and musically, these discs convey maturity and seriousness of purpose even as their musical textures and rhythms, as well as Sheba's still-youthful vocal timbre, proclaim a celebratory soulfulness.

Mr. Sam

Sam Fallie exemplifies the kind of singer who still "tells stories" in his songs. His "12 Steps for Cheaters" saga, for example, which extends over the course of at least two CDs, revisits the theme of a recovering addict trying to reclaim his life, except in this case, he's a compulsive womanizer who's been in treatment and now wants to reclaim one of his old paramours. Everything comes to a head in the song "Voicemail," in which her new lover (sung by Floyd Taylor) warns Mr. Sam's character away. On stage, "Voicemail" expands into a minidrama in which Sam's tormented protagonist eventually pulls a gun on his rival, played by one of his backup singers. Then there are his ballads of heartbreak, such as 2008's "Picking up Pieces" and the more recent "Long Goodbye"; delivered in Sam's anguished tenor croon, they're pearls of songcraft that exemplify southern soul at its best.

Peggy Scott-Adams

Vocalist Peggy Scott-Adams's career extends back to the late 1960s, when, as Peggy Scott, she scored a few hits with Jo Jo Benson on SSS International. In the early 1990s, she and Ray Charles collaborated on his sides "Back to Love" and "If You Give Me Your Heart"; a few years later, former Charles songwriter/arranger Jimmy Lewis brought her to his Miss Butch label. The result was "Bill," her out-of-nowhere 1997 hit that combined sly irony and smoldering rage to portray a "down-low brother," a gay man who closeted himself with a wife or girlfriend but continued to have a male lover on the side. "Bill" stayed on the national R & B charts for ten weeks and even made the pop listings, almost unheard-of for a southern soul record. Scott-Adams has also addressed domestic violence ("Spousal Abuse") and cultural dissolution ("I'm Willing to Be a Friend"), and even her love songs and cheating songs ("I'm Getting What I Want") are undergirded with power and pride. Her fire-and-velvet vocals can cut and soothe with equal aplomb, and although in recent years she's focused mostly on gospel, she remains a beloved figure in southern soul. In 2012, she returned to secular music with the CD *Life After Bill* on her own Nora label; she's touring again, and it looks as if she's back to stay.

Floyd Taylor

Not long after Johnnie Taylor's death in 2000, Malaco signed his son Floyd, a stylish showman with an uncanny vocal and physical resemblance to his father. Although his loving (and eerily spot-on) re-creations of John-nie's hits remain the centerpiece of his live performances, Floyd has also amassed an impressive recorded catalog of newer material. His vocals are muscular and toughened by his hip-hop–flavored phrasing, and the lyric content he favors is streetwise and knowing without descending to clichéd gangsta thuggery. Like many others, he chafes at being categorized as a "southern soul" entertainer; nonetheless, and despite the up-to-date R & B feel that characterizes much of his recorded output, that's the field in which he's best known; he's a mainstay on the annual Blues Is Alright tours, and several of his songs have become radio and club hits along the circuit.

Nellie "Tiger" Travis

Nellie Travis's taut, quivering vibrato takes some getting used to, but it's worth the effort; she laces it with a torrid emotionality that harks back to vintage blues, even when she's conveying modern-sounding ideas. "Slap Yo' Weave Off," for instance, from 2008's *I'm a Woman* on CDS, is a wick-edly satisfying dollop of bad-girl signifying; "Don't Talk to Me," from the same disc, finds the singer kicking her ex to the curb with a resolve so intense and anguished it's almost overwhelming. In 2011, as if to show she could still pull it off, Nellie unleashed the more traditionally Chicago-styled *I'm Going Out Tonight* on the Benevolent Blues imprint. Featuring "Koko," her tribute to the late Koko Taylor, it included some of Nellie's most heartfelt lyrics and singing, and it exemplified her stylistic versatility.

Artie "Blues Boy" White

A full-length profile of Artie White is in my previous book, *Chicago Blues: Portraits and Stories*. Born in Vicksburg, Mississippi, in 1937, White landed a minor chart hit in 1977 with the Bob Jones–penned "(You Are My) Leanin Tree." Since then, he's recorded for such labels as Ronn, Ichiban, the Malaco subsidiary Waldoxy, and his own Achilltown imprint. Even by soul-blues standards, White is pretty old-school; his thick, vibrato-heavy vocals reflect his early gospel roots, and he's made few concessions to modernism—most of his recordings are "natural," with a minimum of electronic embellishment. Although he never charted again after "Leanin Tree," he remained a dependable presence on both southern soul radio and chitlin' circuit stages until ill health forced him to retire a few years ago.

Karen Wolfe

Karen Wolfe's sister-in-law is Denise LaSalle, and her manager is Anna Neal Coday, widow of Denise's former protégé Bill Coday. Karen's breakout CD was 2009's *A Woman Needs a Strong Man*, which featured "Man Enough," an Omar Cunningham composition that deftly recast the famous punch line from Ray Brooks's "Walk Out Like a Lady": "If you're man enough to leave," Karen sang in a voice that both smoldered and glinted with steel, "I'm woman enough to let you go." Her follow-up, 2012's *Telling It Like It Is*, included throw-downs like "You Ain't No Player" and "Grown Ass Man" along with such declarations of womanly power as "Don't Play with Me" and "A Hard Man Is Good to Find." Although she's less flashy than some others, Karen Wolfe delivers the goods with a winning combination of grit, sensitivity, and sass.

• • •

Stuff You Got to Watch

Scuffling and dues-paying are still the norm when it comes to getting known in the soul-blues world. All along the circuit are artists—some newcomers, some with years of experience still seeking that first big break—who have become local stars and have the potential to assume their place among the nationally known figures discussed in this book. Once again, this brief sampling is meant as an appetizer—it's far from comprehensive. To keep up with who's coming up, who's getting hot, and who's beginning to break out, consult the sources mentioned previously; if you're fortunate enough to live in or near a soul-blues stronghold, go out to where the music's playing and discover some of the newer names for yourself.

Booker Brown

Booker Brown has recorded a few small-label CDs worth checking out, but to experience his full force you've got to catch him live. The performance I witnessed in a Memphis, Tennessee, nightclub a few years ago rivaled anything I've ever seen from a deep-soul artist: coaxing the house band into a swaying 6/8 ballad pattern, Brown improvised an extended mediation on love, loss, and redemption that ascended from a whisper into a soul-shredding scream. He topped it off with a version of "A Change Is Gonna Come" that almost eclipsed Sam Cooke's gold-standard original; where

Cooke had sung it as a freedom-bound pilgrim, Brown portrayed a man both cornered and desperate as his voice exploded with anguished fury, sounding like nothing so much as a fist thrust into the face of God himself.

Ms. Nickki

Nicole Whitlock's first club gigs were in the early 1990s at the now-defunct Hard Luck Café on the corner of Third and McLemore in Memphis. Since then, she's appeared at various Beale Street locations, in northern Mississippi casinos, overseas once or twice, and, most regularly, at Wild Bill's, Memphis's famous urban juke on Vollintine Avenue. Sounding like a higher-pitched Denise LaSalle but with phrasing and textural nuances all her own, she delivers bad-mama throw-downs and pleading entreaties with equal facility; her signature song, Toni Green's "Where the Big Girls At?" is the testimonial of a plus-size juke-joint queen unafraid to celebrate life, love, and lust to the fullest (she's included it on a couple of self-released CDs). With her sure-toned vocal prowess, playfully brazen stage presence, and strong repertoire (both borrowed and original), Ms. Nickki is a soul-blues diva-in-waiting.

Uvee Hayes

Uvee Hayes's supple, girlish warble belies both the ladylike dignity she projects on stage and her status as a St. Louis blues and soul-blues veteran. Her performing career extends back to the 1960s, and she's been recording since at least the mid-1980s, but for some reason—maybe her day job as a psychological examiner for the St. Louis public schools has compelled her to stay close to home; maybe the ladylike dignity that distinguishes her onstage persona is ill-suited to today's sexpot-glutted pop music marketplace—her reputation remains limited to a small circle of die-hard admirers. Nonetheless, her meld of soul, contemporary blues, and pop-tinged jazz is both distinctive and satisfying; despite the callow-sounding sweetness of her timbre, she brings life-tested urgency to ballads and barn burners alike.

Jeannie Holliday

Jeannie Holliday, who divides her time between Milwaukee and Chicago, is in command of a stylistic palette ranging from a fluttery pop-jazz melisma to a soulful, blues-inflected wail. As she showed on her 2010

Figure 35. Jeannie Holliday, 2011 Chicago Blues Festival. Photo by Gene Tomko.

debut CD, *You Can't Blame Me* (on the Chicago-based Blast label), she's also deft at spicing up her phrasing with a shape-shifting, hip-hop–influenced rhythmic dexterity. She roughens her sweet soprano mewl to add bite to offerings like the signifying, score-settling "Betrayal" and "Hatin' on Me" as well as "A Change Has Come," a meditation on both the triumphs and the responsibilities implied by Barack Obama's historic victory in the 2008 presidential race. Jeannie's overall sound may be closer to mainstream neosoul/pop than the grittier cadences and emotions of contemporary southern soul-blues, but her emotional honesty and blunt, sometimes confrontational lyric storytelling place her firmly in the soul-blues mold.

Theo Huff

Theo Huff's voice, reminiscent of Johnnie Taylor in his prime, is remarkably developed, especially considering his age (he's still in his twenties); his phrasing is steady and unforced, and his stage presence blends sensitivity and cocksure flamboyance. His resonant vocals, confident onstage demeanor, and sassy call-and-response churchiness invariably get even Chicago's most soul-seasoned clubbers to their feet—including, when she's in the house, Tyrone Davis's widow, Ann, a sure sign that a torch is being passed. Huff's 2010 debut CD on Blast, *Now Is the Time,* consisted entirely of original songs, a few of which he occasionally inserts into his sets. If he can put together more fresh material and then summon the confidence to perform it more consistently, Theo Huff has it in him to play a major role in restoring Chicago's place on the blues and soul music map.

Lola

Lola Gulley was born in New York and raised mostly in California, but she got her professional start in Mobile, Alabama, where she played trumpet, drums, and keyboards in a funk band led by her father, a career military man. She also played and sang in church, and she eventually joined Johnnie Taylor's revue as a keyboardist. Now based in Atlanta (where she can be found hosting the weekly Monday night jam sessions at the Northside Tavern on Howell Mill Road), she records for Stax veteran William Bell's Wilbe label. She favors production that's hardened by tough postfunk aggression, and her vocals combine gospel melisma and bluesy, soul-baring intensity charged with hip-hop–era attitude—exemplifying the kind of old-school/new-school blend that increasingly characterizes southern soul-blues as it adapts itself to remain relevant and marketable to contemporary listeners.

• • •

"The Clock on the Wall Says It's Time to Go . . ."

. . . but the music is far from over. As I've noted, these listings are not definitive; they represent my attempt to select a sample of artists, both famous and lesser known, who exemplify at least some of the richness and diversity of the still-evolving blues/soul/soul-blues continuum. A quick perusal of the sources I cited at the beginning of this section—or, even better, a Saturday night sojourn to your local juke, show lounge, or "hole in the wall"—will reveal many more, most of whom are at the height of their powers and virtually all of whom could have qualified for inclusion here.

"The music," as Peter Guralnick has assured us, "is out there." It's up to us to find it. Look, listen, and discover!

Notes

Introduction

1. It hit the airwaves, but not the R & B singles charts. Malaco never released "Down Home Blues" as a single, preferring to let the song's radio- and jukebox-based popularity drive sales of Hill's album *Down Home,* which ended up selling over 500,000 copies and remaining on the *Billboard* soul album charts for nearly two years.

2. Tommy Couch Jr., telephone interview with the author, October 14, 2011.

3. Disparaging comments about the excesses of rap and hip-hop are common among southern soul-blues artists. "If it's done in a positive way," says Sir Charles Jones, "not hurtin' nobody, you're not promotin' no violence—I'm all for it." But he's quick to add that "a lot of R & B stuff, and all of that hip-hop stuff . . . a lot of the rap artists promoting violence, to shoot and kill and stab out here, that's what bothers me. That really gives it a black eye"; phone interview with the author, February 26, 2011. During a performance at Mr. G's supper club in Chicago around 2011, Bobby Rush tossed out a barb against "saggy-pants" hip-hoppers and then added, "Way to solve that: uplift their minds, and their pants will follow."

4. Bowman, *Soulsville, USA,* 85+.

5. The British hostility to Muddy Waters's amplified sound when he made his first overseas tour in 1958 has probably been overstated, but he did encounter resistance from purists (especially critics) who doubted the "authenticity" of his new sound. Charles Edward Smith, in his biography of Big Bill Broonzy, *Big Bill Blues,* disparaged the "young and knowing (and rock and rolling)" 1950s hipsters who had abandoned authentic bluesmen like Broonzy for electrified urban blues and R & B; Davis, *The History of the Blues,* 187.

6. Compare Brown, *Miss Rhythm,* 113–22; see also Lauterbach, *The Chitlin' Circuit and the Road to Rock 'n' Roll.*

7. Nelson, "Tyrone Davis," 16.

8. One well-known example is Alan Lomax's landmark study *The Land Where the*

Blues Began. It should be emphasized, though, that Lomax's work provided a necessary corrective to generations of racist propaganda claiming, as he put it, that "blacks were contented with their lot" (16) and thus remains valuable and timely despite its occasional myopia.

9. Millie Jackson made these comments at a panel discussion during the 2009 meeting of the Jus' Blues Foundation, an Atlanta-based blues and soul-blues association that hosts an annual awards ceremony and conference in Memphis, Tennessee.

10. Denise LaSalle, interview with the author, January 13, 2010.

11. Emmett Garner, interview with the author, July 8, 2000.

12. I heard the Reverend Green make this statement in June 1994, when I attended a service at his church, the Full Gospel Tabernacle, 787 Hale Road, Memphis, Tennessee.

13. Guralnick, *Sweet Soul Music,* 286.

14. Mayfield, "Woman's Got Soul."

15. For the record, "The Crossroad" here has nothing to do with the cliché about Delta bluesman Robert Johnson's mythical deal with Satan. It is a reference to "I'm at the Crossroad," vocalist Vernon Garrett's 1977 song on the ICA label that has become a southern soul-blues standard.

Part I: Deep Blues, Deep Soul, and Beyond

1. Brown, *Manchild in the Promised Land,* 171.

2. Ibid., 172.

3. Ibid., 173.

4. Compare Floyd, *The Power of Black Music,* 165–67.

5. Yanow, "Soul Jazz."

6. This was not a new perception; see Davis, *Blues Legacies and Black Feminism;* Haralambos, *Right On;* Garon, *Blues and the Poetic Spirit;* Calt and Wardlow, *King of the Delta Blues.*

7. The precise etymology of "I've Got a Woman" is somewhat in dispute. "My Jesus Is All the World to Me" and "I Got a Savior (Way across Jordan)" have also been suggested as possible inspirations for the song. Most sources cite 1954 (perhaps in the summer) as the time of Charles and Richard's moment of epiphany, but Charles told interviewer John Gilliland on Gilliland's radio show *Pop Chronicles,* on KRLA in Pasadena, California, that he'd been performing "I've Got a Woman" for about a year before he recorded it; "The Soul Reformation, Show 15."

8. Compare Guralnick, *Lost Highway,* 77; see also part V of this book, "Soul Stew Revisited," for more on Bland, who should be considered one of soul music's founding fathers as well as a pioneering blues artist.

9. Guralnick, *Sweet Soul Music,* 264.

10. Hirshey, *Nowhere to Run,* 134.

11. Guralnick, *Sweet Soul Music,* 286.

12. Brown made this comment to the audience at the Boston Garden on the evening of April 5, 1968, the night after Dr. Martin Luther King Jr.'s assassination; compare the 2009 documentary *The Night James Brown Saved Boston,* directed by David Leaf (Shout! Factory); Brown et al., *James Brown, the Godfather of Soul,* 187; Guralnick, *Sweet Soul Music,* 354.

13. Hirshey, *Nowhere to Run,* xvi.

14. Pruter, *Doowop,* 3–4.

15. The quotation in the subhead is a favorite catchphrase of Chicago vocalist

Sharon Lewis, who staunchly maintains her identity as a "blues" singer despite her inclusion of soul and pop standards in her performances and on her recordings.

16. See, for instance, Davidson, *The African Genius;* and Zahan, *The Religion, Spirituality, and Thought of Traditional Africa.* In terms of how these holistic perspectives have informed African American (and other American) music and ritual, both secular and sacred, Dixon, *Digging the Africanist Presence in American Performance;* Fine, *Soulstepping;* Palmer, *Deep Blues;* Lomax, *The Land Where the Blues Began;* and Stuckey, *Slave Culture* represent only a small sample of valuable texts. Davis, in *Blues Legacies and Black Feminism,* notes the deleterious effects of "traditionally Christian dualism, which defines the spirit as 'good' and the body as 'evil'" (131), and she suggests that the blues "were part of a cultural continuum that disputed the binary constructions associated with Christianity . . . [and] blatantly defied the Christian imperative to relegate sexual conduct to the realm of sin" (123).

I might go further and argue that this dualism has represented one of the most pernicious and corrupting legacies of the imposition of Anglo-European theological and existential biases onto peoples of the African diaspora. It is exactly this kind of dichotomous thinking, I believe, that has led many blues musicians to sordid and untimely ends. Alienated from "respectable" society; judged by a church-driven moralism that betrayed African cultural roots in its mania for dividing the cosmos into Good versus Evil, God versus Satan; caught between the options of either submitting to an oppressive social order or embracing the blues life (i.e., playing the "Devil's music"); encouraged further into excess by their isolation from moderating influences and social institutions; and sometimes consumed, as well, by guilt over their fallen spiritual status, too many have succumbed to the very demons their ancestors may have ecstatically summoned in ritual and dance. Thus they fulfill the prophecies of the churchmen and moral absolutists who originally cast them out. A similar phenomenon, I suggest, may be seen today in the embrace of nihilism that characterizes the more extreme elements of hip-hop culture.

17. Other musicians also acknowledged this link. Jazz pianist Thelonious Monk spent some time as a young man playing piano for a Pentecostal evangelist, and he described the music played during her services as "rock and roll or rhythm and blues . . . only now they put different words to it"; Hentoff, *At the Jazz Band Ball,* 35.

18. Neal, *What the Music Said,* 70–71.

19. Although Taylor repudiated the word *blues* in some interviews, in private he sometimes embraced it, or at least accepted it for what it was. "Johnnie Taylor told me, 'Don't let nobody tell you not to sing the blues,'" Chicago vocalist Artie "Blues Boy" White said in 2002. "[He said], 'You ain't gonna get rich, but you gonna keep eatin'"; interview with the author, May 1, 2002.

20. Bowman, *Soulsville, U.S.A.,* 152.

21. Ibid., 180.

22. *Daddy B. Nice's Southern Soul RnB.com,* "Simeo, Daddy B. Nice's #83 Ranked Southern Soul Artist."

Chapter 1. Latimore: "I Capture the Feeling"

1. I conducted two interviews with Benny Latimore, both by phone. The first was on April 4, 2010. The second, a follow-up interview, was conducted on January 25, 2011. All biographical information and quotes are from these two interviews, unless noted otherwise.

Discographical data were drawn from Whitburn, *Hot R & B Songs, 1942–2010.* Biographical and discographical information on Steve Alaimo is from McClane, "Steve Alaimo"; background on Henry Stone and his labels is from Stone's official Web site, *Henry Stone Music* (http://www.henrystonemusic.com/history.htm). Historical information about radio station WLAC is from Lowe, *WLAC Radio* and Van West, "WLAC." Descriptions of Latimore's performance style are taken from my own personal observations.

2. Actually, Randy's Record Shop. This confusion comes up in quite a few accounts, probably because another record outlet, Ernie's Record Mart, was also a well-known sponsor on WLAC.

3. Louis Brooks was born Louie O'Neal Brooks in Nashville, Tennessee, on March 19, 1911; De Heer, "Louis Brooks."

4. O'Neal and O'Neal, "*Living Blues* Interview: Latimore," 15.

5. Pieper, "Excello Records Discography."

6. Not to be confused with the late tenor saxophonist of the same name.

7. O'Neal and O'Neal, "*Living Blues* Interview: Latimore," 16.

8. Whitburn, *Hot R & B Songs, 1942–2010,* 281.

9. Not to be confused with soul vocalist Freddie Scott, who had the No. 1 hit "Are You Lonely for Me" on the Shout label in 1966–67.

10. Singer/guitarist Little Beaver (born William Hale in Arkansas in 1945) had a No. 2 hit record, "Party Down," on Henry Stone's Cat label in 1974.

11. As Benny Latimore; he didn't start getting billed as Latimore until he moved to the Glades label in the early 1970s.

12. O'Neal and O'Neal, "*Living Blues* Interview: Latimore," 23.

13. Ibid., 24.

14. Latimore has since moved, but his values and perspective remain the same; he now lives in a "nice, quiet subdivision" outside of Tampa Bay.

Chapter 2. Denise LaSalle: Still the Queen

1. Denise cited this date in Freeland, *Ladies of Soul,* 11. I interviewed Denise LaSalle on January 13, 2010, in Jackson, Tennessee. I also conducted several brief follow-up interviews via telephone to confirm certain facts and details. Unless noted differently, all of LaSalle's quotes are from these interviews. Discographical information, unless otherwise specified is from Whitburn, *Hot R & B Songs, 1942–2010.* Pruter, *Chicago Soul,* was a valuable resource in fact-checking and confirming details about the Chicago soul music scene during the years of LaSalle's early career. I also thank writer and historian Bill Dahl, author of *Motown: The Golden Years,* for his assistance.

2. I thank Robert Pruter, noted R & B historian and author of *Doowop* and *Chicago Soul,* for this information.

3. "So I met Bill Jones in 1967, and we got married, 1969"; Freeland, *Ladies of Soul,* 13.

4. Pruter, *Chicago Soul,* 332.

5. Freeland, *Ladies of Soul,* 13.

6. In 1971, the Rolling Stones had included the song "Bitch" on their LP *Sticky Fingers,* but the Stones were a self-consciously transgressive rock-and-roll band whose predominantly white fans glorified in their rebelliousness. This also applied to other rock groups that arose out of the white counterculture, brandishing their obscenities like freedom flags. Both culturally and demographically, their stance was far from

what most commercial soul music and R & B represented, at least to most of its core African American audience, at the time.

7. It's styled as "My Tu-Tu" on some versions.

8. Although LaSalle may very well have come up with the term *soul-blues* on her own, it predates her career. "Soul Blues" was the title of a jazz instrumental by Coleman Hawkins in 1958. In 1969, a blues harp instrumental with that title by Little Hite (with Magic Slim on guitar) appeared on the Ja-Wes label.

Journalists and writers have also used the expression. On May 23, 1964, a review of Johnny Nash's "Talk to Me" in *Billboard* magazine's "Hot Pop Spotlights" column referred to Nash's song as a "soul-blues ballad." The term also came up in a September 1970 review of an Ike and Tina Turner LP by Mike Leadbitter in the British magazine *Blues Unlimited,* and in November of that same year, in another *Blues Unlimited* article, this one a review of a Little Milton LP by Gary von Tersch: "If you dig the soulblues [*sic*] of Aretha Franklin, then you'll like this one by Milton." In 1971, it appeared in reviews by Jim O'Neal in *Living Blues* magazine; O'Neal used it again over the course of the next few years. Cary Baker used it as well, in 1972, in reviews for *Blues Unlimited.* I thank Jim O'Neal, co-founder and former editor of *Living Blues* magazine, for this information.

9. LaSalle, "Cry of the Black Soul," 2001.

10. Wolfe and LaSalle. *Denise LaSalle's Inspirational Site.*

Chapter 3. J. Blackfoot: "Don't Give Up—Tighten Up!"

1. I interviewed J. Blackfoot by telephone on January 27, 2010; I also conducted several brief follow-up interviews for fact-checking purposes. Unless specified otherwise, all Blackfoot quotes here are from those interviews. Discographical data are from Whitburn, *Hot R & B Songs, 1942–2010.* Cantor, *Wheelin' On Beale,* provides an indispensable—if somewhat cheerleaderish—history of WDIA's evolution as the first American radio station to adopt an all-black format. When considering the history of Memphis blues and R & B radio, it is also important to remember the contribution of WHBQ's Dewey Phillips, the white disc jockey whose "Red Hot & Blue" show from 1949 to 1958 helped introduce a generation of white listeners to black music; Cantor, *Dewey and Elvis,* is a good source for biographical information on this radio pioneer. Details of Blackfoot's funeral are from my own personal observations.

2. Suosalo, "The Soul Children."

3. Compare Gordon, *It Came from Memphis,* 252.

4. Goggin, "J. Blackoot," 32.

5. Freed appeared, more or less in character, in a series of teen-oriented music films between 1956 and 1959. These films, along with Freed's traveling "caravans" of entertainers, played an important role in spreading the rock-and-roll gospel among both black and white teenagers in the 1950s.

6. McGee's actual first name was Isadore; compare Young and Glassburner, "Bogard Brothers."

7. In fact, Stax co-owner Estelle Axton attended that very show; impressed by the Emeralds' version of "Sunday Kind of Love," she invited them to sign with the label; Bowman, *Soulsville, U.S.A.,*72.

8. Goggin, "J. Blackfoot," 34.

9. For the history of Johnny Bragg and the Prisonaires, see Escott, *Good Rockin' Tonight,* 45.

10. Goggin, "J. Blackfoot," 34.

11. Ibid.

12. Ibid., 36.

13. Rob Bowman, personal correspondence with the author, March 24, 2010.

14. Goggin, "J. Blackfoot," 36.

15. Suosalo, "The Soul Children."

16. In 2007, Blackfoot and West got back together, along with Ann Hines and Cassandra Graham, to form a new version of the Soul Children. The following year, the reconstituted group released an album, *Still Standing* (JEA/Right Now), that garnered positive reviews. Katrenia Jefferson has since replaced Graham.

17. *Daddy B. Nice's Southern Soul RnB.com,* "J. Blackfoot: Daddy B. Nice's #32 Ranked Southern Soul Artist."

18. Hayes and Porter, "The Sweeter He Is."

Chapter 4. Bobby Rush: Behind the Trickster's Mask

1. Lame Deer et al., *Gift of Power,* 162.

2. I interviewed Bobby Rush twice for this chapter: in person, in suburban South Holland, Illinois, on October 30, 2010, and by phone on January 3, 2011. All quotes, anecdotes, and biographical information are from these two interviews, unless otherwise noted. The introductory section is modified from an article I wrote entitled "Bobby Rush: The Song and Dance of a Modern-Day Trickster," which appeared in *Living Blues* in 2003. Although most sources spell his given first name as "Emmit," he confirms the spelling used here.

The direct lineage from African trickster myths to the African American folk tradition, including the persona of the blues hero (or antihero) as trickster, has been widely discussed.

See, for instance, Gates, *The Signifying Monkey;* Floyd, *The Power of Black Music;* Spalding, *Encyclopedia of Black Folklore;* and Watkins, *On the Real Side* (from which I gleaned my examples of "John," Br'er Rabbit, et al.). Additional background on trickster mythology, especially that of the *heyoka,* is found in Lame Deer et al., *Gift of Power.*

Discographical data on Bobby Rush are from Whitburn, *Hot R & B Songs, 1942–2010.* Bill Dahl's liner notes to Rush's CD *Rush Hour* (Westside's 1999 reissue of Rush's debut 1969 album of the same name on Philadelphia International) supplied additional historical detail. Descriptions of Rush's performance style are from my own personal observations.

3. Haralambos, "Well Well It's . . . Bobby Rush," 13. More recently, Bobby has modified this story, suggesting that perhaps the club owner did know what was going on but decided to let Bobby get away with it as long as he was bringing in money.

4. Lauterbach, "Bobby Rush," 31.

5. Compare Watkins, *On the Real Side,* 36–41; 237–40, 259–62.

6. Blues photographer, archivist, and promoter Dick Waterman recalls that in the early 2000s a college-sponsored festival in Kentucky canceled a Bobby Rush appearance because "they got reports about Bobby's show and got nervous as it approached" (email message to the author, January 7, 2011). As noted previously, European audiences were initially hostile to him; compare Haralambos, "Well Well It's . . . Bobby Rush."

7. Recently, in fact, he has begun to allow them a few words during some of his routines.

8. Bobby may be mistaken about where this occurred. The Apex, located at 13624 Claire Boulevard in Robbins, was a popular venue for blues, jazz, and R & B artists. It seems unlikely that a nightclub in what was already a predominantly African American township would maintain such a policy. On the other hand, earlier-era "black and tan" clubs and some auditoriums in urban African American neighborhoods had long featured black acts performing for segregated white audiences (albeit in full view). So it's possible that the Apex booked shows for whites only as late as the 1950s. Bobby's recollection of weeknight soirees where African American women were made available to white men definitely reflect the "safari"/"slumming" mentality that some establishments in black communities capitalized on to attract white patronage.

9. Compare comments by Willie Dixon and Malcolm Chisolm, quoted in Guralnick, *Feel Like Goin' Home,* 162–63, 231; Dixon, *I Am the Blues,* 195.

10. Mississippi Legislature, 2000 Regular Session, Senate Resolution 43.

11. This song appeared as "In My Dippins" on Bobby's 2012 CD *Show You a Good Time,* issued on his own Deep Rush imprint.

12. This core tenet of African-rooted religious and philosophical thought and its lasting effect on modern styles of both oral and written discourse have been widely discussed; see, for instance, Davidson, *The African Genius;* DuBois, *The Souls of Black Folk,* 339; Floyd, *The Power of Black Music,* 8 and passim; Mbiti, *African Religions and Philosophy,* 73 and passim; see also Calt, *I'd Rather Be the Devil,* 44.

13. Bobby Rush's paeans to black physicality may seem anachronistic. However, scholars and advocates have made similar claims in less vernacular terms. For a discussion on the distinctive kinesic styles, both in performance and in everyday life, among people of the African diaspora, see Dixon, *Digging the Africanist Presence in American Performance.* The late African American playwright, musician, poet, and social activist Oscar Brown Jr. wrote a paper, commissioned by Chicago State University in 1982, in which he drew examples from dance, sports, other entertainment fields, and children's games (e.g., double Dutch jump rope) to reach conclusions not dissimilar to Bobby's; see Brown, "Oscar Brown Jr. Describes His Study of Black Bodies in Motion."

Chapter 5. Willie Clayton: Last Man Standing

1. I interviewed Willie Clayton twice: on March 23, 2012, and again by phone on April 3. Unless noted otherwise, all of the quotes here are from those two interviews. Discographical information is from Whitburn, *Hot R & B Songs, 1942–2010.* I gathered additional information on Willie's Kirstee releases from Mike Ward's liner notes to the LP *Forever,* Timeless TRPL 127, 1988.

2. Whiteis, "Not So Smooth Operator."

3. Ibid.

4. Kelly, "Darryl Carter—Looking Straight Ahead."

5. It was also issued in 1985 on the Chicago-based Nuance label as "Happy Time."

6. The very first Willie Clayton CD to appear on Malaco, also in 2005, was *Full Circle,* a reissue of a CD he had issued on the End Zone Ent. label earlier that year.

7. "Love and Happiness" wasn't released as a single right away; it finally debuted in 1977. Although today it's considered one of Green's classics, it barely made the charts, peaking at No. 92.

Chapter 6. Sweet Angel: Lessons in Life

1. I thank John Ward for providing me with a video of this performance.

2. I interviewed Sweet Angel and Mike Dobbins at the Ecko studio in Memphis, Tennessee, on August 16, 2010. I also conducted a few brief follow-up interviews with Sweet Angel by phone to check facts and details. Unless otherwise specified, all quotes from Sweet Angel and Mike Dobbins are from these conversations. Information on songwriting credits and session personnel on different Sweet Angel recordings are taken directly from the CDs being discussed.

3. This routine can be seen on YouTube: "Marvin Sease—Sit Down on It."

4. Email from John Ward, April 22, 2011.

5. Quoted on Sweet Angel's Web site, *Sweet Angel,* http://www.sweetangel.org.

6. This was the same birthday show referenced at the beginning of this chapter. Her debut performance of "A Girl Like Me" was that night's encore.

7. Email from John Ward, June 15, 2011.

8. Ground Zero has, in fact, booked southern soul-blues stars such as Denise LaSalle and Bobby Rush. When I spoke with vocalist O. B. Buchana in Memphis in August 2010, he said that when he performed at Ground Zero he had "a mixture" of whites and African Americans in his audience. Guitarist and vocalist Preston Shannon, who also has a foot in both "traditional" blues and southern soul, has performed often at Ground Zero.

Chapter 7. Sir Charles Jones: "Is There Anybody Lonely?"

1. Compare Mitchell, *Black Preaching;* Crawford and Troeger, *The Hum.*

2. I interviewed Sir Charles Jones over the phone on February 26, 2011. Unless otherwise specified, all quotes are from that interview. The Lufkin, Texas, performance is documented on Charles's DVD, *Sir Charles Jones: His Life and Times: Undisputed King of Southern Soul!* Quotes from Charles's voice-over on that DVD are in subsequent notes. Other descriptions of Charles's performance style are from my own personal observations.

3. The All-Stars were formed in the late 1950s at Elizabeth Baptist Church in Akron, Ohio. They recorded singles for various independent labels such as Designer and Process. More recently, a reconstituted version of the All-Stars has been affiliated with the Akron-based Lion of Judah label.

4. *Sir Charles Jones: His Life and Times.*

5. Early in the morning of September 15, 1963, members of the Birmingham, Alabama, Ku Klux Klan planted a box of dynamite under the steps of the Sixteenth Street Baptist Church. Later that morning, the bomb exploded, killing four girls who were in the back of the church putting on their choir robes for the service: fourteen-year-old Addie Mae Collins, eleven-year-old Denise McNair, and Carole Robertson and Cynthia Wesley, both fourteen. The incident shocked the nation and galvanized support for the civil rights movement.

6. Some of America's most historic civil rights struggles, including the famous Birmingham Children's Crusade in May 1963, occurred in or near Kelly Ingram Park.

7. *Sir Charles Jones: His Life and Times.*

8. Ibid.

9. Ibid.

10. Ibid.

11. Ibid.

12. Biographical and discographical information on Marvin Sease found in O'Neal, "Marvin Sease."

13. "Hep' Me: The Senator Jones Story."

14. Denise LaSalle, interview with the author, January 13, 2010.

15. Tommy Couch Jr., interview with the author, October 14, 2011.

16. *Daddy B. Nice's Southern Soul RnB.com*, "Sir Charles Jones: Daddy B. Nice's #12 Ranked Southern Soul Artist."

17. Personal interview, in Chicago, March 9, 2010. The artist has requested not to be identified.

Chapter 8. Ms. Jody: "Just a Little Bit Won't Get It"

1. I thank John Ward, president of Ecko Records in Memphis, Tennessee, for allowing me to view this video in his office.

2. I interviewed Ms. Jody by phone on April 28, 2011. Unless otherwise specified, all quotes here come from that interview.

3. Hildebrand, "It Really Is . . . A Ms. Jody Thang!," 21.

4. Ibid., 23.

5. Ibid., 25.

6. Ibid.

7. Ibid.

8. Ibid., 23.

9. John Ward, interview with the author, August 8, 2009.

10. Ibid.

11. *Daddy B. Nice's Southern Soul RnB.com*, "Daddy B. Nice's New CD Reviews 2009."

12. Hildebrand, "It Really Is . . . A Ms. Jody Thang!," 25.

13. O. B. Buchana, interview with the author, Memphis, Tennessee, August 16, 2010.

14. Hildebrand, "It Really Is . . . A Ms. Jody Thang!," 25.

15. Compare *Daddy B. Nice's Southern Soul RnB.com*, "Ms. Jody."

Postscript: The "Raunch" Debate: Hoochification or Sexual Healing?

1. Compare Minges, *Far More Terrible for Women*, 17.

2. Ibid., 14.

3. Compare Hurmence, *My Folks Don't Want Me to Talk about Slavery*, 80.

4. Davis, *Blues Legacies and Black Feminism*, 4, 45; emphasis added.

5. It wasn't just sexuality per se that was recast as a trope of empowerment. Songs such as Lucille Bogan's "Tricks Ain't Walkin' No More" and Ma Rainey's "Hustlin' Blues," while lamenting the struggles and poverty suffered by prostitutes, also portrayed the women sympathetically, if not approvingly, as workers trying to earn a living by seizing control of their own bodies as means of production. Some songs, such as "If I Can't Sell It I'll Keep Sittin' on It" (recorded by Georgia White in 1936 on Decca and performed as recently as the 1990s by the late Ruth Brown, who first sang it in the 1989 Broadway musical *Black and Blue*), forthrightly extolled sex for money as an empowering and enriching arrangement for the woman.

6. Compare Big Bill Broonzy: "I wonder, when will I get to be called a man / Do I have to wait 'til I get ninety-three?"

7. Gordon, *Can't Be Satisfied*, 103.

8. Ibid., xix.

9. Many historians and musicologists have commented on what Odum and Johnson, *The Negro and His Songs*, called the "absence of the higher ideals of love and virtue" in the blues tradition. This Dionysian bias may have been overstated in some analyses; see, for instance, Oliver, *Blues Fell This Morning*, 79–84. There is little doubt, though, that the increased emphasis on marketing pop music to teenagers in the 1950s played a role in the heightened romanticism of lyric themes in post–"I Got a Woman" R & B and the concomitant decline of the blues in popularity during these years. As Stephen Calt suggests: "The failure of blues song to concoct anything other than a coarse, unsympathetic narrator mandated its obsolescence in the 1950s, when romantic rhythm and blues ballads came into vogue"; Calt, *I'd Rather Be the Devil*, 226.

10. Jahn, *The Story of Rock from Elvis Presley to the Rolling Stones*, 146.

11. On November 25, 1967, for example, a show at the Knoxville Civic Coliseum in Knoxville, Tennessee, starred Pickett, Thomas, and the Staples along with Laura Lee and the Box Tops, among others; *Rock Prosopography*, November 2, 2010; http://rockprosopography102.blogspot.com/2010/11/box-tops-family-tree.html, accessed September 3, 2012.

12. Sease, "Candy Licker."

13. Tommy Couch Jr., interview with the author, August 3, 2009.

14. Little Milton, interview with the author, March 17, 2005.

15. Sir Charles Jones, interview with the author, February 26, 2011.

16. Bobbye "Doll" Johnson, interview with the author, October 29, 2011.

17. Denise LaSalle, interview with the author, January 13, 2010.

18. Quoted in Hildebrand, "It Really Is . . . A Ms. Jody Thang!"

19. John Ward, interview with the author, July 8. 2009.

20. Even Marvin Sease, the one who helped start it all, expressed dissatisfaction at being pigeonholed as the modern godfather of raunch. He told an interviewer in 1996 that "I think it's time to let the Candy Licker rest"; Suosalo, "Interview with Marvin Sease."

21. Tommy Couch Jr., interview with the author, October 14, 2011.

22. Calt and Wardlow, *King of the Delta Blues*, 119.

23. Recalled by a Mississippi Delta resident who saw Wolf perform in the late 1930s; Segrest and Hoffman, *Moanin' at Midnight*, 48. Another example of Wolf's showmanship is a photo taken of him at the 1960 WDIA Starlight Review in Memphis, Tennessee, showing him brandishing a soup spoon as a phallic symbol during his song "Spoonful," which he had just released on Chess Records.

24. This has been widely reported. Harpist Charlie Musselwhite gives a firsthand account of this routine and then adds wryly, "This isn't a show you'd see at a folk festival"; see Calemine, "Charlie Musselwhite."

25. "'Put Yo Foot in It,' Feat. Mr. Sam and O. B. Buchana." The reader should not get the wrong idea about Mr. Sam from this one vignette. See the final section of this book for more on this gifted Memphis-based songwriter and singer.

26. One notable exception was the Dew Drop Inn on LaSalle Street in New Orleans, which used to hire top Crescent City musicians to accompany its featured drag shows. Vocalist Bobby Marchan emerged from these drag revues to become a successful singer during New Orleans's R & B heyday. Chicago's Wilbur "Hi Fi" White was another professional cross-dresser who made a name as a vocalist.

Perhaps a mention should also be made of the late Chicago-based singer Arlean Brown, who bragged in her song "I Am a Streaker" about having a "chest like headlights on a pimp's car" and spiced up her stage act with a Streakers' Revue of scantily clad exotic dancers.

27. Some singers, like Kansas City's Lottie Kimbrough and probably Lucille Bogan herself, performed in red-light districts. Bogan's "Shave 'Em Dry" was a virtually unmitigated torrent of obscene sexual boasts and insults drawn from the tradition of the "Dozens"; it's one of the few recorded examples of a woman engaging in this famous folk art of profane invective.

28. White critics often responded to the Ike and Tina Turner Revue in terms that would probably have been considered egregiously racist in any other context. Philip Norman described Tina as Ike's "half-naked Zulu princess wife"; Norman, *Sympathy for the Devil*, 317. Rolling Stones biographer Stanley Booth virtually drooled over Tina and the Ikettes dancing "in their near-Egyptian way" and wearing skirts "almost high enough to reveal the heavenly mink-lined wet black cunt," and he extolled their "mad nigger poses [and] crotch flashing"; Booth, *The True Adventures of the Rolling Stones*, 128.

29. Sheba Potts-Wright, interview with the author, August 7, 2009.

30. Ibid.

31. Ibid.

32. "Whip It to a Jelly," Clara Smith vocalist, recorded May 25, 1926, Columbia 14150-D.

Part IV: Introduction

1. Waiters and Calloway, "Smaller the Club."
2. Tommy Couch Jr., interview with the author, October 14, 2011.
3. Sir Charles Jones, interview with the author, February 26, 2011.
4. Tommy Couch Jr., interview with the author, October 14, 2011.
5. Larry Chambers, interview with the author, November 19, 2011.
6. Stan Mosley, interview with the author, Chicago, August 8, 2000.

Chapter 9. Blues with a Feeling: Writing Songs for the Market and the Heart

1. I interviewed George Jackson, Harrison Calloway, and Frederick Knight during a visit to the Malaco studios in Jackson, Mississippi, on August 3 and 4, 2009. Unless otherwise specified, all quotes here from Jackson, Calloway, and Knight are from those interviews.
2. Goggin, "George Jackson," 35.
3. Ibid.
4. Tommy Couch Jr., interview with the author, October 14, 2011.
5. Floyd Taylor, interview with the author, April 1, 2010.
6. Bob Jones, interview with the author, November 9, 2011.
7. Sir Charles Jones, interview with the author, February 26, 2011.
8. Bowman, *The Last Soul Company*, 55. That women make up the primary market for blues records has been standard industry wisdom for decades. Leonard Chess, among others, was widely quoted as affirming this belief.
9. Bob Jones, interview with the author, November 9, 2011.
10. Actually, it was Clark's second album; his first, *The Blues Doctor: Operating on the Blues*, had been issued on the Jomar label in 1997. Clark had used the Blues Doctor as his radio disc jockey handle for several decades. Sir Charles takes credit for suggesting the new stage name to him during the recording of *Doctor of Love*.

11. Sir Charles Jones, interview with the author, February 26, 2011.

12. Quoted in Jansson, "Mr. Sam."

13. Ibid.

14. Bob Jones, interview with the author, November 13, 2011.

Chapter 10. Music and the Marketplace: Getting Heard, Getting Known, and Staying on Top of the Game

I interviewed Larry Chambers by telephone on November 19, 2011; my interview with Bobby O'Jay, also by phone, was conducted on November 28, 2011. I had several telephone conversations with Kim Cole, the most in-depth on December 14, 2011, not long after T. K. Soul signed with Universal. Unless otherwise noted, all quotes from these individuals are from these interviews.

1. Sir Charles Jones, interview with the author, February 26, 2011.

2. Ms. Jody, interview with the author, December 3, 2011.

3. Kim Cole, telephone conversation with the author, November 16, 2011. Cole's skepticism about radio, however, does not stop her from recognizing its practical value in at least some situations, as her subsequent comments quoted here illustrate.

4. Radio does still perform this role, but usually only on certain programs and for a subset of its overall audience. Many of these programs are syndicated talk shows with far-flung listenerships, and they address issues of national, rather than local, concern.

5. Floyd Taylor, interview with the author, March 9, 2010.

6. Bob Jones, interview with the author, November 9, 2011.

7. Harrison Calloway, interview with the author, August 3, 2009.

8. Benny Latimore, interview with the author, April 7, 2010.

9. Millie Jackson, interview with the author, February 21, 2011.

10. Sweet Angel, interview with the author, August 16, 2010.

11. Tommy Couch Jr., interview with the author, August 3, 2009.

12. Beck, "Why Arbitron Is Helping Terrestrial Radio Shoot Itself in the Ear."

13. Small and Astor, "What Works in Direct Response Radio Advertising?"

14. Strategicmedia, "About Radio Advertising: Targetability."

15. Country, of course, is well known for its popularity among diverse demographics; few radio programmers would have to be convinced of its moneymaking potential. Quite a few southern soul-blues artists and songwriters I've spoken to have pointed to country music—once stigmatized, as the blues were, as unsophisticated, rich in vernacular tradition but marketed as mainstream pop, stylistically flexible, popular among fans of all ages and most geographic regions—as an example of what southern soul could accomplish with the right kind of marketing and industry support.

16. *Market Research: African-American,* "Black Radio Today."

17. Floyd Taylor, interview with the author, March 9, 2010.

18. Raymer, "Bon Iver, the Grammys, and the Indie Stockholm Syndrome."

19. Lomax, *The Land Where the Blues Began,* 414.

20. Buddy Guy, interview with the author, January 2006.

21. Travis Haddix, interview with the author, April 18, 2005.

22. Tommy Couch Jr., interview with the author, October 14, 2011.

23. Millie Jackson, interview with the author, February 21, 2011.

24. Bob Jones, interview with the author, November 9, 2011.

25. Boylan, "End of the Century," 31.

26. As it turned out, T. K. Soul did decide to exercise this option. He is again a fully independent artist, no longer affiliated with Universal.

Chapter 11. Evolution: A Look toward the Future

1. Russonello, "A New Day in Harlem," 38.

2. "T. K. Soul," *Soul Blues Music.*

3. *Daddy B. Nice's Southern Soul RnB.com,* "T. K. Soul: Daddy B. Nice's #17 Ranked Southern Soul Artist."

4. Kim Cole, interview with the author, December 14, 2011.

5. Brown, *Manchild in the Promised Land,* 272.

6. Sir Charles Jones, interview with the author, February 26, 2011.

7. If I may interject a personal observation: I teach English composition at City Colleges of Chicago. My students are urban, mostly young, and very attuned to what's on the radio and the Internet. I constantly hear complaints from them about what they perceive as negative messages and/or lack of imagination in popular music. When I've had the opportunity to play them songs by some of the artists mentioned in this book, their reaction has been one of astonishment, similar to what Stan Mosley said he has seen at his shows: "Why can't I hear this stuff on the radio?"

Chapter 12. Leading Lights

1. Haggard's original title was "If We're Not Back in Love by Monday."

2. Hirshey, *Nowhere to Run,* 59.

3. "Johnnie Taylor," *Soul Blues Music.*

4. *Daddy B. Nice's Southern Soul RnB.com,* "Johnnie Taylor: Daddy B. Nice's #1 Ranked Southern Soul Artist."

5. Johnnie Taylor usually gave his year of birth as 1938. His gravestone inscription reads "May 1937–May 2000." However, his Social Security file documents that he was born Johnnie Harrison Taylor, May 3, 1934; email from Eric LeBlanc, February 19, 2011; Rogers, "Johnnie Harrison Taylor (1934–2000)."

References

"Artie 'Blues Boy' White." *Soul Blues Music*. 2011, accessed September 14, 2011, http://www.soulbluesmusic.com/artiebluesboywhite.htm.

Beck, Chris. "Why Arbitron Is Helping Terrestrial Radio Shoot Itself in the Ear." *26DotTwo*. November 1, 2011; accessed November 30, 2011, http://26dottwo.com/2011/11/01/arbitron-radio-shoot-itself-in-ear/

Booth, Stanley. *The True Adventures of the Rolling Stones*. Chicago: Chicago Review Press, 2000.

Bowman, Rob. *The Last Soul Company*. Booklet accompanying the CD set *Malaco: The Last Soul Company: A Thirty-Year Retrospective*. Malaco MCD-0030, 1999.

Bowman, Rob. *Soulsville, U.S.A.: The Story of Stax Records*. New York: Schirmer/Simon and Schuster MacMillan, 1997.

Boylan, J. Gabriel. "End of the Century." *The Nation*, January 11/18, 2010, 31–34.

Brown, Claude. *Manchild in the Promised Land*. New York: Signet, 1965.

Brown, James, Bruce Tucker, and Al Sharpton. *James Brown, the Godfather of Soul*. New York: Basic Books, 2002.

Brown, Oscar. "Oscar Brown Jr. Describes His Study of Black Bodies in Motion." *HistoryMakers Digital Archive*, 2010, accessed October 8, 2011, http://www.idvl.org/thehistorymakers/iCoreClient.html#/&s=1&args=N1%253BP-1%253Bids%5BOscar%20Brown%252C%20Jr.,%20Story%2020:15441%5D.

Brown, Ruth, with Andrew Yule. *Miss Rhythm: The Autobiography of Ruth Brown, Rhythm and Blues Legend*. New York: Penguin, 1996.

Calemine, James. "Charlie Musselwhite: The Master of Smokestack Lightning." *Swampland.com,* 2009, accessed November 12, 2010, http://swampland.com/ articles/view/title: charlie_musselwhite_the_master_of_smokestack_lightning.

Calt, Stephen. *I'd Rather Be the Devil: Skip James + the Blues*. New York: Da Capo, 1979.

Calt, Stephen, and Gayle Dean Wardlow. *King of the Delta Blues: The Life and Music of Charlie Patton*. Newton, N.J.: Rock Chapel Press, 1988.

Cantor, Louis. *Dewey and Elvis: The Life and Times of a Rock 'n' Roll Deejay*. Champaign, University of Illinois Press. 2010.

Cantor, Louis. *Wheelin' on Beale: How WDIA-Memphis Became the Nation's First All-Black Radio Station and Created the Sound That Changed America*. New York: Pharos, 1992.

Concord Music Group. "Soul Children." June 1978, accessed April 18, 2011, http://www.concordmusicgroup.com/artists/Soul-Chidren/.

Crawford, Evans E., and Thomas H. Troeger, *The Hum: Call and Response in African-American Preaching*. Studio City, Calif.: Abigon, 1995.

Daddy B. Nice's Southern Soul RnB.com. "J. Blackfoot: Daddy B. Nice's #32 Ranked Southern Soul Artist." Last modified November 30, 2011, accessed January 20, 2012, http://www.southernsoulrnb.com/artistguide.cfm?aid=66.

Daddy B. Nice's Southern Soul RnB.com. "Johnnie Taylor: Daddy B. Nice's #1 Ranked Southern Soul Artist." Last modified January 21, 2011, accessed February 17, 2012, http://www.southernsoulrnb.com/artistguide.cfm?aid=22.

Daddy B. Nice's Southern Soul RnB.com. "Ms. Jody: Ms. Jody's Keepin' It Real (Ecko) Two Stars** Dubious. Not much here." Last modified April 21, 2011, accessed September 18, 2011, http://www.southernsoulrnb.com/artistguide.cfm?aid=219.

Daddy B. Nice's Southern Soul RnB.com. "Simeo: Daddy B. Nice's #83 Ranked Southern Soul Artist." 2012, accessed February 21, 2012, http://www.southernsoulrnb.com/artistguide.cfm?aid=415.

Daddy B. Nice's Southern Soul RnB.com. "Sir Charles Jones: Daddy B. Nice's #12 Ranked Southern Soul Artist." Last modified January 4, 2010, accessed October 6, 2011, http://www.southernsoulrnb.com/artistguide.cfm?aid=55.

Daddy B. Nice's Southern Soul RnB.com. "T. K. Soul: Daddy B. Nice's #17 Ranked Southern Soul Artist." Last modified October 1, 2009, accessed January 17, 2012, http://www.southernsoulrnb.com/artistguide.cfm?aid=93.

Davidson, Basil. *The African Genius: An Introduction to African Cultural and Social History*. Boston: Little, Brown, 1969.

Davis, Angela Y. *Blues Legacies and Black Feminism*. New York: Pantheon, 1998.

Davis, Francis. *The History of the Blues: The Roots, the Music, the People from Charley Patton to Robert Cray*. New York: Hyperion, 1995.

De Heer, Dik. "Louis Brooks." *Black Cat Rockabilly*, accessed February 7, 2011, http://www.rockabilly.nl/references/messages/louis_brooks.htm.

Dixon, Brenda. *Digging the Africanist Presence in American Performance: Dance and Other Contexts*. Westport, Conn.: Praeger, 1996.

Dixon, Willie, with Don Snowden. *I Am the Blues*. New York: Da Capo, 1990.

DuBois, W. E. B. *The Souls of Black Folk*. In *Three Negro Classics*, edited by John Franklin Hope. New York: Avon, 1963.

Escott, Collin, and Martin Hawkins. *Sun Records, the Discography*. Vollersode, Germany: Bear Family, 1987.

Escott, Colin, with Martin Hawkins. *Good Rockin' Tonight: Sun Records and the Birth of Rock 'n' Roll*. New York: St. Martins, 1991.

Fine, Elizabeth C. *Soulstepping: African American Step Shows*. Champaign: University of Illinois Press, 2012.

Floyd, Samuel A. *The Power of Black Music*. New York: Oxford University Press, 1995.

Freeland, David. *Ladies of Soul (American Made Music)*. Jackson: University Press of Mississippi, 2001.

Garon, Paul. *Blues and the Poetic Spirit*. San Francisco: City Lights, 1996.

Gates, Henry Louis. *The Signifying Monkey: A Theory of African-American Literary Criticism*. New York: Oxford University Press, 1988.

George, Nelson. *The Death of Rhythm and Blues*. New York: Penguin, 1988.

George, Nelson. *Where Did Our Love Go? The Rise and Fall of the Motown Sound*. Urbana: University of Illinois Press, 1985.

Goggin, Martin. "George Jackson: From the Heart." *Juke Blues* 50 (2002): 30–35.

Goggin, Martin. "J. Blackfoot: Soul Child." *Juke Blues* 57 (2004): 32–37.

González-Wippler, Migene. *Tales of the Orishas*. New York: Original, 1985.

Gordon, Robert. *Can't Be Satisfied: The Life and Times of Muddy Waters*. New York: Little, Brown, 2002.

Gordon, Robert. *It Came from Memphis*. Boston: Faber and Faber, 1995.

Guralnick, Peter. *Dream Boogie: The Triumph of Sam Cooke*. New York: Little, Brown, 2005.

Guralnick, Peter. *Feel Like Goin' Home: Portraits in Blues and Rock and Roll*. New York: Harper and Row, 1989.

Guralnick, Peter. *Lost Highway: Journeys and Arrivals of American Musicians*. New York: Harper and Row, 1979.

Guralnick, Peter. *Sweet Soul Music: Rhythm and Blues and the Southern Dream of Freedom*. New York: Harper and Row, 1986.

Hamberlin, Floyd Jr. "Mississippi Woman." Malaco Music, BMI. Released on *Denise LaSalle: Pay Before You Pump*. Ecko ECD 1097, 2007.

Haralambos, Michael. *Right On: From Blues to Soul in Black America*. New York: Drake, 1975.

Haralambos, Michael. "Well Well It's . . . Bobby Rush." *Juke Blues* (Winter 1996/97): 10–18.

Hayes, Isaac, and David Porter. "Soul Man." East-Pronto Music, BMI. Stax 231, 1967.

Hayes, Isaac, and David Porter. "The Sweeter He Is." Birdees Music, ASCSAP. Stax 0050, 1969.

Hentoff, Nat. *At the Jazz Band Ball: Thirty Years on the Jazz Scene*. Berkeley: University of California Press, 2010.

"Hep' Me: The Senator Jones Story." *Ponderosa Stomp*. Last updated May 2005, accessed October 11, 2011, http://www.ponderosastomp.com/blog/2010/05/hep-me-the-senator-jones-story/.

Highwater, Jamake, *The Primal Mind: Vision and Reality in Indian America*. New York: Meridian, 1981.

Hildebrand, Lee. "It Really Is . . . A Ms. Jody Thang!" *Living Blues* 205 (February 2010): 20–25.

Hirshey, Gerri, *Nowhere to Run: The Story of Soul Music*. London: Southbank, 2006.

Hurmence, Belinda, ed. *My Folks Don't Want Me to Talk about Slavery*. Winston-Salem, N.C.: John F. Blair, 1984.

Jahn, Mike. *The Story of Rock from Elvis Presley to the Rolling Stones*. New York: Quadrangle, 1975.

Jansson, Tommy. "Mr. Sam: The Songwriter Who Became an Artist." *Jefferson,* no. 156 (June 16, 2008). Accessed July 9, 2011, http://www.jeffersonbluesmag.com/mr-sam.

"Johnnie Taylor." *Soul Blues Music.* 2011, accessed February 26, 2012, http://www.soulbluesmusic.com/johnnietaylor.htm.

Keil, Charles. *Urban Blues.* Chicago: University of Chicago Press, 1966.

Kelly, Red. "Darryl Carter—Looking Straight Ahead." *The B Side: A Celebration of the Other Side,* January 31, 2012, accessed April 3, 2012, http://redkelly.blogspot.com/2012/01/darryl-carter-looking-straight-ahead.html.

Lame Deer, Archie Fire, and Richard Erdoes. *Gift of Power: The Life and Teachings of a Lakota Medicine Man.* Rochester, Vt.: Bear, 1992.

Latimore, Benjamin. "Let's Straighten It Out." Sherlyn Music, BMI. Glades 1722, 1974.

Lauterbach, Preston. "Bobby Rush." *Living Blues* (November/December 2003): 22–35.

Lauterbach, Preston. *The Chitlin' Circuit and the Road to Rock 'n' Roll.* New York: W.W. Norton, 2011.

Lomax, Alan. *The Land Where the Blues Began.* New York: Delta Books, 1995.

Lowe, Jim. *WLAC Radio.* Last modified May 15, 2003, accessed February 17, 2011, http://www.yodaslair.com/dumboozle/wlac/wlacdex.html.

Market Research: African-American. "Black Radio Today: How America Listens to Radio." MichaelD. Communications. July 1, 2010, accessed December 4, 2011. http://michaeldcommunications.com/insights/resources/market-research-african-american/.

"Marvin Sease—Sit Down on It." *YouTube.* Last modified February 24, 2011, accessed April 16, 2011, http://www.youtube.com/watch?v=86kUZCIrUoI.

Mayfield, Curtis. "Woman's Got Soul." Curtom, BMI, ABC/Paramount 45–10647, 1965.

Mbiti, John S. *African Religions and Philosophy,* 2nd ed. Oxford: Heinemann, 1969.

McClane, Ben. "Steve Alaimo." *McLane and Wong Entertainment Law.* 1996, accessed February 17, 2011, http://www.benmclane.com/alaimo.htm.

Minges, Patrick, ed. *Far More Terrible for Women: Personal Accounts of Woman in Slavery.* Winston-Salem, N.C.: John F. Blair, 2006.

Mississippi Legislature. 2000 Regular Session. Senate Resolution 43. "A Resolution Commending the Career and Humanitarianism of Nationally and Internationally Known Blues Singer Mr. Bobby Rush." Accessed July 9, 2012, http://billstatus.ls.state.ms.us/2000/pdf/history/SR/SR0043.htm.

Mitchell, Henry. *Black Preaching.* New York: J. B. Lippincott, 1970.

Moore, Raymond, and John Ward. "The Better the Goods the Higher the Price." Ecko South, BMI. Released on *It's a Ms. Jody Thang!* Ecko ECD 1111, 2009.

Neal, Mark Anthony. *What the Music Said: Popular Music and Black Culture.* New York: Routledge, 1999.

Nelson, David. "Tyrone Davis: I Am Not a Blues Singer." *Living Blues* 105 (September/October 1992): 12–17.

Norman, Philip. *Sympathy for the Devil: The Rolling Stones Story.* New York: Simon and Schuster, 1984.

Odum, Howard W., and Guy B. Johnson. *The Negro and His Songs: A Study of Typical Negro Songs in the South.* Chapel Hill: University of North Carolina Press, 1925.

Oliver, Paul. *Blues Fell This Morning: Meaning in the Blues.* Cambridge: Cambridge University Press, 1960.

O'Neal, Jim. "Marvin Sease: The Candy Licker: Interview by Jim O'Neal." *Living Blues* 134 (July/August 1997): 18–27.

O'Neal, Jim, and Amy O'Neal. "*Living Blues* Interview: Latimore." *Living Blues* 24 (November/December 1975): 13–30.

Palmer, Robert. *Deep Blues: A Musical and Cultural History of the Mississippi Delta.* New York: Penguin, 1981.

Pieper, Thilo. "Excello Records Story." *Excello Records Discography.* 2001, accessed August 16, 2012, http://www.aryan88.com/whiterider/rebrebel/discographies/excellodisco.html.

Pruter, Robert. *Chicago Soul.* Chicago: University of Chicago Press, 1991.

Pruter, Robert. *Doowop: The Chicago Scene.* Chicago: University of Chicago Press, 1996.

"'Put Yo Foot in It,' Feat. Mr. Sam and O. B. Buchana." *YouTube.* October 24, 2009, accessed February 21, 2012, http://www.youtube.com/watch?v=Ef9Jpui3AkM.

Raymer, Miles. "Bon Iver, the Grammys, and the Indie Stockholm Syndrome." *Chicago Reader,* December 8, 2011, accessed January 12, 2012, http://www.chicagoreader.com/chicago/bon-iver-justin-vernon-holocene-grammys-kanye-skrillex/Content?oid=5148438.

Rogers, Bryan. "Johnnie Harrison Taylor (1934–2000)." *The Encyclopedia of Arkansas History and Culture.* August 6, 2010, accessed August 16, 2012, http://www.encyclopediaofarkansas.net/encyclopedia/entry-detail.aspx?entryID=637.

Russonello, Giovanni. "A New Day in Harlem." *Jazz Times* 42, no. 1 (January/February 2012): 34–39.

Sease, Monnie M. "Candy Licker." DafTon Music, SESAC. Released on *Marvin Sease* London 888–798-7, 1987.

Segrest, James, and Mark Hoffman. *Moanin' at Midnight: The Life and Times of Howlin' Wolf.* New York: Pantheon, 2004.

Sir Charles Jones, His Life and Times: Undisputed King of Southern Soul! Produced and directed by Sir Charles Jones. Mardi Gras Records, MG 228 DVD, 2008.

Small, Jeff, and Brett Astor. "What Works in Direct Response Radio Advertising?" *Strategic Media,* 2009, accessed December 3, 2011, http://www.strategicmediainc.com/radio-advertising-articles/what_works_in_direct_response_radio_advertising.html.

"The Soul Reformation, Show 15: More on the Evolution of Rhythm and Blues." Part 1, Track 4: Ray Charles. *University of North Texas, UNT Digital Library.* Accessed July 9, 2012, http://digital.library.unt.edu/ark:/67531/metadc19764/m1/.

Spalding, Henry, ed. *Encyclopedia of Black Folklore.* Middle Village, N.Y.: Jonathan David, 1972.

Strategic Media. "About Radio Advertising: Targetability." 2009. Accessed December 3, 2011, http://www.strategicmediainc.com/radio-advertising.php.

Stuckey, Sterling. *Slave Culture: Nationalist Theory and the Foundations of Black America.* New York: Oxford University Press, 1987.

Suosalo, Heikki. "Interview with Marvin Sease." *Soul Express Online.* Last modified March 4, 2012, accessed July 9, 2012, http://www.soulexpress.net/marvinsease_interview.htm.

Suosalo, Heikki. "The Soul Children." *Soul Express Online.* Last modified March 4, 2012, accessed July 9, 2012, http://www.soulexpress.net/soulchildren.htm.

Sweet Angel. Accessed March 16, 2011, http://www.sweetangel.org.

"T. K. Soul." *Soul Blues Music.* 2011, accessed January 6, 2012, http://www.soulbluesmusic.com/tksoul.htm.

Van West, Carroll. "WLAC." *The Tennessee Encyclopedia of History and Culture.* December 25, 2009, accessed February 17, 2011 http://tennesseeencyclopedia.net/entry.php?rec=1525.

Waiters, Mel, and S. J. Calloway. "Smaller the Club." Delta Boy Music, BMI. Released on Mel Waiters, *A Nite Out.* Malaco/Waldoxy WCD 2835, 2003.

Watkins, Mel. *On the Real Side: A History of African-American Comedy from Slavery to Chris Rock.* Chicago: Lawrence Hill, 1994.

West, Cornel. *Prophetic Fragments: Illuminations of the Crisis in American Religion and Culture.* Grand Rapids, Mich.: Eerdmans, 1993.

Whitburn, Joel. *Hot R & B Songs, 1942–2010.* Menomonee Falls, Wis.: Record Research, 2010.

Whiteis, David. "Bobby Rush: The Song and Dance of a Modern-Day Trickster." *Living Blues* no. 170 (November/December 2003): 36–37.

Whiteis, David. "Not So Smooth Operator." *Chicago Reader,* January 18, 2001, accessed April 4, 2012, http://www.chicagoreader.com/chicago/not-so-smooth-operator/Content?oid=904414.

Wilmer, Valerie. "Monk on Monk." *Down Beat,* June 3, 1965, 20–22.

Wolfe, James Jr., and Denise LaSalle. *Denise LaSalle's Inspirational Site.* 2010, accessed February 4, 2011, http://www.Deniselasalleinspirationals.com.

Yanow, Scott. "Soul Jazz." In *All Music Guide to Soul: The Definitive Guide to R & B and Soul,* edited by V. Bogdanov, Chris Woodstra, and Stephen Thomas Erlewine, 857–58. San Francisco: Backbeat Books, 2005.

Young, Alan, and John Glassburner. "Bogard Brothers." *Just Moving On,* August–October 2009, accessed April 17, 2011, http://www.justmovingon.info/ARTISTS/BogardBrothers.html.

Zahan, Dominique. *The Religion, Spirituality, and Thought of Traditional Africa.* Chicago: University of Chicago Press, 1979.

Index

69–73; 85; childhood in Mississippi, 68–69; collaborations with younger southern soul-blues artists, 80, 81, 82, 84–85; death of, 85–86; discovered by David Porter, 74; dynamism as live performer, 67–68, 85; early musical inspiration, 70–71; on feeling exploited/neglected by the recording industry, 78–79, 85; first recording session (Sur-Speed), 73–74; frustration over lack of radio play, 67, 68, 80–81; funeral of, 85, 86, 252, 281n3; goes to prison, 73–74; musical partnership with Queen Ann Hines, 68, 80, 81, 82, 86; at the 1997 Chicago Blues Festival, 67, 85; personality of, 68, 78–79, 85, 86; with the Prisonaires, 73–74; records "Taxi" as demo for Johnnie Taylor, 79; release from prison, 74; at revitalized Stax label (Fantasy), 78; solo career, 79–85; with the Soul Children, 21, 75–79; at Stax Records, 74–77; street singing with the Intruders (Memphis), 72; vocal style, 67–68, 76–77, 79–80, 81–82

————Albums/CDs: Loveaholic, 80; *Woof Woof Meow*, 84

————Songs recorded under his own name: "I'm Just a Fool for You" (with Lenny Williams), 80; "I'm Just a Fool for You Part 2" (with Sir Charles Jones), 80, 81; "Just One Lifetime" (with Ann Hines), 80, 81, 82, 84, 86; "Meow," 82–84; "Meow (Pussy Cat Remix)" (with The Duchess), 84; "No Ordinary Pussy Cat" (with Ms. Jody), 84; "Respect Yourself," 80; "Taxi," 23, 68, 79–80, 81, 84, 86 (*see also* Jones, Sir Charles); "Tear Jerker" (Ann Hines, lead voc.), 80; "Two Different People" (with Ann Hines), 82, 84

————Songs recorded with the Soul Children: "Can't Give Up a Good Thing," 78; "Give 'Em Love," 76–77; "I'll Be the Other Woman, 132; "I'll Understand," 77; "The Sweeter He Is," 77, 86;

JEA (label), 282n16

Jefferson, Blind Lemon, 179

Jefferson, Katrenia, 86, 282n16

Jerry-O (label), 96

"Jesus Gave Me Water," 71, 167

Jewel (label), 98. *See also* Rush, Bobby

Job, Lionel, 118

"Jody's Got Your Girl and Gone," 152

"John" (slave trickster of myth), 88

John, Elton, 205

John, Little Willie, 16, 112, 257–58

John R. (Richbourg), 32

Johnson, Bobbye "Doll," 189, 268–69; distaste for overly explicit lyrics, 189, 190

Johnson, Ernie, 113

Johnson, Jimmy, 205

Johnson, Leo, 170, 171

Johnson, Lil, 179

Johnson, Robert, 225, 278n15

Johnson, Syl, 42

Jomar (label), 287n10

Jones, Alan, 213

Jones, Blanche (mother of Sir Charles Jones), 147, 149, 150, 151, 155, 160

Jones, Bob, 120, 124, 208, 210, 213, 216, 220, 222, 228, 271

Jones, Charlesia (daughter of Sir Charles Jones), 158, 160

Jones, Charles Sr. (father of Sir Charles Jones), 149, 150

Jones, Denise. *See* LaSalle, Denise

Jones, E. Rodney, 53, 114

Jones, Sir Charles, 7, 25, 80, 81, 82, 162, 188, 200, 201, 207, 208, 212, 214, 222, 223, 225, 226, 231, 233, 246, 277n3, 284n2, 287n10; in Birmingham, AL, 149–51, 158; childhood in Akron, OH, 148–49; controversies surrounding, 158–60; drops out of high school, 150–51; early musical influences, 148–49; on explicit lyrics, 188–89; first recordings and professional success, 153–54, 155; on the Hep' Me label, 153, 156; on his love for his fans, 160; on Jumpin (independent label), 156, 161; as "King of Southern Soul," 143, 147, 154, 158; on the Mardi Gras label, 154, 156, 157; mentored by Marvin Sease, 151–52; multigenerational "crossover" appeal of, 7, 25–26, 145, 153, 154, 187–88, 214, 222, 223; performance style, 143–45, 146–47; performs at the French Quarters (Birmingham, AL), 151, 158; plays in high school band, 151; *Sir Charles Jones: His Life & Times* (promotional DVD), 158; as songwriter, 152, 153, 208, 212; turned down by Malaco, 152–53; works with Senator Jones, 153–54, 212; writes "Slow Roll It" for Lewis Clark (a.k.a. the Love Doctor), 212; youthful involvement in street gangs, 150, 160

————Albums/CDs: *For Your Love*, 156; *Glow* (not yet completed), 211; *Love Ma-*

chine, 145, 154, 155, 156, 157; *My Story*, 157–58; *Sir Charles Jones*, 153–54, 155; *Sir Charles Jones and Friends* (multi-artist compilation), 156–57; *Southern Soul*, 156; "Take Care of Mona" (*sic*: "Mama"), 155; *Thank You for Holding On*, 156; *A Tribute to the Legends*, 158, 160

———Songs recorded: "Ain't No Sunshine," 158; "Better Call Jody," 155; "Blues Spell," 155; "Bring It on Home to Me," 158; "Candy Girl," 155; "Do You Feel It," 158; "For Better or Worse," 153; "Friday," 144, 145, 153, 225; "Hang On," 155; "Happy Anniversary," 157; "I'll Never Make a Promise," 146, 246; "Is There Anybody Lonely?" 7, 45, 46, 53, 56; "Just Can't Let Go," 153; "Love Machine," 145, 146; "Me and Mrs. Jones," 158; "Mom's Apple Pie," 158; "My Taboo," 158; "Never Can Say Goodbye," 158; "Take Care of Mona" [*sic*: "Mama"], 155; "Taxi," 158; "When You Love Someone," 146; "You Are the Sunshine," 158, 160; "You Mean the World to Me," 157; "You're My Latest, My Greatest Inspiration," 158, 155

Jones, Senator, 24, 153, 156, 212. *See also* Jones, Sir Charles

jukeboxes, 2, 3, 112, 168, 199, 201, 224, 258, 277n1

juke joints, 16, 32, 189, 199, 268, 272

Jumpin (label), 156, 161. *See also* Jones, Sir Charles

Jus' Blues Music Foundation (Atlanta), 134, 278n9

"Just a Little Bit Won't Get It," 212

"Just Because He's Good to You," 266

"Just Walkin' in the Rain," 73

Kansas City, 123, 262, 287n27

Kayvette (label), 253

KC and the Sunshine Band, 39

Kelly Ingram Park (Birmingham, AL), 149, 150, 284n6

Kent (label), 256

Killens, Clyde, 37

Kimble, Terence. *See* T. K. Soul

Kimbrough, Lottie, 287n27

King, Albert, 20, 21, 23, 252, 258

King, B. B., 20, 70, 93, 114, 190, 222

King, Ben E., 36

King, Dr. Martin Luther Jr., 31, 51, 75, 149, 278n11

King, Earl, 23

King, Greg, 143, 144

King (label), 222, 257

"King Heroin," 184

Kings of Rhythm, 49

Kirstee (label), 116, 118. *See also* Clayton, Willie

"Kiss You," 255

KKDA (Dallas), 256

Knight, Frederick, 208–10, 212, 252

Knight, Gladys and the Pips, 40

Knoxville Coliseum (Knoxville, TN), 286n11

"Koko," 271

Kool Gents, 266

Kooper, Al, 40

Knight Beat (Miami nightclub), 37. *See also* Latimore, Benny

Knuckles, Frankie, 224

KRLA (Pasadena, CA), 278n7

Ku Klux Klan, 284n5

LaFlore County (MS), 51

Laid Back, 60

LaJam (label), 98, 99. *See also* Rush, Bobby

Land Where the Blues Began, The, 277–78n8

LaSalle, Denise, ix–xii; 1, 2, 3, 6, 7, 110, 113, 154, 159, 168, 200, 209, 214, 256, 272, 273, 278n10, 280n1, 281n9, 281n10, 284n8, 285n14, 286n17, 286n26; Angel in the Midst label, 61, attempts crossover into gospel, 61–62; Chess Records and, 49, 51, 52–53, 186n26, 278n10, 280n1, 281n9, 281n10, 284n8, 285n14, 286n17; childhood in Missisippi, 51; co-owns Crajon label, 54–56; discovers/mentors Bill Coday, 54, 56; early literary ambitions, 49; early reluctance to become a recording artist, 49–51; early years as an R&B singer, 52–54; early years in Chicago, 48–51; first marriage, 51, 52; forms National Association for the Preservation of Blues (N.A.P.O.B.), 60; as inspiration for Ms. Jody, 168; marriage to Bill Jones, 54, 56, 280n3; marriage to James Wolfe, 58, 61, 65; moves to Chicago from Mississippi, 51, 52; moves to Jackson, TN, from Memphis, 58; moves to Memphis from Chicago, 56–57; opinions on synthesized vs. natural instruments, 63, 65–66; Ordena label, 58, 63, 65; performance style, 57, 60–61, 63–64, 185, 192; pre-secular career gospel singing, 49, 52; produced by Willie Mitchell, 54–55; recording ca-

David Whiteis is an author, freelance writer, and educator living in Chicago. He is the author of *Chicago Blues: Portraits and Stories*, and his articles and reviews have appeared in *Living Blues, The Chicago Reader, Down Beat, Juke Blues, Jazz Times*, and elsewhere.

Music in American Life

The Golden Age of Gospel   *Text by Horace Clarence Boyer; photography by Lloyd Yearwood*

Aaron Copland: The Life and Work of an Uncommon Man   *Howard Pollack*

Louis Moreau Gottschalk   *S. Frederick Starr*

Race, Rock, and Elvis   *Michael T. Bertrand*

Theremin: Ether Music and Espionage   *Albert Glinsky*

Poetry and Violence: The Ballad Tradition of Mexico's Costa Chica   *John H. McDowell*

The Bill Monroe Reader   *Edited by Tom Ewing*

Music in Lubavitcher Life   *Ellen Koskoff*

Zarzuela: Spanish Operetta, American Stage   *Janet L. Sturman*

Bluegrass Odyssey: A Documentary in Pictures and Words, 1966–86   *Carl Fleischhauer and Neil V. Rosenberg*

That Old-Time Rock & Roll: A Chronicle of an Era, 1954–63   *Richard Aquila*

Labor's Troubadour   *Joe Glazer*

American Opera   *Elise K. Kirk*

Don't Get above Your Raisin': Country Music and the Southern Working Class   *Bill C. Malone*

John Alden Carpenter: A Chicago Composer   *Howard Pollack*

Heartbeat of the People: Music and Dance of the Northern Pow-wow   *Tara Browner*

My Lord, What a Morning: An Autobiography   *Marian Anderson*

Marian Anderson: A Singer's Journey   *Allan Keiler*

Charles Ives Remembered: An Oral History   *Vivian Perlis*

Henry Cowell, Bohemian   *Michael Hicks*

Rap Music and Street Consciousness   *Cheryl L. Keyes*

Louis Prima   *Garry Boulard*

Marian McPartland's Jazz World: All in Good Time   *Marian McPartland*

Robert Johnson: Lost and Found   *Barry Lee Pearson and Bill McCulloch*

Bound for America: Three British Composers   *Nicholas Temperley*

Lost Sounds: Blacks and the Birth of the Recording Industry, 1890–1919   *Tim Brooks*

Burn, Baby! BURN! The Autobiography of Magnificent Montague   *Magnificent Montague with Bob Baker*

Way Up North in Dixie: A Black Family's Claim to the Confederate Anthem   *Howard L. Sacks and Judith Rose Sacks*

The Bluegrass Reader   *Edited by Thomas Goldsmith*

Colin McPhee: Composer in Two Worlds   *Carol J. Oja*

Robert Johnson, Mythmaking, and Contemporary American Culture   *Patricia R. Schroeder*

Composing a World: Lou Harrison, Musical Wayfarer   *Leta E. Miller and Fredric Lieberman*

Fritz Reiner, Maestro and Martinet   *Kenneth Morgan*

That Toddlin' Town: Chicago's White Dance Bands and Orchestras, 1900–1950   *Charles A. Sengstock Jr.*

The University of Illinois Press
is a founding member of the
Association of American University Presses.

Composed in 10.5/13.5 ITC Berkeley Oldstyle Std
with Helvetica Neue display
by Celia Shapland
at the University of Illinois Press
Manufactured by Thomson-Shore, Inc.
University of Illinois Press

1325 South Oak Street
Champaign, IL 61820-6903
www.press.uillinois.edu